2 - 31654

marie.

4-3012

ALSO BY TONY KORNHEISER

The Baby Chase

✳ PUMPING IRONY ✳

PUMPING IRONY

Working Out the Angst of a Lifetime

TONY KORNHEISER

TIMES BOOKS

RANDOM HOUSE

Originally published in hardcover by Times Books, a division of Random
House, Inc., in 1995.

All of the articles that appear in this work were originally published in *The
Washington Post*. Additionally, some articles also appeared in the author's
syndicated column.

Library of Congress Cataloging-in-Publication Data
Kornheiser, Tony.
    Pumping irony: working out the angst of a lifetime / Tony Kornheiser.
      p. cm.
    ISBN 0-8129-2831-8 (paperback)
    I. Title.
  PN4874.K67P86 1995
  814'.54—dc20   95-21256

Random House website address: http://www.randomhouse.com
Printed in the United States of America on acid-free paper
9 8 7 6 5 4 3 2
First Paperback Edition

For Karril,

Elizabeth,

and Michael

CONTENTS

THE LONG-AWAITED
INTRODUCTION

Originally, the title for this book was *Dave Barry Is Dead*. I thought that would help me sell books to two important book-buying constituencies:

1. The millions of people who like murder mysteries;
2. The millions of people who buy books just because Dave Barry's name is on the cover.

However, it was pointed out to me by Dave's best friend that Dave might not like being called "dead" in print, and might therefore refuse to give me a favorable blurb.

So I changed the title to *THE BEST OF DAVE BARRY . . .* —which would be in capital letters splashed across the cover, and then, in really small type at the bottom of the page— *. . . is better than anything in this tepid collection by Tony Kornheiser.*

This had the advantage of accuracy. But it was still a cheap, obvious attempt to pander to Dave Barry fans and cash in on his name. Dave liked both the title and the impulse, but thought his publishers might not. He asked where I got the idea, and I told him—(take note how I'm subtly insinuating a true friendship with DAVE BARRY, hoping to make you think that since I'm his buddy, I'm probably as funny as he is, and you ought to buy this book)—about the album that was released when the Beatles were at their height, called *Best of the Beatles*. Millions of people bought it, thinking it was an album of Beatles tunes; in reality it was an album of horrid songs by Pete Best, who was the Beatles' first drummer and got dumped for Ringo Starr.

Anyway, I had to come up with another title. I sat around with a legal pad and scratched out titles by the hundreds. I started with long ones, the kind Lewis Grizzard used. The one I liked best was *Unlike Dave Barry, Lewis Grizzard Really Is Dead and Probably Can't Sue, and He Sold Tons of Books, So Maybe This Will Work for Me.* It has the advantage of getting BOTH *Dave Barry* and *Lewis Grizzard* in the title.

From there I went into my standard refuge, old rock 'n' roll lyrics that were meaningful at the time. I offered *Come and Beat Your Crazy Head Against the Sky*, *She Wouldn't Have a Willy or a Sam* and, of course, *Do The Freddy*. These were all met with blank stares.

Then I got caught up in a gerund thing—and I'm sure I don't have to tell erudite people like you, educated but cheap people who stand around reading books in bookstores instead of buying them, what a gerund is. I think we all know what a gerund is, don't we? That resulted in titles like *Bicycling Toward Antarctica*, *Shish-ke-bobbing John*, and *The Bridges of East Brunswick, N.J.*, which doesn't contain any gerunds, but always struck me as a good title for a book. Nobody liked them either.

Then I tried titles that would appear self-effacing and at the same time suggest humor, like (a) *I Suppose You Think That's Funny, Mister*, (b) *If You Like These, I'll Write More*, and (c) *Read Two of These, and Call Me in the Morning*. But I was fearful reviewers might be cruel and say:

a. No, as a matter of fact, I don't think it's funny.

b. Please don't bother.

c. Thanks just the same, but I'd rather vomit all night.

Now, to fill out the required thousand words of this introduction—and could someone please tell me why I have to write
my own introduction, and why the publisher won't spring for
someone funny like P. J. O'Rourke, Roy Blount, Jr., or DAVE
BARRY to write this?—here are some other titles I suggested.

Filtering the River. (Rejected as idiotic.)

The Mirth Canal. (Rejected as tasteless and idiotic.)

Panhandling at the Petting Zoo. (Rejected as inscrutable and
idiotic.)

My last try was *No One's Using Lew Alcindor Anymore*, and
not a single person I showed that to, including my own personal
self, had even the slightest idea what I was trying to say.

Ultimately it became clear to everyone that I wasn't going
to come up with a good title. I could have told them from the
beginning that I wasn't very creative. I barely wrote any of
the columns in this collection. You will notice that an inor-
dinate number of my columns seemed to be filled with lines
supplied by several recurring characters: My Smart Friend
Martha, Mr. Henry (America's Best-Loved Feature Writer), My
Friend Nancy, Man About Town Chip Muldoon, and My Friend
Gino. You probably assume that this is a classic literary trick to
give my columns breadth by using different personae and voices
that are really alter egos for myself. You would be wrong. These
are pseudonyms of real live persons, colleagues of mine who are
far funnier than I am. Roughly 92 percent of everything I write is
stolen from them. I would put their real names here and finally
give them the credit they so richly deserve, but, hey, then I
might have to share royalties.

Anyway, the title we finally settled on was *Pumping Irony*,
which was written by Vicky the Layout Person. We chose this
because it seems to most accurately describe my *oeuvre*, which
relies on the subtle juxtaposition of incompatible frames of reference in a manner reminiscent of Benchley and Thurber and

my fabulous close personal friend and intimate, MISTER DAVE
BARRY, and because it sucked a little less than the others.
    Thank you.

Tony Kornheiser
Washington, D.C.

NURTURING A MESS

*

Pumping Irony

Since my body began to sag under the weight of all my midlife crises, I have joined a gym.

I have a personal trainer. His name is Tom. I hate him because he is my age, and looks twenty years younger. He is, as we say, ripped. You could hang draperies from his pecs. Even the bags under his eyes have definition.

Tom is very excited about training me. To fitness trainers, I am what a lump of clay is to a sculptor. Actually, I am more like what a lump of sugar-cured ham is to a schnauzer. Trainers want to strip me to the bone.

They measured my body fat the other day. I am human Häagen-Dazs. I could charge six bits for a lick of my elbow.

"I'm glad you're doing this," Tom told me on my first visit to the gym. "What made you decide to start working out?"

"I'm getting older, and I don't want to be buried in a piano case," I said.

He asked me if I'd ever lifted weight, and I told him I was pretty sure I could get 205 pounds off the ground. Then I jumped in the air.

But seriously, folks . . .

Before we began training, Tom preached to me about the

benefits of water; he told me to drink at least one hundred ounces of water each day, that it had many, many therapeutic benefits. I've been drinking lots of water for a week now, and it has taught me the important therapeutic principle that when you consume large volumes of water, it makes you pee like a cow.

Tom thought I ought to start on my upper body; I told him that within the last few years it had moved to my lower body. So he stood me in front of a mirror and handed me some ridiculously light weights—three pounds apiece—and told me to lift them slowly. There I am lifting these baby Day-glo dumbbells that look like a starter set for Arnold Schwarzenegger's daughter's Barbie dolls, and the guy next to me, who just happens to be Rene Knott, the likable sportscaster on Channel 7, who is built like a condominium, is lifting a two-hundred-pound dumbbell with each hand. Standing side by side we looked like a "Far Side" cartoon.

Caption: "At that moment, Anthony finally understood he would never realize his dream of wrestling as The Human Threshing Machine."

I can't tell you how odd it felt for me to walk around using all the different exercise equipment. When I was young, a gym was someplace where fat, middle-aged men went to escape from their wives. They took steam and they played cards; nobody actually exercised. There was only one exercise then—you went to the garage, picked up a barbell, and lifted it over your head. Gradually you raised the weight until Vinny came over. Vinny spent all his time in metal shop, making bullets; he was on the fast track to Attica. Vinny put three hundred pounds on the bar, bent down, grunted like a garbage truck downshifting on an ice floe, and lifted the bar over his head. Case closed. Nobody ever suggested to Vinny that he ought to try low-impact aerobics.

I looked around at all these young men with their broad

shoulders and big chests, and I thought to myself—why do they all want to look like Mae West?

At that point Tom began his pep talk. He told me I wasn't in nearly as bad a shape as I thought, and that I had to start thinking positively. He said I had displayed great motor skills in my last exercise. "I wouldn't have started most people on something so advanced," Tom told me. I recalled that all I had done was move a small weight by lifting up my leg; I was quite sure a Border collie could have done it.

"How long until I get big muscles like you?" I asked.

"It's not about big muscles, it's about lifestyle," Tom said evasively. "Goals are fine, but this is a never-ending journey."

I don't want it to be never-ending. I'm looking for a finish line.

Hey, I'm looking for a punch line.

My problem is that I'm old already. I'm formed. I'm fat and bald and I have rolls on my stomach like a shar-pei. I'm never gonna have great deltoids; what do I know from deltoids, anyway? I thought deltoids were little airplanes. I'll tell you what a pathetic girlie-man I am: Tom had me doing exercises without weights—just pantomime exercises, and I'd start using weights in them later—and *they* hurt! My heart was beating like a rabbit's, and all I'd done was Kabuki theater.

So what's the best-case scenario for me? Say I do this for five years—bulking up on water, working on my endorphins, eating the kinds of food you see lying at the bottom of the monkey house—what's it gonna get me? I'll look like somebody stapled Charles Kuralt's head onto Joe Piscopo's body. What am I gonna do, quit the newspaper and become a furniture mover?

Not that I have any chance of getting muscles anyway, if my experience on the treadmill is any indication. Tom wanted me to get a "cardio" (that's workoutese for cardiovascular, just as "glutes" is shorthand for "Help! I glued my tuchus to the NordicTrack''), so I got on the treadmill and began walking at a comfortable pace for me, something like one mile every three weeks.

Directly in front of me was an aerobics class, and I hope it doesn't sound sexist of me to suggest that there were some total stacked hardbody babes in that class, and, as I say, they were working out directly in front of me. And I, uh, kind of got animated, and began walking faster than I should have. And not looking where I was going, I walked right up the treadmill, hit the retaining bar and fell over the side! What kind of motor skill is that? I've got to be the only person in the gym who needs a spotter on a treadmill.

I was discouraged by my klutziness, so Tom has encouraged me to exercise with a female partner. "It can be a very intimate experience," he promised.

Fine. I'm game. To preserve my dignity, though, it will have to be someone at my fitness level.

I've got a call in to Estelle Getty.

A Promising Thought

Of the many differences between men and women when it comes to making New Year's resolutions, the most striking difference is:

Men don't mean any of them.

Not a single word. Consider the issue of family finance in recessionary times.

A woman will resolve, "I'm going to keep to a stricter budget this year."

A man will resolve, "I'm going to earn six hundred million dollars this year."

Or say a couple feel something important is lacking in their lives.

The woman: "I resolve to attend church regularly."

The man: "I resolve to become pope . . . by Friday."

Do you notice a pattern here? Women try to be honest with themselves. This is because women view life as a novel, something by Proust maybe, with shadings and subtleties, elaborate character development, Byzantine subplots, all leading to a satisfying denouement based on emotional and spiritual growth.

Men see life as a daily series of three-panel cartoons: Situation. Resolution. Exit line. Thanks, you've been a great audience, see ya tomorrow. This makes for short attention spans, shocking inattention to detail, and unrealistic goal setting—particularly if it involves the use of power tools.

Woman: "I resolve to be kinder to my children."

Man: "I resolve to build my children a three-story treehouse with flush toilets . . . by Friday."

What a great idea! Any kid would want one of those. However, here are the steps this resolution takes in real—not cartoon—life:

a. The man buys the wood.

b. He goes to store the wood in the garage.

c. He can't open the garage because the door is blocked by the tiles he bought for the swimming pool he was going to build last year. And by now his back hurts from schlepping all this damn wood.

d. He gives the kids money and tells them to go to the mall.

Women make smaller, more reasoned resolutions. They actually write them down. They puzzle over them and try desperately to adhere to them—at least through the middle of January. Invariably women make resolutions about their weight. All women think they weigh too much, even the ones who look like they can use a vacuum hose as a sleeping bag. My friend Nancy makes the same resolution every year, "to lose a few pounds just so I can get into a bathing suit." Not to look like Ellen Barkin. To lose *a few pounds*.

Here's the man's take on that: "I resolve to exercise two hours a day for the rest of my life so I can look like Steven Seagal."

There are two reasons why a man would make this resolution:

1. To bag some babe.

2. See Reason No. 1.

Of course the resolution is thoroughly preposterous, since no man alive has any notion of time beyond next Tuesday, and may as well be committing to eating a weasel in Macy's window as to doing anything for two hours a day *for the rest of his life.*

But apropos of that resolution, I'd like to share with you, verbatim, a conversation I just made up:

Sonny: You really think you can look like Steven Seagal just by exercising? You couldn't look like Steven Seagal with plastic surgery and a hair weave.

Tom: I'm definitely joining a health club.

Sonny: Do you have any idea how silly you'd feel in a health club, with all those young kids around? They've got bodies you see in those Calvin Klein ads. They'll take one look at you and start laughing. You're a schlub, Tommy, you got back hair. You'll walk in the door, and they'll start dialing 911.

Tom: Maybe I could start jogging.

Sonny: For what? So you can drop dead on the side of the road, and they'll haul you away like road kill?

Tom: I've got to do something healthy.

Sonny: Start dating a nurse.

Personally, I don't make New Year's resolutions anymore. I can't afford the lumber.

Adipose Complex

Ready or not, the pool season is upon us. Oh sure, the water feels great on a suffocatingly hot summer day. The problem is, you have to wear a bathing suit. Like most of you, I don't look good in a bathing suit. I look like a cantaloupe with back hair.

It's not that I weigh so much more than I did when I was younger—well, okay, maybe a few pounds more, thirty-five pounds isn't so much, is it? You'd hardly notice it on, say, an adult rhinoceros. But it all seemed to settle in one place: my front. I take off my shirt and sit down on a lounge chair, and I look like a shar-pei. My kids bring their friends around and say, "We can tell how old our daddy is by counting the rings on his stomach." Most people get tan lines where their bathing suits end. I have permanent pale creases on what used to be my chest. It looks like I take sun through a venetian blind.

I try not to let it show, especially around the women. If I'm standing when a woman passes by, I suck in my stomach and hold my breath. But it's a problem if she stops to chat, because after holding in my stomach like that for a long while, when I finally speak, my voice sounds like I've swallowed helium.

I love the guys who wear the tight, skimpy bathing suits—

the ones that look like a Ped attached to a rubber band. The last thing in the world I want is something revealing. If I hauled the waistband of my suit up any higher, I'd be wearing my jock over my Adam's apple.

There are different types of people at a swimming pool. There are the psycho lappers, who blow by like Flipper on bennies; the paddlers, who regularly get in the lappers' lanes and come away with punctured spleens; the divers, who preen on the board and then hit the water with the grace of a penguin dropped from a cropduster; and people who don't swim, they stand. I'm a stander. In my pool there's me and all the women who've just come from the beauty parlor. I'm easy to recognize. I'm the one with the stretch marks.

Each winter I tell myself I ought to get in better shape for the opening of pool season to avoid this anxiety. Apparently I am not alone. My friend Nancy is dreading her Hawaiian vacation, because she'll have to spend ten straight days in a bathing suit. "If you could just swim in black tights and culottes," she sighed. "My husband, bless his heart, wants me to buy a two-piece. I told him I was way past the age of doing that." I asked her, what's the age when a woman can't buy a two-piece anymore? "The age of reason," she told me.

What's the point of dieting, anyway? (Incidentally, my idea of dieting is to use small utensils. I once ate a porterhouse steak with a cocktail fork. If you think that was tough, try having a bowl of wonton soup with a coke spoon.) A report this week in *JAMA, the Journal of the American Medical Association* said that if we reduced our dietary fat intake to meet federal recommendations, the average life expectancy would increase by three to four months. That's an awful lot of dry, disgusting rice cakes for three measly months. (My dietitian used to tell me I was eating rice cakes the wrong way, because I slathered cream cheese over them. "You're supposed to eat them plain," he insisted. "*Gandhi* wouldn't eat these plain," I said.) The kicker is: These three extra months come *at the end of your life*! They call that living? You've got no teeth. You've got no hair. You're impotent. You get wheeled around, and left sitting in the sun like a duck. And you're getting three *more* months. I don't want three more minutes at the end. I want the three months tacked on to my junior year in college, when I can do something useful with them, like driving naked.

By the way, the *JAMA* study said that in a best-case scenario, with all Americans reducing their fat intake to the proper level, we'll get "about 60 million years of additional life."

Talk about idiotic statistics that no one can relate to. It's like saying how old George Burns is in dog years. Who cares?

Talk to me in terms I can understand. Don't give me aggregate life spans of everyone who starts eating low-cholesterol, low-sugar, low-salt, no-taste foods, such as I-Can't-Believe-It's-Not-Cauliflower. Talk to me about what it does for me at my pool, now, when I need it.

You want to make a deal on life span? I'll trade you three months to get rid of this back hair and this ear hair that has come upon me in midlife like the very blanket of death. I'm becoming *furry*! I feel like one morning I'm going to wake up and start eating my meals from a dish on the floor.

Of course, by then I'll be 2,309 years old in dog years.

God only knows how much I'll weigh in dog pounds.

Bookshelf to Heaven?

Just when you thought you'd run out of fabulously appropriate surprise fortieth-birthday gifts, along comes Keith Tibbetts of Windsor, Massachusetts, with a mail-order showstopper: a personalized multipurpose coffin that doubles as a bookcase and wine rack. That's right, it's the Life Coffin, which is sure to become a family conversation piece—especially if your family is the Addams Family.

"My, what an interesting, uh, *coffin* you have in the middle of your living room. Sort of a postmodern Transylvanian decor, isn't it? Where'd you do your furniture shopping, Gawler's Funeral Home?"

These are coffins that can be ordered with adjustable shelves for your books and personal mementos, and a twelve-bottle wine rack—so you can not only age your wine, you can take it with you. (The worst-case scenario is that you die, and your wife says, "I've really grown fond of that wine rack," and she buries you in a Glad Bag instead.)

Tibbetts, a forty-year-old woodworker, writes in his brochure, "Death is an inevitable part of our life. Buying a coffin now can help begin a process of education and acceptance. By seeing your coffin every day, you will be reminded of the preciousness of your physical life. . . . And when all is said and done, you can rest peacefully, knowing that you're enclosed in a coffin to which you have added personal meaning." (Previously, I hadn't thought about having a personal relationship with my coffin. It's not that I don't respect my coffin. I just don't spend much time dwelling on it—sort of the way I feel about Jonas Salk.)

This is an old idea that's been resurrected, so to speak. In ancient Egypt, for example, the pharaohs used to be buried with their household goods and some of their favorite things—bad news for the pharaoh's dog and the upstairs maid. Tibbetts began building his Life Coffins more than a year ago. Thus far he has sold eighteen of them (at $350 and up), mainly to older people. "Younger people think they're invincible," Tibbetts sighed. Most buyers order the shelves. The coffin comes with a hook on the back to hang the lid. It has been suggested to Tibbetts that he attach legs to the lid, so it can be used as a card table—presumably on the theory that while death eventually comes to us all, in the meantime, how about a game of bridge?—but as yet no one has specifically requested that. A person might even sleep in his Life Coffin; since most people die in bed anyway, this would help streamline arrangements at an awkward time for the family.

Tibbetts's work has led to interesting, if brief, conversations. "Sometimes at parties," Tibbetts explained, "people who don't know me will ask me what I'm working on these days. And I say, 'I make coffins that people use as a bookcase until they die.' Usually, there's about five seconds of silence after that." Coffins clearly don't make for the smoothest conversation. But they haven't always foreshadowed gloom and doom; in *Moby-Dick* it's an empty coffin bobbing in the seas that carries Ishmael away from the *Pequod* and to life. Still, it's hard to imagine a coffin not, shall we say, altering the mood.

"Your teeth are like pearls."

"Oh, Roger."

"Let me put on this Johnny Mathis album."

"That's an interesting record cabinet, Roger."

"Thanks. It's my coffin."

"I, uh, have to be back at the convent by nine."

You have to admit though that having a coffin in your house, and throwing a big party while you lie in it, appeals to the universal fantasy of being present at your own wake and hearing what your friends say about you:

"He looks so natural."

"He should. He's not dead yet."

I might buy a Life Coffin, but there are certain creature comforts that I'd want: It doesn't come with a liner. I have to have a liner. Something soft, and in a soothing color. I'd consult a mortician for what my best color is, though I suppose that might change after awhile. I'd want the ice maker, definitely, and temperature controls I could turn on with the Clapper, because my hands will be in that position. A tanning lamp; most dead people I've seen look absolutely awful. A subscription to the Sunday *Times*, for the death notices, to see who's moving into the neighborhood. (Just to confound those insufferable archaeologists who find a toenail clipping in a peat bog and reconstruct it into the Cro-Magnon man, I'd put in a picture of me and a dinosaur, captioned "Me and Mom, at left.") What else would I put in? Hmmm. A periscope, certainly. A cordless phone, because you never know, right? Maybe Houdini *could* have spoken from the great beyond if he'd only had the technology. By the same token, I ought to have a fax, too; someone might want me to bring something back. Above all I want double-hinged doors, in case a tragic mistake has been made.

The truth of the matter is that if I could have anything I wanted in my own coffin, it would be anything but me.

A Garden of Versus

 I was working on a column of monumental intellectual significance, likening the ascension of multiculturalism to the postindustrial decline of structuralism in the visual arts, when suddenly my friend Gino walked in and said:

"Okay, boxing match: Mike Tyson versus Ivan Lendl."

He paused theatrically, the way George C. Scott might.

". . . But Lendl *gets to use his tennis racket*."

I regarded him as if he were a penguin.

"Fourteen seconds, including the referee's count," I said. "Tyson gets a small welt on his shoulder. Lendl is on the canvas, twitching and drooling."

A chastened silence. "Okay, okay. Tyson versus Yogi Berra. But Yogi has a chain saw."

Hmmm.

This new wrinkle required me to step outside my office and into the *Post*'s main newsroom, a cavernous, gravely serious place where journalistic giants were hunched at their desks, laboring over matters of global import.

I made a general announcement: "Tyson versus Berra, but Yogi has a chain saw."

It was like ringing Pavlov's bell. Every man within earshot stopped what he was doing.

"Tyson, within two."

"Berra, the ref stops it on cuts."

"Does Yogi get to fire that sucker up *before* the bell, or does he have to fiddle with it while Tyson's rushing across at him?"

"Toro or Black & Decker?"

The most astonishing part of this debate is that it was conducted deadpan, in utmost seriousness. Men are accustomed to pointless cerebrations involving hypothetical performances by athletes in handicapped mismatches.

"Tyson versus Joe Theismann, but Joe has a can of Mace."

"Babe Ruth versus Michael Jordan . . . playing squash."

"Tyson versus Navratilova, but Martina has a Rottweiler."

"Tyson versus David Brinkley."

"David Brinkley?"

"Yes, but Tyson is blindfolded."

"Is Brinkley wearing aftershave?"

"Why?"

"Because if he's got on aftershave, then Tyson lays back against the ropes and *smells* Brinkley coming at him. Brinkley throws a jab, Tyson gets the scent, fires out a combination. Referee counts to ten. Less than a minute."

"No aftershave."

"Okay then, the smell of fear. Same thing. Thirty seconds max."

Can you imagine women doing this? Of course not. Women are not idiots.

Take the average weekend. Your average woman will go to the dry cleaner. She'll putter around in the garden. She'll go grocery shopping, making sure to buy meals that are not only nutritionally balanced but contain the requisite amounts of fiber and "good" cholesterol. She'll take the children to a handicrafts

fair as a method of instilling a respect for the dignity of indigenous peoples worldwide. She'll finish writing her novel.

This is how your average man spends his weekend: burping
in front of the TV, watching anything with a half-time.

I am convinced that men become obsessed with athletics as
a way to avoid having to deal with anything else. If you are talking about sports, you do not have to develop relationships with
other people beyond the ability to discuss sports. For example,
this is what I know personally about my editor, a man with
whom I spend at least ten harrowing hours a week:

1. He likes the Yankees.

2. He is willing to endlessly debate whether Wilt Chamber-
lain could beat Sandy Koufax in the hundred-yard backstroke.

3. He has a wife. I think.

Men's conversations are vastly different from women's. An
example: A woman is at home, and her phone rings. It's her
cousin's first wife's former au pair. They talk for more than an
hour about relatives, about kids, about schools, about death,
about the high price of housing, about the most intimate details
of their personal lives. The women get off the telephone feeling
like they've become closer than ever. Now, the same thing happens to a man. The phone rings. It's his brother! He says, "Hey,
how ya doing? Look, I got the ballgame on. Hey, as long as I got
you on the phone, lemme ask you. Seriously, who do you think's
a better bowler—Lou Gehrig or Chris Evert?"

Except for sports, men have no attention span. A woman
can watch a TV show and tell you everything that happened,
everything. You'll ask, "Look, I missed *L.A. Law* this week—
what happened?" A woman will start at the top and go word for
word through the show, even adding stuff that she thinks was
implied by the characters' glances. It will take a man about thirty
seconds to realize that he's in for fifty-nine more minutes of this
stuff, and he'll say impatiently, "Look, did anybody die? Because if nobody died, I'd like to watch the O's." (If you reverse

this scenario, and ask a man to recap an entire *season* of *L.A. Law*, all he will tell you is who got naked.)

I think the world would be a lot better off if women engaged in the same kind of stupid hypothetical arguments as men—even if they're not about sports, as long as they're some idiotic comparison. Involving, say, *relationships*. Someday I want to walk in here and hear women say:

"Okay, Meryl Streep and Bruce Willis."

"Get outta here. She could cut her IQ in half and still pound him into dust. Streep and Bill Hurt."

"Too much woman. Hurt goes crying to Mama in two days. Streep and Alec Baldwin."

"Streep as a Dane or an Australian?"

"Forget Meryl Streep. Geena Davis, and she's driving cross-country, and she gets to run over one person and get away with it. Who?"

"Okay, okay, John McLaughlin."

This Stinks

Smells made the news this week. A team of "fragrance scientists" reported that a sniff of peppermint appears to enhance concentration and attentiveness.

Excuse me . . . fragrance scientists?

This is how we're meeting the challenge of the new world order?

"Hi, I'm Billy. I'm in the sixth grade, and I want to be a scientist, so I can develop a rocket ship to take us to the distant reaches of space."

"I'm Molly. I want to be a scientist and help develop a cure for cancer."

"I'm D'Artagnan. I'm going to become a fragrance scientist, and devote myself to making the world safe for honeysuckle."

My smart friend Martha says this whole thing falls under the heading of "aroma therapy," which she claims has been going on for three thousand years. The title of my next book, *I'm Always the Last to Know*, explains why I've never heard of it. (Cher's an actress? You're kidding me. Since when?)

Last year Martha underwent aroma therapy in London. An aroma therapist put some basil oil on her face. Martha thought she'd been dipped in pesto sauce. "I bought different aromatic oils to pour into my bath. They're supposed to relax you. Sage was the best; I felt like I was dead and rotting in a shallow grave. The problem was, my face began to break out. All the stress left my body, but it showed up on the part that wasn't underwater."

My editor here at *The Washington Post*, whom I will call Nancy (she calls me Ramon), remembered doing something similar in the '60s. She took baths in almond-scented oil and got out smelling like marzipan. "Bees followed me everywhere I went. No men, just bees."

All this fragrance research has a commercial application: to manipulate you in the workplace. It's well known that automobile dealers spray the inside of a new car with "new car smell" and try to get you into the front seat, thinking the smell will entice you into buying the car. Some years ago, Bob Howsam, then the president of the Cincinnati Reds baseball team, tried aroma therapy to lure new customers into his ballpark. Howsam was convinced folks couldn't resist the smell of a bakery; whenever they'd pass one, they'd go inside. Howsam got a scientist to reproduce "bakery smell" and lathered Riverfront Stadium with it. Unfortunately, it didn't attract new customers—and many of the old ones who had come to the ballpark quickly left to buy crullers.

You're nobody without your own personalized perfume these days. Liz Taylor has one. Joan Collins has one. Mikhail Baryshnikov just got one; I'm guessing it smells like mare's sweat. This preoccupation with smells reminds me of the old *New Yorker* cartoon with the two dogs, and one says, "Isn't it a cruel irony that we have the greatest sense of smell in the world . . . and dog breath?"

So this is where we're headed, into the brave new world of dollars and scents. Supermarkets are already gearing up. When you're in the detergent aisle, you'll smell dirty socks. The lottery will offer a scratch-n-sniff ticket that smells like new money.

Personally, I want to spray everything in my house so it smells like Annette Bening.

Office productivity might be enhanced by peppermint, but it would plummet if you misted in the scent of musk. No work would get done. All you'd hear would be the sounds of sighing, followed by office doors slamming shut; the first question at a board meeting would be, "J.P., instead of new desks, why don't we order sofas?"

The truth is, the nose is the organ of the '90s. And here's the nightmare: You're sitting at your desk, and you notice nobody is coming near you. So you ask, "Hey, what am I, chopped liver?" And you might well be.

Making No Concessions

Man About Town Chip Muldoon phoned the other day with another amazing tale of life in the big city. It seems he was enjoying a leisurely meal—he'd gotten through the relish tray, the cheese board, and an order of clams casino and was about to start on his prime ribs—when much to his chagrin an intense flash of light hit him squarely in the eye, startling him so, he dribbled au jus all over his new Perry Ellis shirt.

"Sir, what's that you're eating?"

It was the movie gourmet police!

"Uh, nothing," Muldoon stammered, trying to hide his plate.

"Smells like roast beef," one policeman said.

"A bit overcooked at that," observed his partner.

Hmmm, Muldoon thought, what've we got here, Lt. Columbo and Julia Child?

"Sir, did you purchase that food at our concession stand?"

"I'm afraid not," Muldoon conceded. "I wanted your popcorn. But to buy the smallest bag—I believe you call it the Whole Earth size—I'd have needed a home equity loan."

"You'll have to come with us."

"But Joe hasn't gotten to the volcano yet."

Man About Town Chip Muldoon's plea fell on deaf ears. He was evicted from the movie. This was his second offense. A week ago he was caught with a drumstick from Popeye's hanging out of his mouth, and tried unsuccessfully to argue it wasn't a leg of chicken at all, but a traditional Ecuadoran folklore thermometer.

"My photo's up in every K-B, Odeon, and AMC theater in town. I can't watch a first-run movie without submitting to a strip search," Muldoon moaned.

The Film Food Feud is escalating.

Coming attraction: nacho-sniffing dogs.

Movie theaters may have the right to toss patrons for bringing in unauthorized food, but none of this brinkmanship would have happened if theaters weren't greedy. The colossal gall of Cineplex Odeon to sell its cheapest bag of popcorn for $2.45! And what's with these giant boxes of candy? People used to go to the movies because the stars were bigger than life—not the boxes of candy.

Moviegoers now routinely stop in at 7-Eleven before going into the theater, which is incredible considering 7-Eleven's prices. But people like their malted-milk balls by the ounce, not the metric ton. Don't you love movie flacks telling us they sell nine-pound bags of M&Ms because "we want to give the customer the best value possible." Does this mean we'll be able to buy bulk toilet paper and do-it-yourself furniture in the lobby of the Avalon Theater? That would alleviate your stress at having to choose between *Pretty Woman* and Shoppers Food Warehouse.

Of course people smuggle in food. Most women carry it inside their handbags to avoid detection. My sister smuggled halves of a salami sandwich in the shoulders of her Liz Claiborne T-shirt, where the pads normally fit. "Where did you buy that shirt," I asked, after catching a whiff of her the next day, "the Carnegie Deli?"

My editor devised a brilliant ruse: Some time ago she bought popcorn at the Wisconsin Odeon *and saved the bag.* Now she microwaves popcorn at home, packs it into the Odeon bag and smuggles it inside a big purse. "Open the purses of half the women who go to movies," she says, "you'll find enough food to keep Mitch Snyder in high cotton."

People like to eat at movies—except *The Cook, the Thief, His Wife & Her Lover.* Going to a movie is strenuous enough without making food a crime.

When was the last time you went to a kids' movie? That's a real treat. By 5 P.M. on a weekend, either the aisles are so sticky from spilled soda that it feels like you're walking on flypaper, or so slippery you take one step and slide all the way down to the screen. They don't need a vacuum between shows, they need a Zamboni.

And how about the people who like to talk through an entire movie? Really, *the entire movie.* It's unbelievable. Continuous conversation, like they're in their living room, which is annoying enough, but it gets worse—at critical junctures they start shouting at the screen.

"Don't go through that door, fool."

"No! No! He's in there. He'll slash your lips off."

"Don't you see him? DON'T YOU SEE HIM?"

Boot goofballs like these from the movies. Leave the eaters in peace. The flacks have to stop peddling their phony baloney about "the odor" of hot food bothering the customers. You can't stand within five blocks of any theater without gagging at the overpowering aroma of buttered popcorn, so who's kidding whom?

Face it, the notion of the movie theater as chapel is history. The genie is out of the bottle. This whole Film Food Feud is a consequence of home movie rentals. Through the magic of the VCR, we've learned it's easy to watch a movie and eat a good meal at the same time. Jujubes won't cut it anymore, and nobody is going to pay black-market prices for popcorn. Theaters are going to have to offer menus, and not simply yuppie grazing items such as blue corn chips and Evian. Man About Town Chip Muldoon is predicting Domino's delivering pizzas to the K-B Fine Arts, and promising he'll be there in person when the first Ridgewells catering truck pulls up at the Avalon.

Perpetual Parenthood

My friend Dan, who is my age—which is to say, much too old to be comparison shopping for Huggies and Pampers—just had a baby. This is Dan's second wife and second family. He'd had two babies previously, during the Nixon administration, so it has been a while between spit-ups.

Courtney is two months old, and not yet sleeping through the night. And so the other night, Dan found himself with a warm bottle in his hand at 4 A.M. as new fathers often do. "I was rocking her," he said, "and she was almost asleep, and I thought if I sang to her, that might do it. Then I realized the only song I know is 'Thunder Road.'"

Anyway, men being pigs, I asked Dan why he was doing the 4 A.M. feeding.

The first time around, in the Nixon administration, Dan's wife handled the 4 A.M. This was the standard arrangement in those last-gasp days of the single-income household, when men were the providers and women were the nurturers. It worked passably well for five thousand years, until the invention of the summer home.

Now everyone works and everyone feeds.

Dan and Meg have arrived at a *changer* and *feeder* system. The changer is the preferable role, as you hand off to the feeder, having amused the baby while the bottle was being prepared. As most men would, Dan has tried everything to become the permanent changer, a sort of designated hitter of parenting. He has offered lame reasons, such as "She drinks better with you," and inspired reasons, such as "She's so beautiful and looks so much like you, that I weep when I feed her, and the salt from my tears will get in her mouth and cause colic." Needless to say, nothing has worked, which is what you get, I say, for marrying a Harvard woman.

All this talk about babies got me thinking about lies we tell ourselves about being parents—like how we'd never give our children pacifiers. Pacifiers, yeeccchh! Not only do they look awful, but they'll push the kid's teeth out of line. And they only work for a few minutes, if you've got the Gerber baby. The rest of us are trying to Black & Decker the pacifier into Junior's mouth. "So he'll get braces, okay?"

And you swore you'd never smack your kid, right? Oh God, no, hit a child! Never. I'll reason with mine. I'll never resort to force. Which is fine, until you paint yourself into this corner:

"Okay, Billy, time for bed."

"Billy, bedtime."

"Now's the time, Bill. Go to bed."

"I'm not going to ask you again, William."

"Look, Billy, you either go to bed now or I'm gonna crack you."

Whoops! Did I say that? Did I actually put myself in the put-up or shut-up position with a four-year-old? Gaaaackkk! (This is why it's always better to use this last line: "Billy, if you don't go to bed right now, I'll kill the dog.")

Having had to smack the kid to save face, you now spend the next half-hour cozying up to him trying to convince him you aren't the monster you seemed when you gave him a *zetz*. "Can

I make it up to you, son? Would ice cream help? C'mon, let's go get some ice cream. Tell you what, let's go to Paris and get some ice cream. We'll go to Paris, we'll get some ice cream. Your mom said you were annoying her, and I asked, 'What do you want me to do about it?' And she said something that sounded like 'Spank him.' I thought it was spank. It could have been spahn-kee, a cold-water fish they serve in Stockholm. Anyway, it hurt me more than it hurt you.''

And is there anything quite as terrifying as having to discipline your kid in a public place? Which is, naturally, the only place they'll drop straight to the floor and begin howling, straight out of the last scene in *Carrie*. It does no good to say to the people who have gathered around, "I didn't even touch him. Honest." My advice is to head for the frozen foods and pretend it's somebody else's kid. Eventually, he'll either calm down or join the army.

Scenes like this are why, when I take my children shopping, I only go to stores I don't care if I ever go back to again. Like a discount food warehouse. Who cares what your kids do there? You'll never see any of these shoppers again unless it's at a police lineup. The floor there, busted melons everywhere. It looks like Beirut after a thunderstorm. And above the din, this is what you hear clear as a bell, the words you've come to say so often, though you swore you never would: "Because I said so."

Dining at Chez Tray

Ladies and gentlemen, I propose a toast to American ingenuity: Let us raise our Styrofoam cups and celebrate the fortieth anniversary of the TV dinner!

Now, in honor of Swanson, which sent the press release that made this column possible, let's chew and eat our plastic foam cups.

Which actually taste better than Salisbury steak.

(The allegedly edible Salisbury steak can be described as something that, if you stared at it, you'd realize looks like something your dog found in the backyard.)

"Ooooh, Salisbury steak," Mr. Henry, America's most beloved feature writer, said recoiling. "What was that shine on top of the Salisbury steak? That sort of oil slick?"

Ah, the memories.

That crust around the edge of the mashed potatoes that left a pasty rim of white clinging to the aluminum tray and gave you an uneasy feeling that something had gone wrong in the test kitchen; the tray itself, the way the taste of metal got into everything, particularly the gravy, and made you feel you were munching on a ball of tinfoil; that little scream your fork made as it cut through the soggy turkey and scraped along the bottom of the tray. My teeth hurt just thinking about it.

TV dinners proved this about Americans: We'll eat *anything* as long as it's easy to prepare.

The TV dinner was born in the post–World War II convenience boom, when for the first time American homes were casually being stocked with washers, dryers, and other modern appliances, like that little blue thing they hung inside the gas station toilet bowl. The fact that somebody came up with a prepackaged dinner to be eaten specifically in front of a TV acknowledged the TV as the only worthwhile thing in the house—including your parents.

You can tell I grew up on TV dinners, because to this day every time I see a piece of fried chicken, I think of *Sea Hunt*.

The TV dinner was supposed to be great for the family, because:

1. It would give Mom more free time.
2. It would bring everyone in the family together for dinner.

Well, it did give Mom more free time, which she used to read Betty Friedan, and she figured out what a lousy deal she'd been getting all these years, so she left and took an apartment in the city and left us with a pile of fetid aluminum trays; a hell of a lot of good that did us. Now Mom is an arbitrageur and she hasn't been home in three months. She occasionally leaves a note: "Won't be home for dinner. Stick something in the microwave."

And it did bring the family closer together, because in those days nobody had more than one TV, and the screen was twelve inches wide. And we gathered like little rodents, with our TV dinners perched on those wobbly folding tables with the ridiculous dwarf legs and the tops that were either maps of the states or vaguely Polynesian landscapes, with butterflies and grass. And we watched shows such as *Father Knows Best*—which wouldn't get produced now because (a) there were no single parents in it, no dysfunctional parents, no divorced or dead parents, and no loudmouthed kids turning their backs on their parents and saying, "Kiss my butt," and (b) nobody thinks Father knows *anything* anymore. So it brought the family together, but because the family was watching TV nobody said a word—not even "pass the potatoes," since each TV dinner came with its own portion of potatoes, approximately the size of a pat of butter and with the texture of tile grout.

The early TV dinners weren't that convenient, actually; they took about fifty minutes to cook. Technically, a man could cook them, but when dads came home from work in those days, they often started drinking heavily. A dad could get pretty soused in fifty minutes. By the time the dinner was ready, he'd forgotten all about it. If the timer's alarm bell was real loud, he might think he was back in Anzio, and dive behind the couch.

I remember cooking TV dinners (which I preferred over pot pies, where you needed a chain saw to get through the Paleolithic crust, only to discover there was no actual chicken in there) and not eating them because they took so long to make that by the time they were done I'd already eaten fourteen bags of potato chips. It was a shame, too, because I'd done so much preparation: You had to fork-stab the main course and make a tent of the tinfoil over the potatoes, and with twenty minutes to go, peel the foil back from the apple crumb—you could get second-degree burns doing that.

Sadly, the original concept of the TV dinner is unworkable today. You can't gather the family together around the TV anymore, because everyone has his own TV. Anyway, no family eats together nowadays under any circumstances. The parents are out of town: The dad is in the woods beating his chest and eating pine cones, and the mom is at a commodity-trading seminar. The teenage daughter is a vegetarian and hasn't spoken to her parents since joining People for the Ethical Treatment of Animals and splashing deer urine on the leather sofa. And the teen-age son stays in his room and watches endless repeats of Salt-n-Pepa videos and listens to *Tony Bennett Unplugged*. The last thing intelligible he said was: "Pass the remote." You fear he couldn't tell the difference between *Sea Hunt* and C-SPAN.

I miss the old days.

I miss having my metal tray table collapse twice each meal and having to pick corn from my mohair sweater.

I almost miss Salisbury steak.

What a Way to Get Ahead

We begin today by quoting a wire story that would be a testament to good old American ingenuity—if it hadn't happened in Tokyo: "To gain the minimum height requirement to be a sumo wrestler, a Japanese teenager had six inches of silicone implanted under his scalp. Takeji Harada, sixteen, who had failed six previous eligibility tests, finally made the grade in June—thanks to the huge bulge on his head, which added about six inches to his height."

Hmmm.

Lesser journalists than I might be tempted to poke fun at a story such as this, failing to give due consideration to unfamiliar cultural imperatives. After all, this story originates in a society that remains largely mysterious to most Westerners, and we must resist the urge to draw unfair and insensitive conclusions. Still, the story does raise several intriguing scientific questions. Such as:

1. What will he wrestle as, "The Magnificent Beldar"?
2. What a putz.

Anyway, it's not that I don't feel sympathy for Mr. Harada. I do—though I must admit that if I had the opportunity to add a few strategic inches to one of my body parts, my head wouldn't be my first option. *Note to copy editors: Please delete previous joke so I am not fired. Thank you.* The sumo story notes that Mr. Harada's presurgery height was only five feet two inches, and that is hardly his fault—although I'm wondering what kind of high school guidance counselors they have in Japan; shouldn't somebody have said to him, "Sumo? Jockey!"

But why would there be a height requirement for becoming a sumo wrestler anyway? Please don't tell me there is a deep concern for the health of the wrestlers, because we are talking about men who are literally as fat as cows. They weigh 550 pounds. Their cholesterol count is probably higher than the Nikkei average. If you lined up four 550-pound guys, and three were five eight and one was five two, do you honestly think anybody would point at the five-two guy and say, "Will you get a load of *that* tub of lard!" So I feel bad that Mr. Harada was discriminated against because of his height.

On the other hand, having six inches of silicone implanted under your scalp is a hilarious act of desperation. The boy can't really believe this operation has made him *taller*. All that has happened is that some doctor—and where'd he go to medical school, Kuala *Lump*ur? Hahahaha—turned his head into a speed bump! It's sort of like some kid with a D average and 430 combined on his college boards trying to get into Harvard by wearing an Einstein mask.

What's the attraction of being a sumo anyway? As a sports expert, I can attest to the fact that sumo wrestlers are basically hugely fat men with enormous, jiggly bodies. They tie their hair into buns, and they wear diapers. Their job consists of consuming disgusting quantities of rich foods and competing in maybe two matches a year, matches lasting, at most, four seconds each, and entailing no risk of injury beyond being belly-bounced rudely on one's behind—in return for which they receive gargantuan sums of money, are worshiped as gods incarnate, and must fight off phalanxes of lithe ninety-five-pound vixens who want to have acrobatic sex with them constantly.

I mean, who would want *that?*

Okay, so young Mr. Harada was definitely motivated. But even if he had his heart set on getting these implants to become a sumo—"The Silicone Sumo" does have a ring to it—wouldn't it have been smarter to take the injections in the feet, not the head? If he adds six inches to each foot, he's pretty much living with built-in platform heels, like John Travolta in *Saturday Night Fever*. Worse comes to worst, if the sumo thing falls through, he can put on a Qiana shirt and get a job as the world's fattest disco dancer. Now, with this conehead, all he can be is a coatrack.

Finally, in the interests of science, and with basic human concern for Mr. Harada, I asked my research team to telephone an expert in the uses of silicone, who revealed many valuable and frightening things. First, silicone injected directly under the skin tends to "migrate," which is to say it kind of redistributes itself all over the body, sometimes in vaguely unnerving and embarrassing manners. Let us just say that one day you can have a large and inviting bosom, and the next day you could have a smaller bosom and, say, a tail. So Mr. Harada might soon find himself too short once again to be a sumo wrestler, but, for example, perfectly designed as a unicorn, or a bean bag chair.

On the positive side, my expert mentioned that among its many uses, silicone is a key ingredient of Simethicone, a drug that reduces one's output of flatulence. I don't know how this might affect Mr. Harada, but considering his girth and diet, surely it can't be bad.

Taking the Fourth

I hate America.

I begin this way because that is how many readers are going to interpret this anyway, so why not just give them something solid to kvetch about?

Actually, though, I love America. It's the Fourth of July I hate.

Note to letter writers: Yes, this MUST mean I hate America. Have at me. Thank you.

Here's my take on the Fourth: It's about bug bites, bad food, and blowing yourself up. You have to spend the whole day outside in this miserable, steamy summer heat surrounded by people with striated fat rolls that look like Hostess Ho-Hos and armpit stains that resemble the puddles one might find under a '66 Corvair after a front-end collision. You start drinking *way* too early because (1) you're horrified by the sight of these people—who are ordinarily barred from all public places, including Wal-Mart—and (2) it's the only way to lighten the load of the stupid cooler you're lugging around. So by noon you are in desperate need of a bathroom, and the line for the Porta-John stretches to Tegucigalpa, and as you stand there, *shvitzing* like a poodle, you think to yourself: How has it come to this, that I'm the only one without a tattoo?

And then it is two o'clock, and you're sick of the Frisbees, and you're beyond sunburned and into charred—people are looking at your face, which is the color of a prized beefsteak tomato, and asking sympathetically, "Ooooh, doesn't that hurt?" And after awhile you start saying things like, "Well, it would hurt but fortunately my leprosy has deadened all my nerve endings," and then you sneeze on them. And you cannot look at any more of that hideous yellow potato salad that reminds you of the John Lennon line: "yellow-matter custard dripping from a dead dog's eye." And it occurs to you there are STILL SEVEN MORE HOURS UNTIL THE FIREWORKS!

You're stuck in this shimmering heat, being pecked at by mosquitoes the size of onions. Your kids are yapping, but at least you can bop them upside the head. It's the other people's kids' yapping that's driving you nuts. There aren't enough Handi Wipes in creation to get the watermelon juice off your face and hands. It's gridlock; you can't move because every inch of grass is covered with blankets. There's a tuba band warming up, and it's just what you want to hear—the 237th rendition of "The Stars and Stripes Forever and Ever and Ever." It's like being trapped in a really bad Chevy Chase movie. AND THERE ARE STILL SEVEN MORE HOURS UNTIL THE FIREWORKS! No wonder more postal workers become disgruntled on July 5 than on any other day.

Now let's just once tell the truth about the fireworks.

They aren't any good.

The problem with fireworks is that fireworks technology has not appreciably changed since they were invented six thousand years ago to impress the emperor of China, who wore the skins of dead opossums on his behind, and a jingly hat that looked like Santa Claus's underpants. My point is that, back then, people were far more primitive and easy to please. Now fireworks are passé. Rent any Arnold Schwarzenegger movie and you'll see a man's face disintegrate and melt into a snake, and live chickens fly out his eyeballs. So what's something that goes *boom* compared with that? If the guy setting off the fireworks doesn't blow himself up right in front of your eyes like Tommy Lee Jones, or transmogrify into a dinosaur or a griffin and carry away a baby in his teeth, what's the big deal? This is someone's idea of a good time—staring at a few exploding pinwheels like a dodo, then having the soot settle on you like you're standing at a bus stop under Mount St. Helens?

To try to appeal to more demanding tastes, fireworks makers have moved away from displays that merely explode into clusters of colors and have begun producing gimmicky effects that look like something familiar. Remember during the Gulf War celebration when the fireworks formed all those purple hearts and yellow ribbons? Well, things have gotten a little out of hand since then.

"Oooh, honey, look, it's . . . a, a bagel!"

"Ooooh, a Pez dispenser!"

"Ooooh, health care reform!"

The other thing I hate about fireworks is that they begin around a week before the Fourth, suddenly startling you in the middle of dinner, and the dog gets scared and throws up, and the kids crawl under your bed. It's like living in Beirut—only the bread is fresher. This occurs because people start buying fireworks weeks before the Fourth, as soon as those ghastly wooden fireworks kiosks go up. Every June they spring up, like toadstools. You'll be walking along an elegant tree-lined boulevard, past a Christian Science reading room, with the Washington Monument gracefully towering in the horizon, and suddenly you come upon something that looks like an outhouse from the Ozarks, manned by two people in bib overalls ready to sell your kids more rockets than Kim Il Sung.

Anyway, why do we need to celebrate our independence

from England? England is about the only country in the world that still talks to us without Jimmy Carter going over there first.

We built this holiday in praise of the Revolutionary War, which is definitely not politically correct anymore. Celebrating our independence from another country implies that we consider ourselves better than those people. The sensitive American of the '90s wouldn't want to be independent of the British, he'd want to share our cultural diversity with them. If Patrick Henry made a speech today, he wouldn't say, "Give me liberty or give me death!" He'd say, "Give me liberty . . . or if that offends you in any way, I'll accept a modest cost-of-living increase."

As far as holidays go, I rank the Fourth of July *waaay* down there. In fact, I don't like any of the commonly recognized holidays—too commercial. My three favorite holidays are:

1. The first day every spring when the ice-cream man shows up, because he brings joy to all the little children of the neighborhood (and, uh, also because the ice-cream man's appearance generally coincides with the first day women resume wearing halter tops).

2. The day every autumn when you set the clocks back (it is the only time in life one can actually gain time, outside of prison).

3. July 3, which is National Columnists' Day, where no matter how stinko our copy is, you are obliged to read it all the way to the end, and praise us—and you are not even allowed to object to cheap halter-top jokes.

One Man's Edible Complex

I took my kids to the pool the other day and caught a glimpse of myself in the lifeguard's mirrored sunglasses. (A babe, I might add, so I was actually trying to suck in my stomach; if I had sucked any harder, I'd have inhaled the whole pool.) It was appalling. I was so bald, so fat, so white, I looked like the underside of Free Willy.

Why do middle-aged men get so sloppy? We stand around, exposing our big bellies, and from the side we look like an avalanche.

I think it stems from the way men eat.

Men eat foods that come in slabs.

Slabs and mounds. A slab between two mounds, often yellowish mounds—either by design or age.

This eliminates everything green, everything that swims, and everything that might keep you alive past midnight Wednesday.

It's easy to buy food for a man: Just buy something with a large bone in it that he can wrestle with, and gnaw on, then walk away from with barbecue sauce and flecks of char stuck on his cheek.

Women are not like this.

Women do not enjoy making a display of themselves when they eat.

Women dread it when a man says, "You wanna go for ribs?" (which men always want, because it comes in a slab).

That's the last thing women want—to spend all evening sucking sauce off their fingers and picking corn from their teeth.

Women are like cats. They like to eat from a bowl. They'll eat a little bit, then leave the rest for later.

Men are like dogs. They eat everything in front of them.

Men do not even taste their food. Their task is simply to finish it as quickly as possible.

"Hey, Eddie, what was that thing you just ate, that thing that looked like a piece of fried stuff?"

"I don't know. It was brown, right?"

It is a waste of time for a waiter to recite any of the day's specials to a table full of men. (If it was a waitress, the men would not have listened to anything she said, because men don't ever actually listen to women—they simply wait for a woman to get through talking; then a man understands it is his turn to speak.) Whenever the waiter gets to the last special, say, "fresh sea bass, lightly battered and sautéed in a balsamic vinaigrette, with cilantro and basil, and a bouquet of garden vegetables almondine," a man, realizing he has run out of choices, will say, "Good. Gimme that, and put some nacho cheese on top, okay? And fries."

When men are finished with their food, they pause for a second or so—making a big show of how they are pausing, so you'll understand they are trying to act polite—then they go around the table and eat the food off the plates of the women and children.

"You done with that?" a man will ask impatiently, which reminds me of a joke I cannot tell here, about what Jeffrey said to Lorena.

Women know how this game is played. Women deliberately

leave 20 percent of their food so that men can finish it. Women get their revenge, though, by mixing their foods together.

Men hate this. God, how they hate mixed foods! ("Look, don't put the peas so they are touching the potatoes, okay?")

If a man designed fine china, it would all look like TV dinner trays, with separate compartments for every item in the meal. Men eat one thing at a time.

Every man has a different order, but all men eat purposefully and sequentially. Women eat randomly. (Much the way they shop. They can end up buying *anything*! A man goes in for shirts, this is his task, shirts; he buys his shirts, he leaves.) Women like to mix things. They order premixed things, such as risotto, then mix in more things. They commingle; they create. You look at a woman's plate, it looks like an artist has painted it. You look at a man's plate, it looks like Rin Tin Tin has licked it.

Watch how differently men and women eat at a cocktail party. A woman will "plate-hop." She will circle once. She will take something from this tray, and something from that tray, and a couple of things from the table in the center of the room, and she will put all these things on a small plate and nibble at them for the rest of the party. A man will go straight to the swinging doors and camp there, a toothpick in hand, picking off whatever comes out on a tray, like he's defoliating the jungle. He will put nothing on a plate—he isn't even holding a plate—he will stand there, sniping away. Get him a shovel.

Women know this. And still, women care about how they look eating in front of men.

"Women don't eat at all on the first date," my friend Annie told me. "We don't want a guy to think we're pigs. We order something light, something we can pick at; psychologically we're trying to show him that we're picky with food, and we're picky with men—also, we don't want to give him the impression that if he stays with us, he'll wake up one day twenty years down the road and see he's married to Bossy the Cow. A woman never orders spinach on a first date, because it sticks to your teeth, and it's always there when you smile; never garlic or onion; never spaghetti, even if you like spaghetti, because you don't want to eat anything that might hang out your mouth. Never order dessert either, don't even take a bite when he orders two."

"Aren't you hungry?" I asked.

"Starving!" Annie said. "The moment he drops you off, you head straight for the Häagen-Dazs and sit there in a housecoat, stuffing yourself just like . . ."

A man.

The Sexual Life
of the Sponge

Once again we visit the war between the sexes. Today's topic is: residential hygiene.

The other night my friend Walt was hosting a poker game. Walt is no longer married, a condition that becomes apparent when you smell the sponge in his kitchen sink—which you can probably do right now, from where you are sitting. Men are not hung up on sponges. Men will buy a new sponge only after the previous one disintegrates into little wads and falls down the drain. (I can say proudly that I have had to change sponges just twice since 1989.)

Walt also does not go to extreme lengths to tidy up for company. Walt did what most men do to prepare for other men coming over: not a damn thing. He left the small piles of dust in the corners, the rotten fruit on the countertop, the caked-on Prego sauce on the floor, and the newspapers on the kitchen and dining-room tables.

"You saving these for any particular purpose?" I asked Walt.

"I got a lot of reading to catch up on," he said.

"I guess so," I said, holding up a paper with the headline REAGAN FIRES AIR TRAFFIC CONTROLLERS.

Men can do disagreeable stuff if they want to. They will slice a fish from head to tail and scoop out the guts with their bare hands. They would eat a bowl of maggots if they thought it would get them tickets to the Super Bowl. (Some schlemiel in Buffalo, N.Y., actually did this, in a radio promotion. He didn't win. The winner had jumped into a vat of horse poop.) But men will not take the hairball out of the bathroom sink.

The other day, after getting in touch with my feminine side, I went on a cleaning binge. I bought an aerosol can of bathroom cleaner and sprayed it all over. I made the fatal error of spraying it on the mirror. When I went to wipe it off, it left a cloudy film you couldn't get off with a sandblaster. The mirror is now ruined, and I don't consider this my fault. I was doing a good deed by cleaning the bathroom, and I bought something specifically labeled a bathroom cleaner. There should have been a note attached that said: "Tony, Do Not Buy This Product. *You Are Too Stupid to Use It."*

Take towels. A man will use the same bath towel forever. He figures: I take a shower. My body is then clean. I wipe off my clean body with a towel, then drop it on the floor. Therefore, the towel remains hygienically pure for infinity.

I asked my friend Richie: When do you change towels?

"When the old one has a big hole," he said.

He then called me back to add this: "I forgot about the dog. I'll change the towel if I use it to dry off the dog a few times. I'll let the kids use it a few times after that—but not me."

It's pretty much the same with sheets. A guy will sleep on the same sheet for, oh, six to eight months—or until he becomes concerned that the color has changed in the middle. Then he can turn it over and get four more months out of it. Oh sure, lying down on a new, crisp, cool sheet is a delightful feeling. But you can get that same feeling by just opening the window.

Men are always fascinated when they go to their mother's

house and see thirty-two sheets in the linen closet. What can she be thinking? Who's coming over, the Dallas Cowboys? The most anybody needs is two sheets: one on the bed, and one to replace it. Man About Town Chip Muldoon has narrowed it down even further: "It only takes a couple of hours to wash and dry a sheet," he says. "So I do it in the afternoon, when I'm not using my bed. If I get tired, I nap on the couch."

Towels, sheets . . . dishes. If there were no women in the world, one thing that I am certain of—aside from the fact that there would be no reason for anyone to ever take a shower—is that the fine china industry would not exist. All plates, bowls, serving trays, and even punch bowls would be made out of cardboard. This is because men don't wash. Men throw out and buy new. Cost is not a problem. Men would simply factor into their budget $260 a week for "paper products."

A woman I know complains that her husband never picks up his socks. "He drops them all over the house," she says. "Why can't he pick them up and put them in the hamper?"

The answer is simple: He is making a pile. This is high art, for the male gender. Men love to make piles. (However, men don't sort, nor do they fold.) This starts in early childhood when boy children go into the backyard and make a big pile of dirt— half of which they eat—and girl children respond by making a face and saying, "Eeewwwww!"

Piles are part of the male birthright. It's a hunting-and-gathering response—an instinct, like channel surfing to find naked women. In my room I have piles of clothes on the chair, the bed, and the top of the cedar chest. I haven't worn some of these clothes in years. It's possible they aren't even *my* clothes—they may have come with the house. But being a creature of habit like most men, I can't imagine my room without them. So when I go to sleep I gently move the pile from the bed onto the chair. Or when I want to sit on the chair, I gently move that pile of clothes to the bed. In this way, I suppose, I could be called a nurturer.

Noting how much time I have spent through the years moving the piles, a woman once asked me why I simply don't put the clothes in my drawers.

How naïve. Then where would I put all my paper plates?

THIS IS
THE MODERN
WORLD

*

Call Me, Ishmael

Once upon a time the telephone was your friend. It connected you with the world at large and filled your life with happy, carefree sounds of friendship.

It was a wondrous machine. It was made of the same dense, black material as a bowling ball. The receiver weighed as much as an unabridged thesaurus; if you dropped it on your foot, you were in traction for a month. It sat on its own special table, because if you put it on the wall, the wall would collapse. It was simple and direct: It rang, you answered.

Now your phone looks like Lieutenant Uhura's instrument panel, in tasteful pastels. You're filled with dread each time it rings—like hearing a knock at your front door. Nobody in his right mind opens his door. Who comes to your house anymore? Either a Bible study group or an ax murderer. Everybody else phones.

It could be the office wanting you to do more work. (Can you ever remember, even once, when they called to give you less work?) It could be your child's school telling you little Stevie has green phlegm, and he's hawking it into the water fountain, and the girls are shrieking, and you must come and get him *now*! It could be another infernal computerized recording, offering you credit cards, or vacation homes, or an organic banana that cures manic-depressiveness.

All calls are bad. So you stop answering. You have Caller ID to identify who's calling, and reject them. You have Call Block to preempt certain callers from ever getting through. You have an answering machine so you can sit there and screen calls. The more sophisticated your phone service, the less you have to talk to people. The ultimate goal in the '90s is no conversations, only messages. I know a guy who has an answering machine on his car phone! Now, you know that guy is ducking your call, because a car phone isn't activated unless someone's in the car. Why won't he take your call? He's too busy talking to a jack-in-the-box at a drive-thru?

I am a misanthrope. I do not want Call Waiting. I do not want a phone in my car. I do not want Call Forwarding. Send me a postcard. (I want Call Far-Forwarding, so I can send your calls to Yugoslavia, and you pay the charges.) I do not want Call Trace. I'm not bucking for a Junior G-Man badge.

Mine is the only house in America that does not have an answering machine. I just take the phone off the hook, and you get a busy signal. Why should I let robbers know I'm not home? Don't you love the people who have a message on their machine that says "I can't come to the phone right now . . ." as though this inspired bit of caginess is going to hoodwink a burglar. "Duh, Spike, we better not hit the Kornheiser home. He's there, but he can't come to the phone. He's probably in the bathroom."

(Oh, you don't think robbers call first? You think they just take a chance and show up? You think you're smart enough to have all these high-tech sensors on the windows and the shoot-on-sight armed response, and they're so dumb they come in with a crowbar, like in *Home Alone*? Grow up. If I did have a machine, I'd record a message that said: "I'll be back in five minutes. I'm picking up a mail-order AK-47 at the post office. Why don't you come over and wait for me? Don't worry about the Doberman. I'm pretty sure I fed him this morning.")

I hate answering machines. Everybody's either a comedian or a disc jockey. "This is John. I'm not here right now. But my friend Jimmy Cagney is, and he'd like to speak to you. You dirty rat, Looie, you killed my brudder. And whoa! Look who just walked into the room. It's Jimmy Stewart. Wu-wu-wu-wuhhh, well, John's not here right now, but if you leave a mu-mu-mu-muuuhhh, message, he'll get back to you." Then you hear this moronic music, often the theme from *The Flintstones*, which goes on for fifteen minutes. By the time it's your turn to speak, the call has already cost you $2,000. This is clever? This putz doing imitations really thinks he's clever?

I don't have Call Waiting, either. Maybe I'm old-fashioned, but if I want to have every third word interrupted by clicking, I'll dial Jiminy Cricket. So now they have Silent Call Waiting. All you hear is dead air. I don't believe there is such a thing as Silent Call Waiting. I believe the person you're talking to just goes off and makes a slice of toast. I think they have Toast Waiting. And when they come back they always say, "Look, I've got to take this other call." No problem. Have a nice lunch.

Now there's Repeat Call to redial the last number you called if it's busy—in almost the same amount of time it would take you to actually do it yourself. I don't need Repeat Call. I might like Petite Call, for short conversations. Or Conceit Call, for recorded messages about how fabulous I am. Or even Discreet Call, for how fabulous we might be together.

They have Select Forward so you can choose which calls will be forwarded. My select forward is Charles Barkley. (Taking calls is much easier than making calls. To call people from a public phone with a credit card you have to dial a thirty-nine-digit code to make contact with the appropriate operator. Then you punch in the number you want and the number of your credit card. That's twenty-four more numbers. You have to be Rain Man to use a pay phone.)

There is also Priority Call, which lets you pick up six telephone numbers that will "ring in a special way." What do they mean, special? Like, if it was somebody really fat, would the phone moo? I want the ring to sound like another five hundred bucks being flushed down the toilet, so I'll know it's my deadbeat brother Stanley calling.

The most intriguing new offering is Call Block, which lets you stonewall six numbers completely. They never get through. I don't know where the calls go, and I don't care. Let them all go to Larry King.

I want callers to hear, "Tony Kornheiser requests that you suck wind."

Here's the ones I block:

My editor. No way am I coming in to rewrite this column.

Anyone to whom I ever said, "Please call if you're in town."

My cousin Marsha's husband Wally, the forensic taxidermist.

Sally Jessy Raphaël. Because I've had it with those glasses.

King Hussein.

ChemLawn.

And, of course, Cliff Robertson, Candice Bergen, and James Earl Jones. Don't call me, I'll call you.

Sorry, I Don't Do Windows

I finally did it. I went out and bought a home computer. It's absolutely *fabulous*. You won't believe all the things it can do. It can do budgets and banking. It can make maps. It can do my taxes. It can play CDs. It can speak Creole. It can make malteds.

Unfortunately, I can't use it.

I've had it for a month. I can plug it in. I can turn it on. After that I'm lost. I sit there staring at a blank screen, waiting for it to do something magical on its own, like it's the Oracle at Delphi. The only thing I can do on that screen is Windex it.

Here is what the screen says:

C:>

That's it. That's as far as I've gotten. The colon, I sense, is telling me I am expected to do something.

So I type in: Help.

Now the screen reads C:> Hepl.

Oop. I am not good at this. I get nervous and make mistakes. So I correct my spelling, and hit Enter.

The computer answers: Bad file name.

So I type in something else.

Now the screen reads: C:> Please, Please, Please Help.

The computer answers: Bad file name. Abort?

I want to abort. God, I want to abort. I want to abort this whole mission. I am unworthy. I am a squashed skunk on the information superhighway.

It's a funny story how I got the computer. As you know, I type columns for a living. I've been doing it for twenty-five years. A few weeks ago my typewriter broke, and I went out to buy another one. The last one I bought, an Olivetti Lettera 32, cost about $80, so factoring in inflation, I figured a new Olivetti would be about $110—which it would have been if anyone in the world made typewriters anymore. Asking for a typewriter at an office products store is like going into a Rite-Aid and asking the pharmacist for leeches. They look at you like you are a virus.

Which is how I came to spend $2,500 on the world's most expensive typewriter.

The computer came with an instruction book the thickness of *Roget's Thesaurus,* only with smaller printing. I started to read it, and stopped after about ten minutes. I felt like Fabio leafing through Kierkegaard.

So I called the store and said I was computer-illiterate. They said I could buy a video that would take me through the steps of the computer's operations—and I'd do that, except I don't know how to use my VCR.

As you may have guessed, I am technophobic. I still don't own a portable phone. I don't have direct deposit. I cut up my ATM card because I was afraid that if I ever used it, it would somehow transfer all my money to a butcher shop in Paraguay. I'm sure that if I had been alive when the wheel was invented, I'd be the last yutz dragging a caribou carcass with a rope.

My children come in, and they start playing around with the computer fearlessly, the way people my age used to play with a hula hoop. They create files effortlessly; they vary typefaces and colors; they play games against the computer. (I thought a hard drive was when you had to clear 180 yards of water off the tee.)

I watch my eleven-year-old daughter fly around the Windows program, and it occurs to me that the way I look at her, in utter amazement, must be the way my parents looked the first time they saw Mr. Pitagorsky's brand-new Philco television set. Good Lord, Rhoda, how did Garry Moore squeeze himself into that little box?

I'd like to be part of the swinging computer crowd. I'd like to have an "address" on the Internet where I would have a swell sign-on like anthonikorn@boomshakkalakkalakka. I'd like to be able to share in the joke when the punch line is, "So I downloaded, see, and it runs an uplink and comes up star bat dot CMD!" I know funny, and that's funny.

But I am hopeless.

(And I'm not the only one. Recently my smart friend Martha could not get her computer to work. She'd turn the machine on and the screen would fill with small, fuzzy shapes, like a Jackson Pollock painting that had been thrown in the toilet. When the repairman came over and removed the top of the computer—which they refer to as "opening the pizza box"—he found, to Martha's horror, so much matted cat hair that it looked like a muskrat was lodged in there.)

At *The Washington Post*, I am famous for my ineptitude at the computer. The newspaper has a giant computer system that everyone in the building, including the janitorial staff, has mastered except for me. I have learned how to sign on and type stories. I don't know how to sign off because I never absolutely had to learn, since the computer signs you off automatically after ten minutes or so of no typing. This is fine, except this means that for ten minutes or so after I have already gone home, my computer is sitting there in my office, signed on as Tony Kornheiser. This means anyone can come in and send E-mail messages to anyone else in the *Post*, and the messages will appear to have come from me.

I know this must happen because periodically I get return

messages from people whom I have not, to my knowledge, com-
municated with. They go like this one, from the Lord High Assistant Managing Executive Publisher:

"Tony: My behind would be even larger than you seem to
think it is, but fortunately I get to exercise it frequently by punt-
ing fat, aging, bald, not-so-funny-anymore columnists out the
door."

Not Lawn
for This World

"What is it with men and their obsession about lawns?" my smart friend Martha wondered. All week she has watched her beau agonize over his "lawn," a six-by-two-foot patch of earth between the curb and the sidewalk in front of their Georgetown town house. "He's aerated it and fertilized it and seeded and Weedwacked it. Can you believe this? He bought a WEEDWACKER for something that's smaller than the plot in which they're going to bury him! He's been out there on his knees for days trying to grow grass and all he gets are these tiny *threads*—like the hairs you get from Rogaine. I feel so sad for him."

It's a masculinity thing. A man defines himself by his lawn. A good, strong lawn equals a good, strong man. A bad, weak lawn equals . . . you know, ice dancing.

You see the pictures in magazines all the time. Another case of greenis envy. A guy with a scrawny lawn, looking jealously over the fence at a guy with a thick one. The caption ought to say: "Is that a rake in your pocket, or do you use Miracle-Gro?"

"A lawn is the only place around the house where a man shows initiative," my friend Nancy complained. "If they took the same initiative with the laundry or the kitchen floor, the world would be a fairer place.'' Yeah, and if Margaret Thatcher had a wheel on her tuchis she would be a unicycle.

Growing a lawn is simply prologue, though, to the continuing thrill of mowing the lawn. At this time of year, in the first explosive warmth after a hideous winter, a lawn is hormonally supercharged and needs to be mowed every seventy-two hours. It is the horticultural equivalent of Richard Nixon's five o'clock shadow. So, like all men, the problem I faced this week was: With what shall I mow?

Option 1: a scythe. This is that huge crescent-shaped thing actually used, so far as I know, only by Mister Death. For some reason, though, they sell these things at my local hardware store. I always vow I will get one, put on a black bathrobe, and scare the bejesus out of the old man down the street.

Option 2: the old-style manual mower like the one my father had, with the rusty blades that can be sharpened only by a ninety-year-old Italian man driving a wooden truck. The advantage to a push mower is that it'll put me in touch with my lawn—help me feel one with my lawn—and provide a complete aerobic workout. The disadvantage is that I would expire halfway through the first cut, and when the paramedics cart off my body, they'll giggle and say, ''What kind of putz still uses a push mower?''

Option 3: the gas-powered mower. This is one you see everywhere. It looks so easy, even a monkey could work it. Alas, I can't. I'm afraid that I'll hang on to the rip cord too long and the engine will kick in and yank the cord back and my arm will fly off at the shoulder stump and sail away like a helicopter rotor into my neighbor's yard and be eaten by his dog, Woofman Jack.

Option 4: the deluxe riding mower with the leather seat, windshield, and cup holder. The reason to use this mower is that driving it has to be the coolest thing in the world. The reason not to is that my lawn isn't exactly the size of the fifteenth hole at Augusta. I could not actually make a turn on my own property.

These things require the turning radius of a Greyhound Super-cruiser. I could fire that mother up and tear forward about nine feet until I wedged myself into the side fence. Then I'd have to sell the monster mower to someone who owns a helicopter and a big magnet.

So I chose:

Option 5: I went to the bank with a large box, had the teller fill it with United States currency, and walked out into the middle of my street and flagged down a truck with a sign that said ESPERT LANSKAPING, and I gave the driver—a man who had muscles with large blue veins and foreign-language tattoos—all my money and pleaded, "Make me a good lawn, because if I have to do it myself I will have nothing but weeds the size of moose antlers."

"You don't got a green thumb?" he asked.

"Mister, I got thumbs like Fast Eddie Felson in *The Hustler*."

So he put my money in a satchel and grunted. I felt I had closed a canny deal, just like Donald Trump.

He came back the next day and put hay on my front lawn.

"This is to protect the grass seed," he told me.

"Oh, good," I said. "I was afraid you wanted to hold the Kentucky Derby here."

Then he surveyed my lawn, mentioned that "someone ought to trim those bushes," and blew his nose on my crape myrtle tree. For this I gave him $11,000 and agreed to pay for all his children's orthodontia.

I told my friend Annie about this wonderful man who was to be my salvation, and she said she would have joyfully dumped hay on my lawn for $300—and thrown in a bag of charcoal.

My friend Gino contends that paying someone to do your lawn is insane, because no one really knows anything about gardening. He is basing this on an experience he recently had. Desperate to get better tomatoes this year, he actually called the county extension office and spoke to a professional horticulturist (a legal term, which means he takes hookers to the opera), who told him to saturate the garden with something called Milorganite. So he went to Hechinger and bought a few hundred pounds of the stuff, and as he was waiting in line the guy behind him sidled up real close and said in a conspiratorial voice, "People poop."

At this point Gino plastered a sick smile on his face and kind of edged away. But the guy followed him.

"You ain't gonna use that stuff on anything you're gonna eat, are you?"

Gino looked at the label. Sure enough, Milorganite is condensed sewage sludge. There was a warning that it should not be used for vegetable gardens—on account of you aren't supposed to eat its main ingredient.

They worked up a great friendship, there in line. On the guy's advice, Gino bought some other garden stuff, and when he got home, he rushed out to put it on the dirt in his garden. Reading the fine print, he discovered he had purchased cow poop. Which, apparently, you *can* eat.

Who knew?

The Hard Cell

When I purchased my cellular telephone, I thought I was getting a great deal. But as soon as I swaggered out of the store with my $70 telephone, I learned that (a) only a complete imbecile would pay *anything* for a cellular phone, since some places let you have them for literally *one cent* because (b) the true cost of a cellular phone has nothing to do with the actual cost of the phone, but is what you pay each month to make and receive calls, which is $4,000 per minute.

Giving me a cell phone is like giving a kangaroo a food processor. The kangaroo might push the buttons, and something mechanical might happen within the big bowl part—but the kangaroo probably wouldn't make a good remoulade sauce.

I am not good at this sort of stuff. I recently ordered voice mail from the phone company for my home phone. For pennies a month, they turn your phone into an answering machine! So after a few days I picked up the telephone in my kitchen and heard a stuttering *beep-beep-beep-beep* sound before my customary dial tone kicked in. I called the phone company and told them my phone was broken.

They told me the choppy sound was the voice mail indicator that I had a message. I expressed surprise.

"How did you think you would be informed you had a message?" the phone company lady asked me.

"Well, my phone at work has a message light, so I figured my phone at home would light up too," I said.

At this point, the phone company lady got very quiet. Extremely slowly, as though talking to a very small and not very bright child, she asked: "Do you see a bulb anywhere on your home phone that could light up?"

"Well, ah," I stammered, "I thought maybe my hall light would flicker or something."

(I should tell you about the message I recorded for the voice mail. The phone company lady patiently walked me through the steps to get me to the point where I could record a message. But I hadn't planned on what I would say, so when it was my actual turn to speak, I wasn't prepared. And this is exactly what you hear when you call my house: "Uh, I, uh, I've, you know, sort of been dragged kicking and screaming into the technological age, so, uh, well, leave a message and see what happens. Is that okay? Did I do that right? Hello?")

Anyway, my first problem with my new cellular phone was trying to figure out which part you talk into. There's no mouthpiece, no familiar grillwork. Below the last row of numbers, there's a tiny slot, no bigger than an eighth of an inch; you couldn't fit a cat's toenail clipping in it. This, I assume, is where you talk. Or maybe I bought the model where you can only listen; you call people and hear them say, "Hello. Hello. Who is this? Is anybody there?" Then they hang up—which is okay, on account of the aforementioned cost of using the phone.

A lot of people tell you they're buying a cell phone for safety. My friend Jeff said he wants to get one so that in case he's carjacked, he can call 911. Like the robber is going to let you make a phone call. This is a carjacking, not *Barney Miller*. (You may be safer not using a car phone at all. Sometimes when my friend Nancy drives to work in the morning, she has one hand holding the phone, one hand holding a cup of coffee, and then she realizes: My God, I'm driving with my knees!)

The truth is, I have no need for a cell phone. I didn't want one for safety. I wanted it so I could look cool. You know how when you see some guy waiting in line at a restaurant and yakking on a cell phone, and you say to yourself, "What a putz!" Well, I want to be that guy. I want the maitre d' to come over and tell me my table's ready, and then as all the seated diners look at me, I sashay by, and I'm holding my cell phone to my ear, laughing like I'm talking to Bob Hope! I want my neighbors to see me standing out on my stoop on a Sunday morning, wearing a Pierre Cardin bathrobe, walking in tiny circles, talking to my agent! Of course what I'd mostly be saying is: "Is it better now? Can you hear me now?" Because on most cell phones you can't hear a word anybody's saying. It's like trying to talk to Boutros Boutros-Rodham-Ghali in the Holland Tunnel.

But that is beside the point. The fact is, I finally have a cell phone!

"How long have you had it?" my friend Gino asked me.

"Two days," I said.

"And how many calls have you made?" he asked.

"It depends on what you mean by calls," I responded, warily. "Do you mean, where I dial a number, and someone answers, and says 'Hello,' and I say something back?"

"Yes, that would be one call."

"Well, by that strict definition—none," I admitted. "But that is because the calls are so expensive."

Gino looked at me. "No it isn't," he said. "It is because you don't know how to make a call. Prove to me you can use your cell phone."

I tried calling the phone on my desk. I punched in the numbers, then hit *send* and waited for the phone to ring. It didn't.

The display on my cell phone informed me my desk phone was "busy." The only thing it was busy doing was making me look like a doofus.

I tried something easier, 411. Nothing.

So, finally, Gino says, "Look, see if your phone is working. Dial your cell phone from your office phone."

"I, ah, don't know my number," I said.

It was hard to hear what he said next, on account of the guffaws and chortles and spittled snorts and gasps, but basically he urged me to call information for the number.

"I can't," I said. "It's unlisted."

Regrettably, everything in this column is absolutely true. Even:

Anthony is an idiot.

The High-Tech Slow Burn

Same-day dry cleaning; twenty-minute workouts; one-hour photos; instant karma. So much in modern life is designed to help us cut corners and save time. I thought about this the other day after waiting ten-deep on line at a McDonald's to get a grinning salesperson who not only screwed up my order twice ("No, not a Big Mac, a Quarter Pounder with cheese; not a vanilla shake, chocolate; if I asked for fries, would you bring me an apple pie?"), but after finally getting it right, happily told me the Quarter Pounders were gone, and I'd have to wait for a new batch. I've often wondered if it wouldn't be better to go to a fast-food place and simply ask, "What do you have that's ready right now?" But it'd probably be the fish filet that's been sitting under the warming light since Memorial Day. There's no such thing as fast food. But if you've been to any of these places, you already know that.

Isn't it ironic that we spend half our lives waiting for things that are supposed to make our lives quicker and easier?

Raise your hand if you've burned half a tank of gas at a bank drive-thru.

Or frittered away an hour on a supermarket express line,

behind people with more than twelve items who say things like, "Will you accept a personal check from a bank in Burma?"

Or stood in the freezing cold at an automatic teller machine waiting your turn, then punched in your code—approximately as long as the first chapter in *The Great Gatsby*—only to be told they're out of cash, come back tomorrow.

Greetings from the Age of Technology.

Take a seat, we'll be with you when we're damned good and ready.

This is all prologue to a story about buying a computer that will underline how the more things change for the better, the more they get worse. After lunch the other day, I went with a friend to buy this basic computer. We walked west on M Street. I remember being across from House of Salad, and in front of Business Land, and thinking: What happened, were we just tele-ported to Planet of the Morons?

Anyway, she finds the store. She goes in, and immediately spots the one she wants. She tells the salesman she also needs some paper and a cable to plug the computer into a printer. She takes out her checkbook to pay the bill.

All this takes one minute.

The salesman sits down at his computer—a hot-shot deal with multicolor type and fancy graphics—to compose the receipt.

This, as they say in the airline game, is where we start circling.

"I need your address," he says.

He types it into his computer, along with his name, the cashier's name (why would you need the cashier's name?), the date, my friend's name, an invoice number, and an account number. The ability to store all kinds of information has led to an insatiable pursuit of all kinds of information—mostly worthless. The food, as we say at the dinner table, is beginning to get cold.

He types in mysterious codes and slashes, romancing the

computer like this is a deliberate process. Our biological clocks are racing.

Eventually, eight full lines appear on screen. Five of these lines describe options she hasn't bought. I suppose they're noted for archaeological purposes.

She looks at the screen and says, "I thought the computer was $729."

"It is," he says.

"Then why does it say $829?"

He looks at the screen where it says $829. "Did I do that?" he asks.

In order to change the bill he has to go back up through all eight lines of type one at a time. (Does the term *glacial thawing* mean anything to you?) By the time he reaches the top, he's apparently forgotten why he's there, because he announces triumphantly, "That will be $884."

"It can't be," my friend says, nonplussed.

Oops. Again, up we go through the eight lines.

All told, the paperwork took twenty-eight minutes.

"You know," I say, "in the old days, before the computer came along to make your life easier, a salesman could have used a pen and written up a receipt and had you out the door in, oh, maybe as long as two minutes."

"The guy wasn't exactly Einstein at the keyboard," she says.

"Yeah, but you weren't exactly shopping at NASA," I say.

Now my seven-year-old wants a computer, and I can appreciate that it would be a good learning tool. But first I want her to learn to write with a pencil in case she ever has to take a phone message when her computer is on the fritz. Whenever people rely too much on computers, they assume machines are right and people are wrong—and burdensome. The more you depend on a computer, the easier it gets to forget how, as they say, to interface with other people.

"You're so low-tech," I'm told. (I don't have Call Waiting.)

"Yes, but so high-anxiety."

Next year in New York, high school students will be allowed to use calculators on their statewide mathematics exams. I took those exams. I had to do the math by myself. As a result, I can check the accuracy of a lunch check without having to locate a supplementary light source for my solar calculator. What's next? If I take the Spanish final, am I allowed to bring in Charo?

JUST PLANE SCARED

*

On a Wing and a Prayer and 35,000 Feet of Air

I wanted to go to Norway for the Olympics. Plain and simple. How else was I going to get there, walk?

So I enrolled in USAir's fearful flyer course. At the least, I figured, I'd get a column piece out of it. At best, I'd get to Norway. (Can you imagine, wanting to solve your fear of flying so you could get to Norway in the *winter*? That's like wanting to get over bronchitis so you could take a job working in a coal mine.)

I'm not actually afraid of flying. I'm uncomfortable flying. I'm *afraid* of crashing.

My fear is quite simple and specific: I believe the plane will break apart in mid-air, and we will all tumble to our deaths in an unspeakable blazing inferno. Other than that, I'm fine.

That fear has been so overwhelming that I have done everything I could to remain earthbound. I won't bore you with a complete recitation of how many times I maneuvered to avoid getting on a plane. But in 1991 I not only started the Bandwagon, but I actually rode the damn thing three full days and 1,500 miles to the Super Bowl in Minneapolis, and then took a twenty-six-hour train trip back to Washington without a shower so I smelled like a goat, and had the standard phoney-baloney fallback line: You never really see the country until you do it on a train. Don't get me wrong, I really do love trains, but I love ice cream, too, and I don't sleep inside a Good Humor truck.

More than 30 million Americans share this fear of flying—though some not as graphically, I suppose. And fifty of them were at National Airport with me taking this course.

You know us. We're the ones who ask, "If flying's so safe, why do they call the building a *terminal?*"

Fear of flying ranks eighth, by the way, on a list of common fears, behind death and ahead of dogs—though I imagine you could go for the quiniella if you were afraid of being bitten to death at 35,000 feet.

I admit I had some trepidation walking into the first class. I thought perhaps I'd be the only one who was really crazy about flying. But I was cheered when we went around the room introducing ourselves and explaining our fears, and the first person the instructor called on said, "I have this fear that the pilot will have a heart attack, and the copilot will panic, because he won't know whether to help the pilot or continue flying the plane." And I thought *I* was crazy.

Surprisingly, almost all the people there were veteran flyers who'd become paralyzed by their fears. Whether they suffered from claustrophobia or a fear of heights or discomfort in giving up control of their lives to a pilot, they were all there for the same reason: They wanted fuller lives. Many had passed up trips. Some had quit jobs because they couldn't get on airplanes. One woman who recently had gotten engaged said pleadingly, "I want to go on my honeymoon."

"You have a disease," Carol Stauffer, the instructor, told us kindly. "The relaxation tape you'll listen to daily and the book you'll read are the medicine."

She laid out the course, the five three-hour sessions culminating in the "graduation" flight—during which, I was certain, the plane would break apart. She said we would get champagne after the flight . . . so, if by some miracle we survived the flight, we could get drunk and kill ourselves on the drive home.

Carol was a social worker, which explains her persistent optimism. She kept talking about the "fun" we'd have. As proof, she introduced a graduate from a recent class, a Mr. Norman Braverman. I muttered: Norman, you're a braver man than I.

As we went around the room elucidating our fears, people recalled episodes of horrifying turbulence that swore them off air travel—like a thunderstorm that bucked the plane so wildly, the flight attendants held hands and prayed. One man said he dwelled morbidly on plane crashes; he read the news accounts and memorized the names of the dead. A woman said she could not fly without drinking, and because her job required her to fly two or three times a week, she was worried she was becoming an alcoholic. Another woman said she cries throughout the flight: "I listen to all the noises the plane makes. When they aren't deafening I feel the engines are being turned off," she said. A man said he panics when people begin to walk around the cabin, because he thinks they will tilt the plane and cause it to turn over in the sky.

When it came my turn, I said, "Boy, am I glad I don't have to fly with you guys. Your fears are so irrational. My fear, on the other hand, makes all the sense in the world: I believe that a giant is going to come along and cut the strings that hold the airplane up."

Frank Petee, a retired pilot, taught the course with Carol Stauffer. He wore his captain's uniform to class, which I found reassuring—though I admit it's a little like Red Auerbach wearing a whistle.

Frank had flown for more than forty years, and offered himself as proof of how safe airplanes are. On an average day, he said, twenty thousand jet planes take off and land, and 99.99 percent of these maneuvers are normal and routine. "You were

in much more danger the last time you stepped out of your bathroom shower than you will ever be in an airplane," he told us
. . . prompting a woman to ask: "Is it the same if you take
baths?"

But statistics are cold comfort if you're up in the air and
you're afraid, as is the claim that "the media blows accidents out
of proportion." When 288 people fall from the sky, it's simply
not the same as a Mazda rolling over the curb into a cappuccino
bar.

Still, Frank did his best to calm us. And in my case it helped
to know that turbulence will not cause a plane's wings to fall off;
that I should think of turbulence in the same vein as driving a car
over a bumpy country road; that even if its engines go out, an
airplane can glide for miles and find a place to land; and that
because of sophisticated onboard computers, a pilot doesn't
even have to see out the window to land the plane. "We can
make an approach without seeing," Frank said. Which is not to
say that I'd necessarily feel relieved to look into the cockpit and
see Ray Charles flying the plane.

Afterward I felt slightly foolish that I had been so afraid of
turbulence for so long. One of the men in the class who knew
my fear sidled up to me and said, "I told you your fear was silly;
planes don't break apart. Once they're up in the air, nothing
goes wrong. My fear is much more reasonable. It's about takeoff."

"What about takeoff?" I asked.

"That we'll fly into a flock of birds and crash."

Like so many pilots, Frank has that reassuring Chuck Yeager
voice that Tom Wolfe wrote about in *The Right Stuff*. When
Frank told us not to worry, that everything would be all right in
the airplane, we all wanted to trust him. For a while I almost
forgot what a group of loons we were. Until the question-and-
answer period, when one of the men asked, "You said that air-

lines would try to accommodate special requests by passengers. What if I liked to fly in a certain seat? Could I do that?"

"Certainly," Frank replied. "The airlines will be happy to give you the row you want, window or aisle."

"I mean the color seat I want. Bold colors make me hyper," the man said.

Oh.

Frank was very positive about maintenance. He said airline maintenance was very good. I'd never given airline maintenance a second thought; I mean, I was taking this course to become a better passenger, not a baggage handler. But it gave me a whole new area to be neurotic about. (What about that plane in Hawaii where the top peeled off? *"Look, honey, we're in a convertible."* How was the maintenance on that baby, huh?)

We had a slide show on maintenance. One slide showed the oxygen masks being released—which we greeted with nervous laughter. Somebody asked: What causes the oxygen masks to come down? Frank said they rarely do come down: "Maybe if a window broke, but I haven't heard of a window breaking in many, many years." Wow, a window breaking! I never thought of that. Something else to add to the worry list.

Part of the mental training of the course was to take control of your own thoughts; they told us we were the gatekeepers of our thoughts, we could associate pleasant thoughts with flying if we wanted to. Toward that end we went outside to examine a plane up close, the theory being we would see how sturdy it really was. But up close the rust and the scruffiness unnerved me. So many bolts. What if just one or two fell out over the Atlantic? I tried to follow Carol's advice and banish the bad thoughts and substitute a pleasant one. But all I could think of was: fiery descent into shark-infested water.

As always, Frank said not to worry. Smiling, he told me, "Go ahead and kick the tires. Bang on the wings." So I banged on the fuselage, and the woman sitting in a window seat by the wing felt the plane move, and it scared the color out of her face. I waved at her sheepishly. I tried to banish the thought that the plane seemed flimsy by chanting the most comforting words I knew of when it came to strong, clunky, reliable transportation: "Volvo station wagon."

Halfway through the course, some of us started flying; one of the women went to New York and back, played the relaxation tape on the plane with her, relying on it throughout the flights, and crowed, "It worked, really, it worked. I thought I was going to fall asleep on the flight!" Now you might say: New York is a short flight, a piece of cake. (Though we would say nothing is a piece of cake when you're up in the air.) But one of the men flew to Germany and back. And not only was his return flight turbulent, but the plane was delayed three hours because of a bomb scare! "I was amazed that I didn't panic," he told us. "All the way across I was thinking—Gee, I'm normally petrified. And yet I'm completely calm." We listened raptly to their testimony, like witnesses at a religious revival. That night, when I went home, I played the relaxation tape twice, and kissed it for good luck.

My turning point was the class when two pilots and three flight attendants came and talked to us. These were people who actually flew the plane. Walt had flown weather reconnaissance in the navy; he'd been in worse weather than I could even imagine. So I felt I could trust him when he said that weather will bounce you around, but it won't break the plane. Listening to Frank was comforting, but he was a retired pilot. Joe and Walt were active—they were going up every day. They were my age, maybe even a bit younger. They had small children. They had *volunteered* to fly us on our graduation night! "They love flying, and they want you to love it, too," Frank explained. Looking into their faces, I asked myself: Why would they do this if it weren't safe?

I can't tell you how reassuring it was to talk with people who flew for a living, who did it out of routine, who put a casual face on it. The flight attendants spoke jovially about their work, telling us they call the preflight recitation of the safety procedures "the singing and dancing." Obviously, all of us in a fearful flyer course feel that safety is the A–No. 1 priority, but humor goes a long way in a classroom like that—like when someone asked Walt, "How do you know when to come over the intercom and talk to the passengers?" And Walt deadpanned, "The rule is: Never interrupt the movie." One man, confessing the fears of us all, asked Bonnie, one of the flight attendants, "Is it all right to tell the flight attendants you're a fearful flyer? Will they look after you?" Bonnie sensed his apprehension and smiled. "And give you free liquor, yes."

Much of what was said I wrote down, because I knew I'd eventually do this story. But one thing Joe said I'd have remembered even without my notes: "An airplane is designed and built to fly. It *likes* to fly."

That night, with Joe and Walt at the controls, we taxied. They told us what they were doing each step of the way. They identified each sound. They showed us the spoilers, and how the wing flaps move. They put the engines in reverse thrust so we could become familiar with that sound. They took us down the runway at full throttle briefly—we were light, and if we'd stayed at that speed for just a few more seconds we'd have been airborne.

I sat on an aisle over the wing, silently mouthing, "Go, go, go."

I didn't want another week to think about it. I wanted to fly already.

Carol said we could bring somebody with us on the graduation flight.

But:

1. Don't bring a fearful flyer.

2. Don't bring a small child.

3. Don't bring a first-time flyer.

4. Don't bring anyone who thinks your fear is silly and this flight is no big deal.

That disqualified everyone but Michelle Pfeiffer. I left a message with her agent, but she never returned it. So I went alone.

As always, we met in the classroom and listened to the relaxation tape as a group. In her last-minute instructions, Carol told us, "Boeing built you right into the airplane. You're part of it. Whatever that airplane does, you do it too. Lean with it, not against it. If there are bumps, don't stiffen up, ride with them." It was such a good speech I thought it would be silly to point out that we were flying a McDonnell Douglas plane.

I actually wasn't supposed to be on this flight. I'd said all along I had a previously scheduled engagement. But at the last minute I decided to bag that and take the flight. I was proud of my desire to fly, though I reminded myself that Amelia Earhart probably felt the same way.

I was nervous driving to the airport, because this time was different. This was not a drill, not a simulation—this time we were going up. Fortunately the weather was spectacular: clear, mild, calm. There shouldn't be any turbulence at all. That helped me relax. And because I wasn't expected, when I showed up the rest of the class applauded, which made me feel great. So by the time we boarded the plane, I felt strangely confident.

Briefly, I asked myself: What the hell are you doing? How can you take a flight you don't *have* to take? Are you out of your mind? Quick, run out the door. Everyone will understand. Heck, they'll probably follow you.

But I was committed now.

I saw Carol and Frank on the plane. On the way in I'd said hello to Joe and Walt in the cockpit. All the folks I'd seen in the class for almost two months were in their seats. It felt like family.

We did the tape one more time.

Then the engines started. And we taxied onto the runway, and we went full throttle. And as I said a silent prayer and closed my eyes, we were up—smooth as satin.

There was some applause at liftoff, though not from me; I thought that was premature, considering the fact that we were in a floating metal tube, and if the engines fell off, we were Spam in a can.

I think it goes without saying that no matter how relaxed I may have felt relative to other times in a plane, I was still not relaxed; I still had the nervous system of Don Knotts in a cyclotron. But I wanted to try to feel calm. Carol and Frank had exhorted us not to sit frozen solid in our seats, but to stretch our muscles and alleviate the tension. So I got up and walked straight for the cockpit. We were still in the climbout. I was walking UPHILL! I must have been out of my mind.

Throughout the flight I chatted like a magpie. I went up and down the aisle asking people how they were doing; I felt like a wine steward. I was never entirely comfortable, particularly the one or two times the plane hit a slight bump in that ocean of air. But I was better than ever before. I never reached for my trusty Valium. I never thought the giant would cut the strings.

We stayed airborne almost forty-five minutes, going south to Richmond, then turning north toward the eastern shore of Maryland, and coming back into National. It was such a perfectly clear night that standing in the cockpit—and we were encouraged to do that—you could see forever. Oddly, when you're in the cockpit, you have almost no sensation of moving. It really does feel as if the plane is being held up by strings.

There were tears in my eyes when we landed (and this time I heartily joined in the applause), I was relieved and grateful and proud; I drank the champagne delightedly. They gave us diplomas, and we all felt we'd earned them.

I won't say I was cured, though. I still felt terrified to get on a plane. Most of my fears were still there. The difference was that now I had a method to help me better cope with them. I had the relaxation tape. I had a positive experience to fall back on. I had a support group I could call anytime; in fact, I've called Frank for reassurance before a number of flights. I had the knowledge I could get on a plane.

A few months later I flew to Norway. And back.

The planes I was on were designed and built to fly. They liked to fly.

And nobody cut the strings.

The Zoom and a Boom

Do you remember where you were at ten o'clock last Tuesday morning? It might help if I give you a hint: sonic boom. (What do you mean, give you another hint? That's it: sonic boom. Look, this isn't an essay question. Tuesday morning at ten was when the SR-71 Blackbird spy plane broke the sound barrier over the Washington area. You didn't hear it? You didn't feel it? What, I'm doing *Tommy* here? There was a sonic boom. Was it as good for you as it was for me?)

I was throwing out the garbage when the noise shook the sky. Instinctively, I narrowed the choices:

1. Nuclear attack—in which case I was toast;
2. Mathematically remarkable coincidence: a flock of birds with heartburn;
3. Sonic boom.

I did what any D.C. resident would do under the circumstances: I telephoned District Cable Vision to find out how many days service would be interrupted this time. I'm still on hold.

Do you know how fast this plane was going? Do you know? Do you know? Do you know? (Yo, Wernher, check it out!) Average speed: 2,112 miles an hour. That's so fast, Tattoo only has time to say, "Look, boss, de . . ." before it's gone.

(The *what*? The miles per gallon? Who cares? Hey, buddy, this isn't a van pool. We're not going for environmentally correct, we're going for zoom.)

The average commercial airliner goes coast-to-coast in four hours, fifty minutes. This baby went coast-to-coast in sixty-eight minutes! (Johnny Carson said, "It broke the old record of sixty-nine minutes set by a Domino's Pizza truck.") Sixty-eight freaking minutes! L.A. to D.C. One hour, eight. Ballgame. You can spend one hour, eight sitting on the runway at National just waiting for your plane to take off.

En route, the Blackbird flew from St. Louis to Cincinnati in eight minutes. Granted, that may not be a favorite route of yours. But if you have to take it, this thing gets you there in eight minutes. You can't fax anything that fast. You're *actually there* before your secretary can get an open WATS line. It's Star Trek. Scotty beamed you up!

As you know, they're mothballing the Blackbirds. Putting them in museums. (To show you how old I am, I thought U2 was a spy plane.)

There they go, swinging low, bye-bye, blackbird.

That's nuts. It ought to be: Blackbird, buy! Buy!

Air Force and industry sources say these planes are good for twenty more years. They shouldn't be in museums. People should be allowed to purchase them. Slap a coat of fresh paint on them—maybe those Braniff flying colors from the solvent days—and let's rock 'n' roll. If you've got an evening, we'll give you the world.

"Honey, get a sitter. We're having dinner in Kabul."

It's an airplane for people with money to spend, but no time to waste.

Air Yuppie.

It will be the first airline with no ticket counters. You can only purchase through catalogs.

Imagine what the conversation would sound like on an airplane filled with yuppies. All those whiny, self-indulgent laments:

"Isn't the food in the Caribbean just awful?"

"That's why we're driving a Jaguar; the seats in the BMW were too rigid, too *achtung*!"

"Dockers? They were last year."

"Can you believe the markup on the vineyard-designated Pouilly Fuisse? It's a well-focused, exuberant wine, but excessively fruity by my taste."

"We used to have a Norwegian au pair. You'll be pleased. But there's nothing quite like an English nanny. We wouldn't trade ours for the world."

"The bench-press muscles are too bulky. I want the Nordic-Track muscles."

Okay, back to the plane. It flies at eighty thousand feet. "It's a real smooth ride up there," the pilot, Lt. Col. Raymond Yeilding, reported.

It gets to eighty thousand feet in about six seconds. You spend the first five or so with your eyes closed wondering how Big Daddy Don Garlits got into the cockpit. Then it flattens out and you know you're at eighty thousand feet, because you look up and your eyebrows are pasted to the ceiling.

Because of the quickness of the trip, the flight attendants serve the meal right away. (All Air Yuppie flight attendants—male and female—graduate from the Al Neuharth Sky Girl Academy. In case of emergency, they chew gum and shriek.) Unfortunately, the speed of the aircraft requires a slight alteration in the style of service. The G-force pins the flight attendants to the back wall for the entire flight, so they load a cart with food, then let it loose down the aisle at about 1,300 miles an hour. We're talking FAST food. You grab what you can. Window seat? Best of luck, babe. Hope you're on a diet.

Bathrooms? Don't ask. It's a short flight. Hold it.

There's not enough time to show a full movie. (On the St. Louis–Cincinnati run, there's not even enough time to put up the screen.) So there's a choice of the titles and credits of a real movie, or the new, unbelievably brief Seven-Minute Evelyn Wood/CNN Headline News Half Hour.

Before you know it, you're there.

Then it's the most fun of all: baggage claim. Coast to coast in sixty-eight minutes, and it still takes four hours to get your bags.

Winging It

Welcome to USAir, where "everything we do begins with you."

Except maybe landings. Which begin with Jane.

Jane Zweber is the off-duty flight attendant who sat in the captain's seat while USAir Flight 528 from Tampa was landing in Philadelphia. (How'd she get a great seat like that? Oh, so this is what they mean by airline deregulation.)

And where was the captain?

A good question. According to USAir, Capt. Jon Swartzentruber was sitting in the jump seat at the rear of the cockpit. I guess he drew the line at pushing the drink cart up and down the aisle. It's so demeaning having to say, "Please pay with one-dollar bills. We're short on change."

Interestingly, not one of the 145 passengers was made aware of this game of musical chairs. Capt. Swartzentruber didn't come on the intercom and announce in those dulcet tones pilots have: "Ladies and gentlemen, this is your captain speaking. We're having a little fun up here. I'm letting a stewardess sit in my seat while I put on an evening gown and prance around like a goat. We'll be landing in Philadelphia within the minute, and don't you worry. Say, how about those honey cashews?"

Now I don't think I have to point out that landing is one of the three most dangerous portions of a flight—the others being (1) taking off and (2) being in the air. What makes landing so dangerous is that a plane traveling at about 650 miles an hour is falling out of the sky and attempting to sit on a patch of concrete a little bit wider than a toaster oven.

I don't know about you, but I don't feel secure about that under the best of circumstances—and even if the copilot is at the stick, I certainly don't want someone who's spent most of her in-flight hours collecting barf bags sitting in the captain's seat, while the captain is in the back anticipating all the laughs he's gonna get telling the boys at the Moose Lodge about this one.

Are you kidding me?

This is like being on the operating table having delicate bypass surgery, and you hear the chief surgeon tell a nurse, "Hey, honey, c'mere and close this guy up for me. It's a snap. Last week Molly from payroll did three nose jobs."

Now we know why the Titanic hit the iceberg. The captain was playing Hide the Grey Poupon with a chambermaid.

USAir (catchy new slogan: "Watch Tiffany Land This Bad Boy!") fired the pilot, the copilot, and the flight attendant, sent every passenger a letter of apology . . . and enclosed a free upgrade to the cockpit for you and Sharon Stone.

I can't believe this actually happened. What were they doing over there, running a game show? "Hi, welcome aboard. I'm Scott, your first officer, and in a moment I'll stick my hand into this drum containing all your names, and I'll pick out our lucky passenger who'll come on up here and *fly this plane!*"

Did you ever see *Airport 1975*?

At the end, the stewardess, Karen Black, was flying the plane. I can still see her crazy cross-eyed grin. It's a nightmare. Doesn't anybody at USAir rent movies?

Until a few years ago they used to let children visit the cockpit during a flight. Now I know why they stopped. The airlines didn't want kids to see that the cockpit was a karaoke lounge. (Speaking of airport movies, remember the hilarious *Airplane!* where Peter Graves played Capt. Oveur? And when young Joey came into the cockpit, the captain asked him: "You ever been in a cockpit before, Joey? You ever seen a grown man naked? Ever hang around the gymnasium? Do you like movies about gladiators? You ever been in a Turkish prison?" I loved that movie. I bring it up because I didn't know it was part of the USAir training film library.)

What is going on in the airline industry today?

First Clinton gets his hair cut on the tarmac at LAX, and stacks up planes from here to eternity. (How many frequent-flier miles do you need to get a *haircut* on a plane? And how many would Hillary need for a leg wax?) Then Delta and American announced they were laying off pilots. Delta and American have seen USAir prove you don't need that many pilots to actually fly the planes—you can use baggage handlers in a pinch.

Just the other day Virgin Atlantic Airways announced it plans to offer its passengers the chance to play video poker, slots, and roulette in flight. Now, maybe it's just a matter of semantics, but I'm not comfortable with the concept of gambling at 35,000 feet. I'm not sure I want to fly an airline that can use a slogan like: "Fly With Us. Maybe You'll Get Lucky." I thought when airlines got slots at the better airports they were talking about routings.

Are the pilots going to have video poker in the cockpit? And are the flight attendants going to ply the pilots with free drinks, like in a real casino? That's all we need, right? We can go USAir, where anybody can fly the plane, or go Virgin Air, where the captain doesn't bother to check velocity because he's already three sheets to the wind.

I don't want to depend on my pilot pulling to an inside

straight as we come into LaGuardia. What happens if he winds up with a pair of fours—are we diverted to Hartford?

I can't see how it's a confidence builder to walk past the cockpit on your way to the lavatory and hear your pilot pleading, "C'mon, seven, baby needs a new pair of shoes."

CARPOOLING TO EXOTICA

*

Nudes on Ice

Sure, we can quibble about what's tastefully done here. You might think the Mirage, with its outdoor volcano that blows piña colada–perfumed natural-gas flames into the night sky every fifteen minutes (except during high wind conditions for fear they'll singe several hundred potential customers who stand and gape), is excessive. Or you might think the Excalibur, a forbidding architectural concept that looks like Disneyland leverage-brokered by Howard Johnson's, with its gigantic red, teal, and gold medieval spires and knights jousting on real horses in the dirt-floor showroom, is excessive. Or you might think the Flamingo Hilton, with its façade of about 72,000 neon pink flamingos, each twelve feet high, blinking in syncopation like some sort of thermonuclear chorus line, is excessive. You might even think that Caesars Palace, with its grotesquely inappropriate but anatomically accurate Roman statuary and its helpful staff's lobby directions—like "Go straight to the naked Nubian slave barge, then take a left"—is excessive. As I said, we can quibble.

But surely we can agree on the quintessential Las Vegas revue, by which I mean, of course, the long-running *Nudes on Ice*, which combines the two critical elements of a Las Vegas revue: a room with chairs, and nudes. In a pinch, you can make do without the chairs.

Mapplethorpe? Bad.

2 Live Crew? Bad.

Nudes on Ice? Kowabunga! ("Barbara and I go every time we're in town.")

Nudes on Ice—okay, they're not fully nude, just topless; Vegas has standards, you know—is performed twice nightly at the downtown Union Plaza hotel and casino (downtown Vegas being somewhat less refined than the Strip, which itself is to refined what two tin cans and a string is to C&P) in a red-carpeted, red-curtained, red-tableclothed showroom that seems to be somebody's idea of a great party in 1880.

(Before I elaborate on *Nudes on Ice*, let me relate a personal story. I arrived there in the evening, tired from the travel. And like most people on an East Coast body clock, I awoke quite early the next morning and flipped on the TV to the predawn news. Though groggy, imagine how quickly I snapped to upon hearing the newscaster giggling that "an underground nuclear explosion of more than one hundred kilotons"—which sure sounded like it could pop me out of a toaster—"will be detonated around nine A.M., so if you're on a high floor, you might want to hold on to something solid." I stared at my room key: 2207, plenty high enough, considering a hotel maintenance worker informed me that the tallest building in the whole state of Nevada was 30 stories. Welcome to Las Vegas. Can I get you anything—coffee, tea, space in a fallout shelter? Needless to say, at nine A.M. I was on the ground floor.)

Okay, to *Nudes on Ice.*

So named, as executive producer Paul Szigety recalls, because "we were thinking about what to call the show, and one of the owners said, 'We got nudes and we got ice, let's go with *Nudes on Ice.*'" And you wondered where the next flash of creative genius would come from.

It opens with ten female skaters, four of them bare-bosomed; believe me, in this cold you can tell which four. But if you needed a hint, the bare-bosomed ones were the ones standing on platform steps at the back of the stage. Oh sure, they're wearing skates, and once in a while they actually go on the ice so they can glide to the platform steps at the front side of the stage, but skating is not why they were hired. "Skaters are easy to find, nudes aren't," said Szigety, who confessed he's happy "just as long as the nudes don't fall down."

Two lead skaters are bare-bosomed as well, particularly "the sexsational" Kelly Hagen, who does stylish minor jumps on the small rink, but not too many spins, since turning her back to the audience would diminish the marquee appeal. Hagen used to be an aerialist at Circus Circus, but grew tired of hand burns and became a skater. How did Szigety persuade her to skate topless?

"Money," he explained.

This isn't a complicated town.

Not that breasts are the entire show. There's a weak comedian and two terrific novelties: a kid juggler and a wild, randy gaucho act. But now that Ed Sullivan's dead, where do you go with those routines? You'll notice they didn't name the show *A Comedian, a Juggler, Two Gauchos, and Some Skaters, All Clothed. Nudes on Ice* knows where its bread's buttered.

So you get nudes on ice in a Ziegfeld number, and nudes on ice in a Russian Palace number, and nudes on ice in a Brazilian Carnival number—wearing costumes quite similar to the Russian ones except the nudes are wearing fruit baskets on their heads—and nudes in a *Chorus Line* finale, this time with headdresses that look like the Chrysler Building. I could tell you that after awhile you don't notice the nudes, but who's kidding whom?

Nudes on Ice has been running for two and a half years; Szigety says 500,000 people have seen it. It's hard to say how many nude skaters got their big break through this show, but you wouldn't believe some of the stuff they run on cable these days. It occurred to me that *Nudes on Ice* might really go over the top if a big-name skater like Dorothy Hamill agreed to star, but Szigety shook his head unconvinced. "It all depends," he said, shrugging his shoulders. "How big are her boobs?"

This Was Just
Inviting Trouble

Several years ago I got a phone call from the White House inviting me to a black-tie state dinner for President Roh of South Korea. Of course a real journalist would have turned it down flat. A real journalist wouldn't want anything to do with these rich, stuffed-shirt, self-important dilettantes who haven't gotten their hands dirty since the trust funds kicked in. And I would have said so, too—except what came out of my mouth was "Seven-thirty? Sure. Do you validate parking?"

Now that I've been to the White House, I can assure the American people that the country's in great shape on the china front. You get a different plate with every course.

The invitation said seven-thirty. Some people, I was sure, would arrive fashionably late. Not me. I'm an on-time guy. In fact, I'd guess I'm probably the only guy ever invited to a state dinner who even *buys* on time.

You drive onto the White House grounds and the Marines valet-park your car. You get a claim check that promises they'll return it, unless war is declared during the cocktail hour, and then it turns into a park-and-lock deal. You walk into the East Entrance, and a Marine announces your name over a loudspeaker. "Mr. Kornheiser." This happens to me all the time, but usually it's followed by "party of four. Your table's ready." You pass by the press, who are safely herded behind ropes—where they belong—and they ask you questions. In my case, it was "Why were *you* invited?" I said it was because Sununu needed a ride home.

Up a flight of stairs, down a marble corridor, and into the East Room for cocktails. What's really cool is that you can walk all over the White House and you don't have to get your hand stamped. A Marine escort (a "handsome hunk" is the politically correct description, according to interoffice memos at the Nation's Newspaper) led us to a group of people and made a few polite introductions. Famous people were scattered about, like Dick Cheney, Jim Baker, and Frank Gifford, but the group I was led to included *another lowly reporter*! I felt like Dorfman in *Animal House* when he shows up to rush the WASPy fraternity and Greg Marmalard steers him over to Achmed, Mfoom, and the rest of the dweebs.

Suddenly, Dan Quayle walked in, and much to his horror, I'm sure, I reached out my hand and introduced myself, and began babbling that I wanted him to give me golf tips for a sports column. Marilyn Quayle came over, and I could tell from the Mona Lisa smile she gave me that she wanted to get to know me better—or have me shot.

The band started playing "Hail to the Chief," and in walked the Bushes and the Rohs. I was no more than five feet from them, and I clutched at the prospect of being first in the receiving line, so I faded back into the crowd. I cut ahead of Indy 500 winner Rick Mears—something I'd never do on the road—and introduced myself, commenting that it was hard to recognize him without his Valvoline suit. Eventually, I found myself just a few steps from meeting the president.

The chief of protocol asked me my name. In retrospect, I should have said "Dr. Morris Fishbein." That way, if the Bushman said, "Nice to see you, Morris," I'd have known for sure he didn't know me from a plate of kung pao chicken. But I said, "Tony Kornheiser," and now I'll never know, because the president said, "Great to see you, Tony," like we were old pals. And I said, "Mr. President, your fly is open." Just kidding. Actually, that morning I'd telephoned novelist Dan Jenkins, Bush's favorite writer, to get something witty to say, and Dan told me this joke about the rabbi, the priest, and the Aer Lingus stewardess, which I couldn't repeat, so I said, "Mr. President, I bring regards from Dan Jenkins." (Watch for that scintillating quote in the next edition of *Bartlett's*.) Bush gave me a big smile and said, "We've got to get Dan and his wife up here for one of these." I thought to myself, get *them* up here? Like, what am I, chopped liver?

Bush passed me along to President Roh, who beamed as I said that I'd spent three wonderful weeks in his country during the 1988 Summer Olympics. (I didn't mention the kimchi aftertaste that haunts me still.) I moved left, to Barbara Bush, who smiled warmly and said something that sounded like "Nice to meet you, Mr. Porthauser." Not a steady reader, I guess. Then, I shook Mrs. Roh's hand, repeated my Olympics comments—you go with a winner, you know?—and I was led out the door and toward the State Dining Room.

There were fifteen tables, ten people apiece. I was at Table 15 on the far outside. Another foot to the left and I'd have been in the Potomac. Dick Cheney and party monster Georgette Mosbacher were the star attractions at my table. I managed to get a few words with Cheney, who said he liked my column—"sometimes." Had I been quicker, I'd have said I liked his wars too, "sometimes." I told Georgette that I recognized her from her photo, which is in the "Personalities" column so often I thought she was an advertiser.

I sat between Richard Solomon, assistant secretary of state for East Asian and Pacific affairs, and the charming Natalie

Kohler, whose family owns Kohler Industries, which I later discovered produces every kitchen and bathroom fixture in Western civilization—and if I'd only known that at the time, I'd have hit her up for a toilet seat. My dinner companions were great—they told me which forks to use and everything. I only made one rookie mistake, dropping the peach bombé and raspberry sauce dessert on my shirt. But it's a rental, so who cares?

Dinner was terrific. Lobster in champagne jelly, grilled veal, free wine. I was a little disappointed we didn't get goodie bags. I pocketed a copy of the menu, a book of matches—they're white, with the words THE PRESIDENT'S HOUSE in gold letters—some mints, and a cocktail napkin. I considered glomming some silverware, but then I remembered the metal detectors downstairs.

During dessert the strolling violins appeared. They played "In-a-Gadda-Da-Vida." Oops, there I go kidding again. We left the dining room and ambled back to the cocktail room for the evening's entertainment: selections from *The Phantom of the Opera*. During the singing I sat next to the ever-gorgeous Frank and Kathie Lee Gifford. I asked Kathie Lee if she'd ever want to sing at the White House. She said, "No, too much pressure." TV stars. What do they know about pressure? Try making the eleven-thirty deadline after a night game, that's pressure.

Then it was mix-and-mingle in the hall. People began drifting down the stairs to get their cars. In the corridor leading out I spotted Jaclyn Smith, who was almost wearing a white dress. The rules of etiquette say that being guests at the same dinner constitutes an introduction, and I was hardly going to pass up this chance. I found that Jaclyn and I have a great deal in common—like we both wear shoes. Though hers probably weren't rented.

"You made a fool of yourself, talking to her," my wife said later.

"How?" I asked.

"You had drool coming down the sides of your mouth. You looked like Lassie."

A Marine delivered my Honda, and I said to him. "The president of Korea, huh? If I'd had more sense, I'd have brought a Hyundai."

So here I am, just plain old Tony Porthauser, in my rented tux, with White House chocolate mints melting in my pocket and a vision of George turning to Barbara in the family quarters and saying, "A friend of *mine*? Honey, I thought he was a friend of *yours*."

Is this a great country, or what?

Having a Gray Old Time

Before I made this trip, folks would come up to me and ask, "Why would you go to Norway in the winter?"

So let's get this straight: I did not go to Norway. I went to *north* Norway. This may not be the end of the earth, but believe me, you can see it from here. The other day the mailman told me I'm the next-to-last person on his route. After me, he delivers to Santa.

Every morning at 8:00, I wake up and look outside, and wonder why it looks like night—then I remember that's because the sun doesn't rise until about 9:15. And it never gets real high in the sky, only about eye level. Then it goes down at 4:20, which I like, because it makes for a good, long cocktail hour.

Actually, it doesn't really matter when the sun rises, or how high it gets, because you can't see it. The sky is always gray, and it's always snowing, so you have to take the sun on faith. I'd never been in a place before where it's so gray you can't distinguish between the earth and the sky. There is absolutely no contrast. It is just total gray. It's like looking into a bowl of glue soup. The snow is gray. The sky is gray. The trees are gray. The ground is gray. If Jessica Tandy had come here, she'd have been invisible.

It is also very cold, and by very cold I mean that you can't just see your breath, you can *write* on it.

Some people might think all this cold and gray is depressing.

In my limited experience this is not so. I have already met two delightfully different kinds of Norwegians:

1. Those who are inebriated;
2. Those who have committed suicide.

(Attention people in the Norwegian embassy, who are furious now: That was just a joke. Not everybody is drunk or committing suicide—some are flogging themselves with tree branches or applying for exit visas.)

As you can imagine—particularly those of you who have seen Edvard Munch's famous, and truly upbeat, Norwegian painting *The Scream*—Norwegians are not a howlingly funny people. Here is a typical Norwegian joke: Arne and Snorri are getting drunk in a bar, and Arne says, "Oof, am I depressed." And Snorri says, "So am I." And Arne says, "Let's kill ourselves with hammers." Ha-ha-ha.

This has been a very hard winter in Norway—not that I have any idea what a mild winter in Norway is . . . I mean, it's not like when there's a mild winter in Norway, all the hotels in Miami Beach are empty. But there has been a pile of snow here, even by Norwegian standards. You can walk out of your third-floor window and hail a cab.

The continuous snow has even depressed the moose population. Thousands of moose are committing suicide by throwing themselves in front of trains. (That is not actually true. What is actually true is that there is so much snow on the mountainsides that the moose are having to come down to flat land to forage for food, and almost seventy of them have been hit on the railroad track by the direct train between Oslo and Lillehammer. I hear they are thinking of renaming the train "The Bullwinkle Special.")

Oof, all this talk about depression has made me depressed.

I am looking out the window at the total grayness, and it occurs to me that the difference between a live Norwegian and a dead Norwegian is that after the mortician gets done, a dead Norwegian probably has a bit more color.

I am so depressed now, I am beyond Norwegian—I am Swedish.

I will cheer myself up by telling you that the McDonald's here in Lillehammer serves McSalmon, yes! Okay, in Norwegian it's *McLaks*, but that's what it means: McSalmon. They even have a McSalmon Value Meal! I believe it comes with capers and a souvenir cup of white wine.

By the way, for those of you who are wondering why I would come here, let me inform you that I am here to cover the Winter Olympics. I am staying in Vormstuen, a section of media housing named after Stanley Eugene Vormstuen, a famous Norwegian herring fisherman who got drunk and killed himself with a grappling hook during a Norwegian winter.

My room is totally white. It has white walls, a white frame bed with white sheets and a white comforter, a white closet, and a white desk. I call the look "contemporary mental asylum."

I must tell you about the shower. It is part of the floor. What I mean by that is that you do not step into the shower—the shower is *actually part of the floor*. The drain is on the floor, a few feet from the toilet. It's all on the same level. You walk to the shower, then pull the curtain all around you. It's like being in a voting booth, only less private.

There is a large squeegee in the shower. I have not yet figured out if you are supposed to use it to squeegee the floor after the shower or squeegee yourself during it. I now think of myself as the Squeegin' Norwegian.

Mini and the Moocher

Last weekend I took my kids to a hotel in New York. After the clerk gave me the room keys, he attempted to press another key into my hand: the key to the minibar. I backed away like John Bobbitt would from a Cuisinart demonstration.

I live in fear of the minibar.

It is a sick seductress. It is the Glenn Close of hotel furniture.

I know I shouldn't open it. I know the prices are outrageous. I know I don't really need a tiny foil bag of nine or ten imported cashews for fourteen dollars; where could they be imported from for fourteen dollars—Phobos, the larger moon of Mars? And I know the Minibar Police will get me. They'll barge into my room at 7 A.M. the next day, carrying a clipboard, and they'll say "Housekeeping, here to check the minibar," and I'll stand there sheepishly as they pounce on the broken plastic seal of the minibar as though it were a vital clue, like that taped-up lock at the Watergate. Then they'll gleefully check off "one bag cashews, $14" on their manifest.

Only a fool would open the minibar. You can *grow* cashews for less. But sometime in the middle of the night every middle-aged man in a hotel room eventually gets up and goes (a) to the bathroom to pee and (b) to the minibar to desperately inspect its contents, which will inevitably include Belgian chocolate dusted with a whitish powder indicating it's been lying there since 1973, and no wonder, because who'd spend twenty-two dollars for a chocolate bar except possibly some idiot like me. (Some of us are weaker than others. My pal Mike Wilbon, the Monster of the Minibar, raids the minibar WHILE HE'S WAITING FOR ROOM SERVICE TO ARRIVE!) So I refuse the minibar key, and go cold turkey—which, by the way, costs $203.50 in the Marriott minibar.

And it's not just myself I fear for. It's my children.

It's every parent's worst nightmare in a hotel with the kids: You'll take a catnap, and you'll awaken and find your kids glassy-eyed on the floor, surrounded by empty bags of the world's most expensive potato chips and macadamia nuts, and empty minia-tures of Chivas Regal and Bailey's Irish Cream—watching, on Spectra Vision, *Toilet Slaves of Bangkok*. Think of the guilt and shame! You close your eyes for twenty minutes, and your kids are drunk and corrupted. Far worse, you're out about ninety bucks.

The minibar simply has to be the world's worst deal for the consumer; it makes 7-Eleven, where they routinely charge forty dollars for a box of Pampers, look like an outlet mall.

Often, a person will check into a hotel for a rate of $79 a day, and when he checks out the next morning the bill is $600, and he recalls only a box of M&Ms, a can of orange juice, a bottle of Heineken, and three phone calls. (Recently, my friend Gino was in Nova Scotia and made two collect calls to Washington. I emphasize, these were *collect calls*. His hotel bill included a $26 surcharge covering a hotel operator's fee, a Canadian Provincial fiber-optic cable assessment, and something he remembers as "depreciation of the queen's machinery.")

I think you ought to be allowed to sample from the minibar at no cost—maybe one cashew, for example—the way you can

sample the porno movies; you can usually watch up to five minutes of something like *Ravenous Bulgarian Stewardesses* without
getting charged, which is why I always travel with a stopwatch—
though I tell people I'm there to cover a track meet.

Gino is forever trying to figure out how to fool the Minibar
Police.

"Like with potato chips," he said. "What if you carefully slit
open the bag so you can't tell it was opened. And after you eat
the chips you replace them with something light but bulky, like
the free shoe-buffing cloth in the bathroom?"

"That could work," I said. "But with liquor, once you break
the seal on the bottles, they'll catch you."

Gino has given that a lot of thought, too.

"The whole key is the plastic doodad on the door of the
minibar," he says. "If that's not broken, they'll never even open
the minibar to see if you took anything. So what you gotta do is
you bring in an acetylene torch, bust into the minibar through
the *bottom*, and empty it out!

"No, wait!" he said, on a roll. "What you do is, buy your
own miniatures at a liquor store for ninety-nine cents a pop, and
substitute them for the ones you drink! They'll never catch
you," Gino said triumphantly.

This diabolically brilliant criminal mind still has not figured
out the teensy logical flaw in his plan: If you bought your own,
why would you drink *theirs*?

Almost as bad as the minibar key problem is the room key
problem. Actually, your room key is no longer a key so much as
a stupid slip of plastic. So, say you are at the National Conven-
tion of Fat Sportswriters Who Drink Too Much, and it is 2 A.M.
and you are ready to go upstairs to bed, and you pull out this
stupid key, and much to your horror you see that it doesn't have
your room number on it; no key does anymore, for security reasons, so if you lose your key, no one can get into your room. But
for some reason possibly related to six frozen Kahlua Kiliman-

jaros, you have momentarily forgotten your room number. So whaddaya do then, pal?

Me, I go to the front desk, and say I'm a guest in the hotel, and hold up my key helplessly and ask, "Could you please tell me which room this key opens?"

And they look at me like I'm Himmler.

So I show them my wallet with my IDs, and ask for my room number.

And they say, "You might have stolen that wallet too, along with the key. How can you prove you're Tony Kornheiser?"

So I tell the blind-date and dog joke from a column I once wrote.

And they say, "Anyone who reads Kornheiser could tell the joke. If you are Kornheiser, you know sports. Who won the 1978 Rose Bowl?"

And I don't know. And since they wouldn't ask me the starting lineup of the 1962 New York Yankees (Richardson, Kubek, Maris, Mantle, Howard, Berra, Pepitone, Boyer, and Terry), I knew I couldn't win here.

So I say, "Look, it's late. Here's a credit card. Why don't you give me another room for the night? And you can keep the key to the minibar."

The Sun Also Riles

Good fortune had me in South Florida last week when a big snowstorm socked the Northeast. True, Washington escaped. But cities farther north weren't so lucky. According to the TV news shows in Miami:

New York got eight feet of snow. All schools will be closed until June.

Philadelphia got fourteen feet of snow. The Rocky statue is ear-deep in snow. It looks like an Easter Island head.

Boston got twenty-one feet. They've dispatched Saint Bernards to find Norm at Cheers.

Forget Pittsburgh. Everybody's dead.

I am exaggerating. Only north Pittsburgh.

The point is that every time it snows up north, the newscasts in Florida go crazy with glee. They *hemorrhage* glee. They need to contract out for glee removal. They devote at least twenty-five of their thirty minutes to the terrible weather elsewhere. They open with two or three of their 450 daily homicides (South Florida being one of the few places in the country where they ask tourists their blood type at the airports) and then immediately go to a live remote of snow in Milwaukee or Syracuse.

Look at that old lady, freezing her *tuchis* off!

Look at that guy, having to abandon his car on the interstate and sliding like a hockey puck, and—whoa!—getting whacked by an eighteen-wheeler!

Ha-ha-ha-ha.

Now stay tuned for our warm, beautiful Miami weather.

The Germans have a word for this. It's *Gerplutzenheimerzetzenpfunff* or something. It means "glee at another's misfortune."

This is what Miami does about weather.

They trot out their poodle-haired TV newscasters—and because it's politically advantageous to be Hispanic in Miami, the newscasters all have these bizarrely hyphenated names like Caitlin McTavish-Ruiz, or Annamaria Gallucci-Gonzalez, or Fong Li-Feldstein-Fernandez, and you are supposed to believe that they are Latino even though the only Spanish words they know are *Gloria Estefan*—who tell you how bad it is where you came from and aren't you glad you're here. (They also do this odd thing where they show you a map of greater Miami, with thirty-five different communities, all within eight blocks of each other, and they give you *each temperature:* "At the airport it's eighty-one and fair, in Coral Gables it's eighty-one and fair, on U.S. One in Hallandale it's eighty-two and fair, on the Tamiami Trail it's eighty-one and fair . . ." Okay, we get the point. It's better than Toledo.

Of course in the summer they get defensive about the weather. (Dave Barry once wrote about this defensiveness, saying that the weatherman will admit, "Okay, true, it's a hundred and seven in the shade here—but that's balmy when compared to the six hundred forty degrees on the surface of Mercury.")

South Florida weather forecasters make no mention of the facts that:

1. They are living with cockroaches the size of Herve Villechaize.

2. It is so hot there that not only do M&Ms melt in your

hand, but you melt into the seat of your car, and when you get out of the car you sound like a seal passing gas.

3. Everyone in the state who is over eighty—which is to say almost everyone in the state—is lined up at three forty-five for dinner, because the early-bird specials start at four, and who wouldn't want to get minestrone, three-bean salad, a piece of veal parmigiana left over from the 1960 Olympics in Rome, and a portion of lime Jell-O for $3.95? (Every bit of food in Florida is cooked soft in case you left your teeth in the glass at the condo.)

4. You're taking your life in your hands every time you get on the roads because the worst drivers in the world are in Miami, their geezer heads barely poking above the steering wheel, going five miles an hour, with their foot locked on the brake pedal, making a screaming hairpin left turn from the extreme right lane.

5. And every European who rents a car winds up on a barbecue skewer. (As I was checking in for my flight to Washington, no fewer than five people—total strangers—told me I was crazy to go back to the snow. Three of them were killed at the curbside check-in.)

No, none of that matters.

Because at least they don't have snow.

This, believe me, is *Gerplutzenheimerzetzenpfunff.*

So is what we do here in D.C. Let's be honest, this is a city that is so boring, so utterly lacking in pizzazz, that a man such as the pale, vaguely frightening Supreme Court justice David Souter, who may well be a vampire, is considered the Most Eligible Bachelor in town. Washington has no style whatsoever. It has people who think they're making an avant-garde fashion statement by loosening their neckties. And so what do we say about New York, a truly vibrant, diverse, sophisticated city? We say, "At least *our* subways are clean."

A friend of mine used to go to Bethany Beach each summer

with her family, and she remembers how her father delighted in looking just a few miles up the Delaware coast at Rehoboth Beach, under a dark, ominous cloud, and gloating, "They're getting it in Rehoboth." That is the very essence of *Gerplutzenheimerzetzenpfunff:* It's not enough that we have sun. *You* have to have rain.

To Live and Cry in L.A.

You can't live here. The people here are too beautiful, and too *built*. It's a petri dish for the gorgeous. How did they all get here? What is there, some sort of gravitational pull that only works on Hard Bodies?

Is it the designer vegetables? I mean, doesn't anybody ever need to see a dermatologist here? Or do they round up the average-looking people and float them out to sea?

Talk about having an out-of-body experience.

If I don't get out of this body and into a size thirty-four waist by sundown, I'm in Idaho.

When I arrived here for the Super Bowl, Man About Town Chip Muldoon, who moved to L.A. a year ago so he could strike it rich without ever having to hear anyone say a three-syllable word, immediately drove me to Venice Beach so I could feel even worse about myself. Suddenly I was surrounded by golden California tans, which made me aware of how cadaverous my own East Coast dead-of-winter skin looks. I feel so pale. I feel paler than Michael Jackson—although, thankfully, I'm not in danger of melting, like he is.

Venice Beach is a promenade composed entirely of T-shirt shops and tarot card readers—the connection apparently being that after a psychic tells you, "You are going to have a life of leisure," you can dress appropriately for it.

It was at Venice Beach where I saw the great new trend that will sweep the East, and I am talking, of course, about the Incredible Wiggling Hand. It is a battery-powered, all-too-lifelike severed hand, sticking out of a plastic garbage bag, that wriggles across the ground. A great gift for preschoolers. Buy your kid one, and maybe he'll grow up to be Freddy Krueger!

Another trend to look out for is self-puncturing. Those of you who thought it couldn't get any worse than nose rings, guess again. Lip rings! Yes, lip rings. Two and three at a shot, right through the kisser. The lip-ring capital of the world is the Melrose section of L.A., where everybody under twenty-five seems to be auditioning for a part in the David Lynch version of *Beverly Hills 90210*. Why not take care of all your puncturing needs by marching down to the local Hertz, finding the warning sign that says DON'T BACK UP—SEVERE TIRE DAMAGE, and simply rolling your face over it?

I'm not going to say *anything* about the nipple rings.

It's like another planet here.

What kind of pick-up line is "Who's your agent?"

You one-up someone in Washington by delaying their bill in committee. You one-up someone in L.A. by having bigger hair.

In Washington, women have three names. In L.A., only one.

In Washington, people are named after distinguished ancestors. In L.A., after shrubbery.

People begin conversations in Washington by asking you where you went to college. In L.A., they ask you what you put in your salad. (One benefit of all the recent rain is that people now have mushrooms growing from their ceilings, so they live in a self-contained salad environment.)

Traffic here is totally impossible. Everybody drives. Nobody moves. Court TV moves faster than the cars on Wilshire Boulevard.

The moment you get into your car, you have to be prepared to stay there between forty-five minutes and forty-five hours. So the intelligent commuter stocks up on good tapes and good food. This is why as you wait at the freeway entrance ramp you see people selling huge bags of groceries. The entrance ramp has become the new stop-and-shop. The current theory is that most of the freeway drive-by shootings are committed by people who have either eaten rotten kiwi fruit or listened to Kenny Rogers.

People go stir crazy in their cars. Up until this week, you could see them constantly yakking into their cellular phones. Now with the cancer scare—what's next, toxic toilet paper?—they're throwing their cellular phones out the window along with the rotten kiwis and working on their personal grooming. In the past two days, Man About Town Chip Muldoon saw a man blow-drying his hair in the car and a woman clipping her toenails *with her right foot on the steering wheel.*

The recession has left a lot of Angelenos out of work, and you can see them standing on the entrance ramps holding up hand-lettered signs offering to work for food—though it strikes me as bizarre to think that, say, a film producer might be cruising the Ventura Freeway looking for an experienced key grip. The offers are indigenous to L.A.: "Will Do the Back-of-the-Cab Scene From *On the Waterfront* for Food," "Give You Arsenio Hall's Home Telephone Number for Food."

L.A. is full of fine restaurants. But don't try to get a dinner reservation between seven-thirty and nine-thirty, unless you're a close personal friend of Jack Nicholson. If Jesus had wanted to eat the Last Supper at Spago's, he'd have had to wait until ten.

L.A. has two kinds of people: somebodies and nobodies. The somebodies are the ones who say, "Well, I was talking to Al, and Al says . . ." And the nobodies are the ones who interrupt to ask, "Al who?" I am a nobody.

The other night a group of us nobodies finally got a table, and my friend Mitch was talking about corruption in the movie business, when a steel-bellied, drop-dead beauty wearing a dress the size of a cocktail napkin walked by, and Mitch said, and I'm quoting now, ". . . and *first* you have to pay off some, uh, some gruh, gruh, gurooomah." I missed the rest of it, because I, too, had become distracted by this woman, and had placed a forkful of creamed spinach in my ear.

You can't live here.

You simply *cannot* live here.

Pardon My French

Je suis scandalisé.

(I am outraged.)

The French are accusing us of spying on them.

Now let's get this straight. We marched in and liberated them from the clutches of Satan. In return, they gave us, like, eels on toast. And now they are accusing us of *spying* on them?

Hey, listen. We should be free to go over there and help ourselves to whatever we want. Not that there's much to take. Truffles? A fungus snuffled out of the ground by pigs?

Anyway, I don't want to get into gratuitous French-bashing. After all, the French have given the world many important people, including Marie Curie and, um, hang on a minute. There's Marie, definitely. She was one important chemistry babe. And . . . Charles de Gaulle! He is famous for signing the "letters of transit" in *Casablanca*. Isn't it funny how we keep coming back to the Nazis?

But I digress.

So anyway the ingrates, I mean the French, want to boot five Americans out of France on the grounds that we have been stealing their technological secrets. Like what, how to make a car that looks like a toaster? Have you driven a Citroën lately? They've actually put in a new option for a "crumb disposer."

Remember Renault's Le Car, which was constantly in Le Repair Shop?

How good can their technology be? It certainly hasn't helped them win any wars. French military technology, now there's an oxymoron. What's the first thing they teach in French war college, how to say "I surrender" in German?

But I digress.

I will say this for the French: They are not pikers. They just spent $20 million building a fabulous state-of-the art yacht for the America's Cup. The keel fell off. You know what that is like, building a boat and the keel falls off? You know how pathetic that is? That is like building a bridge but accidentally making it out of pasta.

It is so typically French to purse their lips and assume that their stuff is so good that we'd want to steal it. We've already got everything good they make. (It was over for the French the day you could buy a Croissanwich at Burger King.)

Bread. Sauce. Wine. Perfume.

Am I leaving anything out?

Certainly not soap.

Please don't tell me about French culture.

The Singing Nun. I rest my case.

I know their movies were good at one time. But like Brigitte Bardot chaining herself to a flock of sheep, they have grown old and tiresome. Every year at Cannes they enter a film that reeks like Limburger and loses to something with Wesley Snipes. The French haven't made a decent movie in years, and of course they blame us for cheapening the art form, which is preposterous considering that they . . . no, I won't even mention Jerry Lewis.

French movies generally feature a young woman running around in her underpants. Sometimes she's in a forest; some-times in a field of day lilies; sometimes she's a stewardess on the

Concorde. All the adults in the movie are smoking Gauloises in
that snotty way where they look as if they're pinching a derriere,
and fretting about whether the Beaujolais nouveau tastes impish
enough. It's quite existential. It's all mood and look. It's called
film noir. The literal translation of film noir is: Get me out of this
theater before I flambé myself until *mort*.

Their language is so prissy sounding that you could be challenging someone to a street corner fight and it would sound like
an Elizabeth Barrett Browning sonnet. What other language
would have a wine named Pouilly Fuisse? Try bellying up to a
bar in Detroit and ordering three fingers of that.

The French will eat anything that's cooked in butter. You
could sauté a Chiclet in butter and slap some béarnaise sauce on
it, and half of Paris would line up. And they're big on glands.
They love glands. If it once was in a body and squirted out goo,
they love it.

"*Oooh, what ees thees?*"

"It's the anal gland of a ferret."

"*C'est magnifique.*"

Possibly I am sounding somewhat embittered. You would be
embittered, too, if you stormed the beach at Normandy, armed
only with an M-16 and a pack of unfiltered Luckies, and a belly
full of churning guts . . .

*Tony, you were no closer to Normandy than you are to Cyd
Charisse's daughter, Myrna, who lives in Istanbul.*

Well, true.

*How can you condemn an entire noble nation of people so cava-
lierly?*

I'll tell you how. When I was in high school, we had a French
exchange student named Chris. (Which he pronounced
Kweeeees.) He had a goatee that made him look like Maynard G.
Krebs. He wore a beret. He couldn't play a single American
sport. He threw like a girl. He never participated in guy talk,
wherein we all sat around and lied about all the thousands of

girls we were boinking. I always had total contempt for Chris. But when I went to my ten-year high school reunion, I got to chatting with the women and discovered that half of them had slept with Chris, including many of the ones who wouldn't sleep with me.

The Gaul of that guy!

Urgent Correction: In the previous discussion I referred to the French in ways some French persons might find offensive, such as saying that the only good thing to come out of France was Marie Curie. This was so wrong and unfair of me that I am plotzing in my embarrassment. It turns out that Marie wasn't French at all, but Polish. I hereby pledge to do my research better in the future.

Why My Vacation Was a Bust

I hereby declare myself a mosquito-free zone. I simply have no more blood to give. After two weeks with the mosquitoes in Portugal, I have less blood than George F. Will.

It's not that I didn't bring mosquito repellent. I slathered it on like mayonnaise on a BLT. I must have been repellent to everyone and everything *but* the Portuguese mosquitoes. They took one whiff of me and brought their families around, like I was the All You Can Eat buffet at Denny's.

Not that the threat from mosquitoes is the scariest thing in Europe—it doesn't come close to the threat from European drivers, who drive fast, crazy, and absolutely everywhere. Oh sure, America has guys who like to go eighty-five on the highway. But would they do it four abreast downhill through an alley? Let me put it another way: The skipper of the Exxon *Valdez* is a better driver than anybody I saw in Lisbon.

To begin with, most city streets in Portugal are no wider than your thumb. Plus, they have cars parked on both sides. You'd swear you couldn't squeeze a tube of toothpaste through there. And here come three cars, barreling down on you like you're the last gas between here and the Red Sea. The cars, incidentally, are itty-bitty tin cans straight out of *The Flintstones*, and somehow they have managed to cram in six people and enough luggage to open up an American Tourister outlet. The visual effect of this is fascinating. You think you've wandered into a Farmer Gray cartoon.

Anyway, with the cars bearing down, your first instinct is to jump as far back on the sidewalk as you can. Unfortunately, this is a difficult maneuver in many European cities, as the sidewalks are already chock full of parked cars. Maybe I just don't travel enough, but it still comes as a shock to me when I walk along the sidewalk and bang into someone's front bumper. It's just something I never expect—like opening up the refrigerator and finding a live muskrat the size of Macedonia eating from a tub of cottage cheese. I don't know why so many cars are parked on the sidewalks in Europe. Maybe the rooftops don't validate.

Checking into a hotel in Lisbon, we couldn't find a parking space on the street, and the concierge had us pull up onto the sidewalk and park directly in front of the hotel lobby, so nobody could go in or out without stepping around our car.

"How long can we leave it here?" I asked, assuming we had ten minutes max to unload.

"Checkout is noon," he said.

Which was great, because it gave me more time at the topless beaches. This was my first time at a topless beach, and I think I behaved properly—other than that one silly little episode with the flash attachment, which I still think the police overreacted to. I mean, it's not like I used the whole roll on that one woman. I was simply trying to take pictures of the ocean from the cliffs with the brand-new $700 telephoto lens I happened to purchase from a man named Juan I'd just met on the street. Could I help it if from where I was standing she was right in my line of sight?

It is hard for me to be politically correct on this one. I'm asking my sisters to cut me a little slack. I mean, look at it from my perspective. (To do that you might want to borrow the dark glasses I also bought from my new best friend, Juan, who, I might add, seemed to be doing a fabulous impulse-buy business.) Where am I gonna see babes like this? They're young, they're healthy, they're doctoral candidates in physics or chemistry, I'm sure, and did I mention they're not wearing any tops? It's hard not to notice. Let me give you an example of what I mean. I was at the beach with my friends Mike and Susie, and as one particularly endowed woman bounced by, Susie happened to comment, "Did you see what a cute thing she's done with her hair?"

And I said, "She has *hair*?"

It was actually safer for me to be on the beach. When I was on the road looking down at the beach, I wasn't paying any attention to where I was walking, and so was in grave danger of either smacking into a series of parked cars on the sidewalk or wandering into the street and being run down by a tourist bus (the second leading cause of death in Portugal, after mosquito attack). I imagined my obituary starting out, "Newspaper columnist Tony Kornheiser was tragically killed yesterday in the Portuguese seaside resort of Lagos. Kornheiser apparently was preoccupied with something on the beach below and inadvertently wandered into the street in front of a tourist bus. Eyewitnesses said Kornheiser died with a sly grin on his face, though his eyes were shielded by cheap dark glasses, recently purchased. Kornheiser's best friend, Mike David, who was walking with him, said, 'What bus? I didn't see any bus. There was a bus? Hey, where's Tony?'"

I grant you I was out of control. I wish I would have been cool like the European men. They sat there like a topless beach was no big deal, like it happens to them all the time. Which, of course, it does.

I need to get to that place, where topless is no big deal. I need to get beyond my immature reaction. I'm told that after repeated exposure one gets used to topless beaches. I owe that to my sisters. Which is why I have bought a thirty-year time-share in a Portuguese condo from my main man Juan.

The Flush of Victory

LILLEHAMMER, NORWAY: In my unceasing effort to ferret out the real news, and not simply the news *they* want you to read, I have uncovered the following scandal, courtesy of a local newspaper (my favorite newspaper here is the Oslo daily *Dagbladet*, because I just love saying, "Here's the news, *Dagbladet*!"). Anyway, according to the newspaper, the sewer system of Lillehammer is dangerously close to overflowing because of EXCESSIVE FLUSHING OF CONDOMS IN THE OLYMPIC ATHLETES VILLAGE!

There is a picture of the manager of the Lillehammer sewer system kneeling beside what looks to be a huge trough of FLUSHED CONDOMS, and he's holding out a small stick, and draped over the far end are—yechhh—two FLUSHED CONDOMS, which, for all we know, may have come from Alberto Tomba's personal supply. I might describe the look on the sewer manager's face as "bemused."

The story said, in part: *"Under OL har nemlig kondomtrafikken blitt manage ganger fordoblet . . . tette til kloakken i Ol-byen."* The problem in quoting from a Norwegian newspaper is that the words are all in Norwegian. Norwegian is a language that uses more than its reasonable share of the letters *t* and *k*, and sounds

like the chunkk-ka-chunkk of ice cubes dropping into your
freezer bin. Norwegian is not a good make-out language. This is
why you will never hear anybody referred to as "the Norwegian
Johnny Mathis."

Upon translation, the key element of the story seems to be
that the Olympic athletes are DOING IT LIKE RABBITS! Usually, the Lillehammer sewer system gets its largest influx of
FLUSHED CONDOMS at 1 A.M. But since the Olympics
began, the flushing goes on TWENTY-FOUR HOURS A DAY!

This does not in any way lead me to the subject of the
next part of this column: *turisthyttene*, which are cabins in the
woods reserved for cross-country skiers. Norwegians love cross-
country skiing. They sold 100,000 tickets, and had a waiting list
of 200,000 names, for the fifty-kilometer cross-country, which
is an event where grown men with icicles in their beards disappear into the pine woods and don't come out until July. There
aren't even *seats* for these events. Norwegians just stand in the
cold and wave their Norwegian flags. Curiously, this is the single
greatest danger you face at the Olympics—getting your eyes
poked out as you walk through the crowded streets passing millions of Norwegian flags that stick out of backpacks just at eye
level.

Anyway, Norwegians love to cross-country ski (Dan Jenkins
once said the reason the Norwegians win all the cross-country
races is because that's how they go to the 7-Eleven), and the
government encourages them by offering them these cabins to
bunk in. There are three classes of cabins. The top class is like a
hotel. You get three meals and full service staff for about $120 a
night—and they validate your parka. Har har. That's a ski joke.
The second class offers beds, cutlery, and canned food, and oper-
ates on the honor system; there is a box for you to leave your
money in. The third-class cabins are spartan; there might be a
bed, or simply a floor where you'd place your bedroll and sleep.

These cabins are literally open to everyone—they have no locks on the doors.

The idea of providing shelter for people is a noble idea, but it strikes me that the cabins underscore some of the cultural differences between Norway and America. We might spring for $120 for three meals and a nice bed—if there were some Marriott points involved. But that "honor system" stuff, I don't know. Where I grew up, in New York, not only would people not *leave* money in the box after they finished eating the food and sleeping in the beds, they would steal the money, and the food, *and* the box. The place would be a crack house in fifteen seconds. In fact, if people in New York read this and realize these cabins are just lying here for the picking in Norway, they'll take up skiing. Personally, I'd be at a loss if I had to leave money in the box. I've been here three weeks and I still have no idea about Norwegian money. I'm not good in math, so it does me no good to know that it's 7 kroner to the dollar; I can't make the conversion in my head. If my dinner costs 230 kroner—and for you weenies in the accounting department, it's always at least that—I have no idea what that is in American money, and I don't try to figure it out, because by the time I do, I'll have missed the bus. To me, 230 kroner is simply two pretty burgundy bills with a picture of a woman from the 1800s, and a smaller green bill with a man with a beard. There are also purplish bills with a picture of the man who wrote the Norwegian constitution, and a blue bill with the composer Edvard Grieg. I love foreign money because it's so pretty. I'll bet in the new, hip countries you can get flaming orange bills, or bills that are black and teal, like those cool Charlotte Hornets hats!

If a sandwich costs 43 kroner, I don't bother trying to come up with the 43 myself, I simply pour all my coins into my hands, hold my hands out like I am the village idiot, and let the Norwegians pick through the small, thick gold coins with King Olaf and the bigger, thinner coins with King Harold, and the tiny wafer coins with the shield or the dog. I trust the Norwegians will take the right amount and not cheat me. How can you not trust people who don't put locks on their cabins?

GETTING TOWED FROM LIFE'S LITTLE PARKING SPACE

*

Born to Raise Heck

So I'm at a dinner party the other night, a casual thing among friends, and the host, the thoroughly suburbanized E. (not his real initial) announces he is buying a truck.

Mouths open.

A what?

A truck, E. says.

Everybody looks at E. He's never seemed to be the truck type. He is wearing a cashmere sweater and velour shoes. And if his eyes were any worse, he'd be a bat. Nobody can imagine E. at a truck stop—except as a hostage.

A truck? Like to haul pipe?

No, E. says. A small truck, a four-wheel-drive truck.

Oh, a *yuppie* truck. A cross between a big Jeep and a Lincoln Town Car. All the big-feet corporate lawyers have them. Whaddya gonna do with it, drive over to Sutton Place Gourmet and hang out with the Range Rovers?

"It's just your age," someone tells E., who's fifty-one (not his real age). "You're having a midlife crisis."

He's having a midlife crisis, someone tells E.'s wife, J. (not her real initial).

J. shrugs.

"Cheaper than a mistress," she says.

Not really, someone says. It only gets three miles to the gallon.

"Well," J. says, "cheaper than a divorce."

How you gonna put it in four-wheel drive, someone asks E., when you can't even go to the self-serve pump without bringing a change of clothes?

What are ya, nuts, someone else says. Whaddya need a four-wheel drive for? You live in Bethesda (not E. and J.'s real town).

"It's a recreation vehicle," E. says.

A recreation vehicle? Who talks like this? And where might we be recreating in our vehicle, where might we journey off-road to traverse the ecological frontier?

"Suppose I want to go hunting and fishing," E. says.

Marty and Karen (their real names—I'm not making fun of them, what do they care?) are laughing hysterically. Since when do you hunt and fish? What are you, Natty Bumppo? You get squeamish holding a can of tuna.

"Who's gonna give you a hunting license with *your* eyesight?" Karen wants to know. "At twenty yards you can't tell the difference between a deer and the Suez Canal. You'll end up shooting cows!"

I try to picture E. driving down Route 270 with a cow strapped across the hood, and a cop stops him and says, "What're you going after next, Deadeye, a Perdue Oven Stuffer?"

Does it really come with a gun rack? somebody asks.

No, J. says. "It's a yuppie truck. It comes with a brie knife."

E. starts ticking off the features: Tinted glass. Power windows. Reclining leather seats. Sunroof. CD system.

What's it called? someone asks.

"It's a Blazer Lake Tahoe," E. says.

A Lake Tahoe? They're naming trucks after resorts now? What's next, a Chevy Club Med?

Why did you do this?

"He wants to go to Vermont and see the leaves turn," J. says.

And he can't take a bus?

There are leaves around the corner. You can walk.

"Haven't you ever wanted to go fly-fishing?" E. asks.

We look at him as if he were a penguin.

You don't know anything about fishing, someone says. You'll go to cast, and you'll hook the back of your neck and bleed to death in the stream.

He'll never get to the stream, someone else says. He has no idea how much power these things have. Talk about going off-road, the first time E. turns on the engine, he'll crash through his garage and into his living room. He'll demolish his center-hall Colonial (not his real house).

Or worse, he'll slip a disk just climbing into the cab.

"This isn't you," Marty tells E. "You're not an outdoors guy. You gotta buy waders to go fishing. Whaddya know about waders? You hear 'wader,' you think you're ordering Chinese."

"The truck will be fun," E. says.

Fun? What fun? The part where you break down on the road, and some Bubbas come over, and say, "Pretty far from Connecticut and K, ain't you, Hoss?"

Haven't you ever seen *Deliverance*?

"We'll go skiing," E. says.

"I don't want to go skiing," J. says.

"Come on. We'll take a vacation and go skiing," E. says. "With a truck like this, we can go anywhere."

"I want to go to the Bahamas," J. says.

He's having a midlife crisis, J. is assured.

You're having a midlife crisis, someone says to E. You'll get a tool belt, and a chain saw, and the next time any of us see you, you'll be living in a treehouse.

"Not a chance," J. says. "He's afraid of heights. Just sitting in the front seat of the truck will be enough to kill him."

That was a couple of weeks ago. E. has since bought the truck. It's maroon (not its real color). He has never carried anything in it, because the bed is exposed, and he's afraid to leave the truck unattended. On the first day he drove it to work at the National Security Council (not his real place of employment), where he advises the president on domestic affairs (not his real job), his ignition key was stolen from the garage.

So now, E. rides the bus to work. He keeps his truck at home, paranoid that whoever stole the key will break into his home, remove his wide-screen TV, his overhead-projector VCR, his rowing and Nautilus equipment, and his Dolby Surround audio system—and haul them away in his spanking-new truck.

The moral of this story is: The older you get, the wiser you get (not my real point).

Shut Up, Barbie

Apparently, Barbie has made a boo-boo. One of the 270 catchy statements the new Teen Talk Barbie is programmed to say is: "Math class is tough!" This has drawn the wrath of the National Council of Teachers of Mathematics, which, when you think about it, sounds like one wild, happenin' assembly of monster party dudes with plastic pocket pencil caddies.

The math teachers' position is, Teen Talk Barbie plays into a stereotype that girls are stupid in math.

Now, I don't want to offend women, many of whom are real babes. And I certainly don't want to hurt the feelings of all the girls out there—one of whom is my daughter—but unfortunately, girls are—how shall I put this sensitively—stupid in math. Everyone who's been through junior high school knows this.

I give you this example. My own personal daughter, who is nine and whom I love dearly, is extremely conscientious about her homework. She will spend a full hour telling me about the books she read that day. However, when I ask her how much is eight times nine, she says: "Dad, please, I'm on the phone."

My feeling is that girls aren't good in math because the cold logic of it has no appeal. Girls are more interested in emotion and sensitivity. They are nurturers.

Let's look at a typical math question: "A bus leaves Pittsburgh at 7 P.M., heading for Cleveland, and traveling 50 miles per hour. If Cleveland is 200 miles away, at what time will the bus arrive?"

I posed this problem to my daughter.

Her answer was: "Are there enough seat belts on the bus, Daddy?"

Girls are bad in math, and boys are bad in English. Boys grow up with no concept of words and their relationships to each other. Let me re-create a typical boys' conversation:

Boy No. 1: Me and Freddy, we were, you know, like, uh, going, uh, with the thing, and, you know, like, what's doing?

Boy No. 2: [grunts].

So when it comes to a test of their language skills, and there are no uhs, likes, and you knows, boys have no recognition of this particular language and can't negotiate simple terrain. They are lost on standardized English tests:

"Good" is to "best" as "warm" is to . . .

Boys write in: "elevator."

What interests me is the notion that Barbie shouldn't be saying, "Math class is tough!"

Help me out here. Why should anybody expect Barbie to say anything but "hunh?"? I mean, what are we talking about? Teen Talk Barbie isn't the only new Barbie this year—there is also Totally Hair Barbie. *Totally Hair Barbie!*

There has been a Surfin' Barbie, a Stewardess Barbie, Beach Blanket Barbie, Barbie Goes to the Beauty Shop. And *now* they're worried about what Barbie says?

What were you expecting, Kierkegaard Barbie?

Barbie is a bimbo.

Always was.

Totally Hair Barbie! (As opposed to Klaus Barbie, the Totally Herr Barbie.)

Look at Barbie's proportions. If you extrapolated her out, and made her, say, five feet five, her measurements would be something like 45-13-40. This is someone who's likely to make conversation about nineteenth-century agrarian reform?

My daughter has many Barbies already, and every birthday and holiday she asks for more Barbies and more Barbie accessories. She and her friends sit and play Barbie for hours. They spend days planning Barbie weddings, Barbie kitchen renovations, Barbie orthodontist appointments. My daughter loves Barbie.

I, on the other hand, loathe Barbie. (I loathe Legos, too, especially in a dark room at three in the morning, with no socks on. But that's a different column.) Every father will understand why I loathe Barbie: Because I walk around the house picking up tiny, stupid pieces of junk from the floor, which I throw out—and which turn out to be Barbie's shoes, or Barbie's purse, or Barbie's contraceptive device. Who knew? (By the way, Barbie's shoes are usually spiked high heels, a great role-modeling device for small girls. Who designs these things, Tina Turner?)

Anyway, throwing these stupid little things out gets me in big trouble with my daughter, who doesn't buy the explanation that I mistook Barbie's black spiked heels for half-eaten raisins, of the kind she and her brother routinely deposit between the cushions on the couch, and she starts throwing a terrible tantrum, which ultimately results in my driving her to the Barbie store ("How nice to see you back so soon, Mr. Kornheiser. Did we inadvertently throw away Barbie's cotillion fan?"), where I am relieved of eighty bucks, and that afternoon I see spread before me on the floor a host of impossibly tiny plastic gizmos that, I am informed, is Barbie Has a Totally Awesome Picnic.

So anyhow, what's the big deal if Barbie thinks math class is tough? Math class *is* tough. Until I was twelve, I couldn't count past ten without taking off my socks.

But if the math teachers insist, let's think about what Barbie *should* say to be relevant in the '90s.

"You know, you really ought to get that looked at."

"Hi, my name is Barbie and I'm a codependent." *("Hi, Barbieeee.")*

"Ken, I am leaving you for Courtney."

"The coefficient of X is inversely proportional to the lateral vector of pi."

"Lower middle class is tough."

And of course:

"Hey, where are my genitals?"

With Liberty and Justice for Gall

As a patriotic American who is saddened by the erosion of values in our communities, I am determined to do my small part to make this country great again. And so I have decided to build an enormous gazebo in my backyard, and to get you to pay for it.

Perhaps this requires some explanation.

"America, the Beautiful" is more than just a song that inexplicably describes mountains as "purple." America the Beautiful is a national credo. Being beautiful is as American as apple pie used to be before the Matsamuto Electronic & Hydraulics Corp. engineered a leveraged buyout of Granny Butterworth's Pies, Inc.

Have you *seen* America lately? Have you checked out the strip malls, the burger joints, the endless parade of car dealerships, the UA Solarplex Cinema 1-2-3-4-5-6-7-8-9-10-11-12-14, where the neon marquee is larger than Mount Rushmore?

Well, I, for one, in a patriotic fervor, have decided to fight back. And I am going to start with my own backyard. The gazebo. A terrace made out of shale chipped from a quarry in Saskatoon. Tiny Japanese bonsai trees, the ones that look like broccoli stuck in dirt. Chinese lanterns hanging from the roof like lollipops. A tethered llama I shall name Maximilian. No expense will be spared. Nothing is too good for America—except, possibly, Jerry Lewis.

And America will get the bill for this because I am applying for tax-exempt status, on the grounds that I am doing my small part to beautify America.

If this sounds a trifle nervy to you, consider the case of William I. Koch, the multimillionaire who rounded up $68.5 million to build a yacht and win the America's Cup—a race nobody ever heard of until ESPN was invented.

You financed his yacht.

Is this a great country, or what?

Koch, whose personal fortune is estimated at $650 million, received tax-exempt status for the America Foundation, which solicited funds to build his yacht, on the theory that he was contributing to the advancement of America's amateur sports effort.

I can see how giving money to cure disease is tax-deductible. I can see how giving money to a school is tax-deductible.

But a *yacht*?

What are we doing here, making the world safe for Blistex?

Is the future of yachting a key national concern?

How many of you yacht?

How many of you have ever had this conversation?

"Hey, Angie, whaddya wanna do tonight?"

"I dunno, Marty, what do *you* wanna do?"

"I was thinkin' maybe we could put on our white ducks and go down to the yacht club, order a dry martini or two, and trim the mainsail."

"Cool. Lemme call Consuela and tell her to have Bitterman bring around the roadster."

Yachting is the least populist sport this side of polo. And it's even less utilitarian. At least in polo, if you get hungry, you can eat the horse. How do you become a yacht skipper anyway? What's the test, parallel-park the QE2?

(While we're on the subject, if it's pronounced "yot," how come they spell it "yacht"? Does anybody say it's "hacht" outside?)

For about 125 years the America's Cup was merely a tin pot that collected dust in a corner of the New York Yacht Club. Every few years a bunch of filthy-rich American bankers and brokers in silly hats and blue double-breasted crested blazers with gold buttons put a boat in the water and raced against a bunch of similarly rich and similarly dressed foreigners, and then drank champagne until they fell overboard and had to be rescued by their chauffeurs and driven home. The world at large didn't care who won. Hardly anybody knew there was a race. Have you ever seen a yacht race? It is not like, say, the Kentucky Derby. You can't even tell which *direction* they're going.

Then one year we lost the Cup, and suddenly it was Armageddon.

Along came people like Dennis Conner and Bill Koch, wrapping themselves in the American flag, braying about how our national honor was at stake—and won't you please send money?

Tax-deductible.

For a yacht.

Defenders of the America's Cup argue that winning it makes everybody in America feel good—although I suspect Sears shoppers could survive its loss, considering that for 125 years nobody even knew we had it. They praise technological advancements, such as lightweight sails. And I suppose that's great . . . if the next time we go to war, we use a fleet of catamarans.

No, yachting is not a valuable American resource, worth protecting. But something else is: the chutzpah that allows a man to tax-deduct his yacht. What could be more of an inalienable American right than gall?

Maledictory Address

Dear high school graduates:

I agreed to address you today because I am concerned for the safety of our republic. As Woody Allen once wrote: "Mankind is at a crossroads. One path leads to oblivion, the other to total destruction. I pray we have the courage to choose correctly."

Many journalists give commencement speeches. We work cheap. We are also considered to be people in the know, filled with canny observations about politics. I will keep mine brief. I love Ross Perot. I admire a guy who thinks he can be president because he ran a successful business. That's why when I want a really good meal, I go to a furrier.

Let me tell you what I remember about my high school graduation twenty-six years ago. We had a speaker who told us to look around at our fellow classmates—because we were the Leaders of Tomorrow. Someday we would be Running the Country.

I'm about the same age as most of your parents. So I want you kids to look at your parents. Are any of them running the country? Your father falls asleep at the dinner table with his mouth open. Your mother plans her whole life around Last Call at Neiman Marcus.

Your parents are such dweebs. They walk around the house humming songs by Wayne Fontana and the Mindbenders! They embarrass you at every waking moment. My daughter is almost ten. She hasn't spoken to me in three years except to say, "More gravy." When her friends come over, she says I'm the gardener. Tell the truth, kids, you can't believe how totally uncool your parents are!

Do they look to you like the Leaders of Today?

You won't be the Leaders of Tomorrow either. You won't Run the Country.

The kids from the St. George Country Day School will.

You should have been smarter.

Anyway, who knows if there'll be a country to run. I've seen so many changes in my lifetime. There's no Soviet Union anymore, no East Germany, no Iron Curtain. Thirty years ago, John Kennedy made his famous *"Ich bin ein Berliner"* speech. Now what would he say? *"Ich bin ein Bosnia-Herzegowinian"*?

I know that most of you plan to go to college and become communications majors. Everybody wants his own talk show. Take my advice, learn to drive a bus. Somebody's got to take all these communications majors to the unemployment office.

Four years from now you'll be back living at home. I lived at home for a while when I got out of school. I was working nights, getting home at 3 A.M. I'd have a snack and sleep until noon. My dad kept telling me it wasn't a hotel—I couldn't keep leaving my dishes in the sink, waiting for my mom to clean them. Soon, Dad actually started putting my dirty dishes in the bed while I was sleeping. I moved out. It took me years to get even. My dad is 82 years old. When he comes to visit, I hide his Depends.

I think back to high school, and I can honestly say almost nothing I learned is of any use to me now—unless I get on *Jeop-*

ardy! and the category is "William the Conqueror." Other than that, I have a calculator to do my math, a computer to correct my spelling, and an editor to correct my syntax, whatever may be that.

The best course I ever took was driver's education. In New York State when I was growing up, you couldn't get your driver's license until eighteen, unless you passed a driver's ed course in high school—then you could get it at seventeen. The first time I ever got in the car, my instructor had me drive up a narrow street in a busy commercial area and parallel-park. I did it. And he said, "Okay, Tony, get out and let Susan Pfeffer drive." I opened the door, and a truck sheared it right off! Boom, the door was gone! Most of my hair fell out right then. The next time I got in the driver's ed car, a girl named Chelsea Nunez-Katz (not her real name) was behind the wheel. Beautiful girl, a cheerleader. My high school was building a swimming pool at the time. Chelsea had just done her nails, and she didn't want to chip the polish on the steering wheel, so she gripped it with her knees and, needless to say, drove us right into the excavation. We were knee-deep in pool water. Chelsea is the only person ever in New York State to get her license and her water safety instructor's card on the same day.

I go to all my high school reunions. I think of my high school friends as the best ones I ever made. They're the ones who knew you when you were the most insecure jerk in the universe, when you couldn't get a date, when you couldn't pass a test. You'll go to these reunions, and people will come up to you and give you a big hug and say, "Gee, your face cleared up."

In closing, let me quote Dean Vernon Wormer of Faber College, and what he said to a student named Kent Dorfman: "Son, fat, drunk, and stupid is no way to go through life."

Thank you.

Good luck.

And drive carefully. I'm out there, too.

This is excerpted from Anthony I. Kornheiser's speech to the 1992 graduating class at Bullis School. Kornheiser will make the same speech to your school for the standard fee of $16,500. But you must send a limo.

Oat Bran Bites the Dust

Boy oh boy do I feel good this morning. I'm sitting down to breakfast with a big smile on my face.

No more guilt.

And no more oat bran.

Praise the Harvard researchers, and pass the butter.

I need a good breakfast today. I have some heavy lifting to do. I've got to go through my pantry and gather up the boxes of oat bran cereal we've bought in the last few years: Post Oat Flakes, Kellogg's Oatbake, Quaker Oat Squares, Oat Bran O's, Oat Bran Options, Cracklin' Oat Bran, Common Sense Oat Bran, 3 Minute Oats Plus Oat Bran, Oh's, Nutrific Oatmeal Flakes, Mother's Oat Bran, Wholesome and Hearty Oat Bran.

Yep, gonna gather them all up. And dump them down the toidy.

And then I'm gonna get a machete and go after Wilfred Brimley. Because it's the *right thing to do*, you old goat? Because it's the *right thing to do*?

Read *The New England Journal of Medicine*, oat breath.

I hate that guy.

Can we be honest about the taste of oat bran?

It was like chewing on a carpet.

Okay, toasted carpet.

That differentiates it from the health food craze of the 1970s, wheat germ, which tasted like sawdust. I resisted the temptation to pour wheat germ on everything including the dog. Why would you eat something called wheat *germ?* By the same token, how does anyone put a spoonful of Mueslix in his mouth? What an awful-sounding word, *Mueslix.* Did you ever see it? It looks like fish food. In our house we have Count Chocula. Maybe it'll kill you, but you'll die smiling.

Nobody actually liked oat bran muffins, you know. (Sorry, I take that back. Secretariat liked them.) "It was like eating a Brillo pad," my friend Jim said. They were the biggest, driest muffins I've ever seen. The first time I saw one, I thought it was a bowling ball for a midget.

The study group was fed five oat bran muffins a day along with their usual diets. Five oat bran muffins a day for six weeks! They don't even eat that many on *thirtysomething.*

And so another cure for high cholesterol bites the dust. Truthfully, I hadn't heard about cholesterol until a few years ago. Nobody ever told me bacon and eggs was death. Stupid me, I actually liked eating steak. Of course, as soon as I learned cholesterol was lethal I immediately started eating foods low in cholesterol, like soybeans, polyester blends, and the cardboard cartons from IKEA. I was particularly conscious of using products fortified with high fiber. My car runs on a high-fiber unleaded gas. I don't know the octane, but after we fill up it automatically pulls over at rest stops.

(What really confused me was finding out there was good cholesterol and bad cholesterol. I was hoping I could get both at the same place—the Carnegie Deli. Unfortunately my HMO doesn't cover pastrami overdose.)

It's a whole new world since cholesterol. I went to a dinner party a couple of months ago where the hostess served nothing but whole-grain breads and water.

"What happens after we eat, does the governor pardon us?" I asked.

"This will reduce your cholesterol," she assured me.

"And I'll live longer?"

"At least five years," she smiled.

"Which five? I'd like to do nineteen over a few times, but if you're giving me eighty-one through eighty-six, save the bread and slap some pork chops on the grill."

I guess oat bran will fall off the face of the earth now. I can assure you the bloom is already off the husk. Yesterday morning, within hours of the news that oat bran was no better at reducing cholesterol than snake meat, my pal John at Bethesda's Chesapeake Bagel Bakery reported that while business was brisk in rye, onion, and plain, there was hardly a dent in his bin of oat bran bagels.

"They're not moving," he said.

"How do they taste?" I asked.

"I put some molasses in to give them flavor. Otherwise, you know, they'd taste like carpet."

On the same day we learned oat bran was a fraud, the *Washington Times*'s wine columnist wrote that heart attacks could be avoided by drinking two to five glasses of wine daily—not exactly hardship therapy. Then, one day later, we're told that if we drink a lot of coffee, our sex life will improve after sixty. (If I drink twice as much, can it start now?) It's like in *Sleeper*, when Woody Allen wakes up two hundred years from now and finds out that chocolate and red meat are actually *good* for you.

Who knew!

"I ate the oat bran to balance the wine that I assumed was killing me," Jim said. "I was hoping to make it to sixty. Now I don't have to eat any oat bran, and if I drink enough coffee, sixty will be the start of my good years. I'm elated."

It's pretty much good food news in the '90s so far—except for you folks who bought Quaker Oats stock recently.

Oat farmers are hurting, but they can convert to wheat or barley. Think of this as the first shot in the Grain Equality Movement.

Yuppie bakeries might be hurt briefly, but the next muffin trend should be rolling by in thirty seconds.

The problem would seem to be disposing of the massive oat bran storage. (I mean, really, how many bird feeders do we have?) Remember when we had all that surplus cheese? We gave it away on street corners—that's probably what started the cholesterol crisis.

Nobody's going to queue up for oat bran. It'll end up as an export. You're familiar with the TV commercial where the two older kids push a bowl of cereal at the little kid and say, "Let's see if Mikey likes it."

Well, let's see if Romania likes it.

Cigarettes and Virile Chicks

Let's hear it for the public-spirited R. J. Reynolds Tobacco Co. Those same geniuses who tried to foist Uptown on black people are at it again with a cigarette brand called Dakota they're aiming at white girls, ages eighteen to twenty, with no education beyond high school and a longing to marry young and have babies.

The phrasemakers for Reynolds publicly call them "virile females." Their studies say VFs are glued to *Roseanne* and nighttime soaps, tag alongside their boyfriends to tractor pulls, and flock together to cruise shopping malls and bars. We can guess what the phrasemakers for Reynolds call them behind closed doors.

R. J. Reynolds should be kidney-punched for marketing this. Like Uptown, Dakota is an unscrupulous attempt to exploit and eventually kill a vulnerable group. In this particular case the sense of outrage is tied to society's protective instinct toward young girls. Symbolically, introducing a cigarette like this borders on molestation. Anyway, we don't really need another brand of cigarette, do we?

Think of the horror parents will face. Bad enough that your daughter comes home smoking. Total nightmare if she comes home smoking Dakotas, the brand of choice of cheap sluts like Kelly Bundy.

"Loretta, is that a pack of Dakotas in your back pocket?"

"What's it to ya?"

"What happened to your neonatology courses? What happened to your dream of attending the University of Chicago and becoming a doctor?"

"That's for losers. I'm gettin' a factory job."

"And I suppose you'll live in a trailer park too?"

"Yeah. Wanna make somethin' of it?"

"Oh honey, I thought you wanted more out of life."

"I do. Someday I want a one-bedroom brick rambler."

I imagine today's virile female sitting at home, spending forty-five minutes a day with hot rollers, a blow dryer, and a curling iron, reading *Soap Opera Digest* and eating bag food. She hopes the trick to cooking is figuring out the gauges on the microwave. She's a little too loud, wears a little too much lip gloss and eye shadow. You've seen her before, Joan Cusack played her in *Working Girl.* She's probably no less honest and no less industrious than everyone else, but when she looks up she sees a lower ceiling. Those marketing geniuses say she likes classic rock 'n' roll (Steppenwolf is my guess). She has a job—not a career—it's something she has to endure until five each day when she gets off and meets her boyfriend, who thinks as short-term as she does. Sha-la la-la-la-la live for today.

I went to high school with girls like this. We called them "hitter chicks," because they liked to hit people, and I adored them for their wild ways. They got in fights, duking it out in the hallways. The guys were astonished at how savagely they fought. Guys never bit or pulled hair or ripped clothing. First thing hitter chicks did in a fight was rip the other girl's blouse off. That's why so many of the boys crowded around.

Their signature look got me crazy: tight dark skirt, black fishnet stockings, and spiked heels. They all dyed their hair either black or blond, and did it up in a rattail bouffant piled high enough to hide a sharp comb inside that they could use as a weapon. They were very big on chewing gum, often grape gum; they'd pop it so loud, it sounded like an air rifle. (The gum you find stuck under chairs and tables? They stuck it there.) They drove Cougars and Camaros with reclining bucket seats and a glove-compartment door that folded down into a tray to hold two large Cokes from McDonald's.

Hitter chicks smoked Marlboros in the red box. ("Marlboro greens only if they were wearing a wedding dress," my friend Henry points out.) Normally they hung out in twos near an outdoor phone booth or a liquor store. On dates, you didn't have to buy a pint to make sure you had a good time, a hitter chick had that covered. Very hetero, very. I used to fantasize about driving to Palisades Park with one for a weekend, knowing if anything went wrong with the car she could fix it.

I rarely took a class with the hitter chicks. (It was hard to major in both Chaucer and stenography.) Once though, in driver's ed, our paths crossed. Three of us in the same car, all sixteen, me, Arthur, and the beautiful Tina. She was quite glamorous. I wanted to go out with her, but she dated much older guys—mostly with criminal records. I believe one of the boys she was pinned to was recently executed.

Other than to practice backing around a church parking lot with my father, I'd never been behind the wheel. Tina had already been driving for four years. She drove to school every day. She owned her own car. I don't know why she was taking driver's ed—she should have been *giving* it. I'd ask, "Tina, how can you drive when you don't have a license? Aren't you afraid of getting in trouble?" She'd French-inhale her cigarette, and laugh and say, "What are they gonna do about it, give me the electric chair?"

They were building a swimming pool at my school then. One day there was an accident. A student drove a car through the barricades and smack into the pool, leaving it hubcap-deep in water at a forty-five-degree angle like a beached freighter. It goes without saying the driver was Tina. She walked away singing "Walking in the Rain."

After all these years, after NOW and ERA and Title IX, isn't it interesting to see the staying power of hitter chicks? After changes upon changes we are more or less the same. I imagine Tina's oldest is about twenty now, just the age the marketing geniuses are aiming at. I hope she doesn't smoke, but if she does, I hope it won't be Dakotas. No second-generation hitter chick should have to buy self-esteem in a cellophane pack.

So Long, Orlon

Orlon, one of the Four Mus-keteers of sportswear along with Dacron, Ban-Lon, and rayon, will breathe no more. (Or stretch. Or wipe clean with a damp cloth. Or whatever it is that synthetic fibers do.)

The Du Pont Co., which created Orlon forty years ago, said the other day that it will shut down Orlon production "as soon as possible."

Bubba, acrylics are history.

I'll wait while you get a tissue.

(And while some of you clean out your closets.)

Orlon—chemically, it's polyacrylonitryl, and by the way it is not, repeat not, melt-stable (I could explain this to you, as a Du Pont chemist explained it to me, but what's the point? How many of you are going to MIT anyway?)—is found in many things, all of which escape me at the moment.

"You won't particularly miss it," the Du Pont chemist told me.

And that's the truth. We won't miss it. We wouldn't miss Ban-Lon or Dacron or nylon either. They're made-up fabrics. One day they're a shirt, the next day they're a landfill. They look like something else. They feel like something else. They act like something else. And in no case are they as good as that something else.

We won't miss them.

We don't need them.

We ought to celebrate their passing.

Orlon's gone.

Hooray.

Though sexless and dull in that utilitarian way of fabrics that were designed to act like other fabrics—only cheaper—Orlon was distinguished as the only synthetic blend to give its name to a rock 'n' roll group. We remember the Orlons of "Don't Hang Up" and "South Street." But we'll never remember the Dacrons, the Lycras, or Danny and the Naugahydes.

Alas, poor Orlon, we knew you well. Once you defined our existence. Once you were our future. Once you were the only miracle fabric we had. (Well, okay, we had nylon, too, but it's all in the family, isn't it, nylon, pylon, Longylon.) And now, what? No one even remembers your washing instructions.

Wash in Woolite.

"No, that was rayon."

Tumble dry.

"No, that was Acrylan."

Do not bleach.

"No, that was the dog."

As a fiber, Orlon was somewhere between Qiana and doubleknit, in the same way that Iowa is somewhere between Pennsylvania and Colorado (Qiana being the scariest of the miracle fabrics, it's so clingy it's almost alive). Orlon was slippery, although not as slippery as Teflon.

"Fabrics and Politics," for $800.

Who was the Orlon president?

"Fabrics and Geography," for $400.

True or false: Burkina Faso used to be Upper Orlon?
Lightning Round: Name four uses of Orlon.
1. To polish Zamfir's pan flute;
2. To coat the tiles on the space shuttle;
3. William Shatner's hair weave;
4. Miss America evening gowns.

Orlon actually was a major component in sweaters in the 1950s, '60s, and '70s. You could recognize Orlon sweaters by how limitlessly they stretched. They stretched so much you'd think that Jackie Gleason sneaked into your closets late at night while you were asleep and tried them on.

"Ever buy anything made of Orlon?" I asked someone.

"Not knowingly," he sneered.

I thought I owned an Orlon golf shirt, but on second thought realized it was Ban-Lon. And I thought I had an Orlon windbreaker, but maybe it was Dacron. Could I have owned Orlon shoes?

Oops, Corfam.

It's so hard to keep the miracle substances straight. You never know which is which. You use one to fasten your shoes instead of laces, another glues your shoes to the ceiling, another lets you hang upside down in your shoes from the ceiling while firming and toning your abdominal muscles, and still another will convert your shoes into a playroom while-u-wait.

Orlon, of course, has become as much a part of America as sugar in the raw and diet chocolate fudge soda. It's virtually impossible to conceive of a world without Orlon. I can remember as a kid when my mom sang to me about "the train they call the City of New Orlons," chugging out of Arkansas with a new crop of Orlon from the plantations, bound for glory and the Milan fashion shows.

Du Pont hasn't announced what it will do with the remaining supply of Orlon, whether it will be donated to the Synthetic Fibers Museum in Reno—and displayed next to John Travolta's three-piece disco leisure suit—or sealed in a cylinder, and buried at sea. (It can't be put into the ground; it's not biodegradable.)

It's funny how things happen. Just the other day I overheard a conversation that started with these words: "They're not making Orlon the way they used to." And now they're not making it at all.

PG-13, NC-17, *Hike!*

Now that we've started to get used to the new NC-17, let's make sure we understand the old movie-rating system, using *Bambi* as a model.

G: No foul language. No sex. The acknowledgment of violence—Bambi's mother is shot off-screen by a hunter—but no visible bloodshed.

PG: Introduction of foul language, but delivered in a cute manner: Bambi's wise-guy kid brother calls Thumper a "----face." Introduction of mature themes: Early one morning Bambi spots a strange pair of antlers outside his mother's door. Consciousness-raising violence: Hunters are shown dropping rabbits into a stew pot.

PG-13: Escalation of mature themes: Bambi's fraternity brothers sit around discussing sex; one young buck resembling Judd Nelson unwraps a condom and shows it to the others. Emphasis on teenage concerns: The hunters—symbolizing typical adult authority figures—are depicted as mean and slothful.

R: Magnification of mature themes: Bambi is a pimp. His sister dances at a topless bar. Gratuitous violence: Bambi's mother is shot with an AK-47.

X: Total depravity: Bambi agrees to be tied up in a deer-slave love tryst. Thumper is sliced up with a chain saw and fed to wolves. Bambi's mother has graphic sex with Smokey the Bear and is snuffed.

Of course we don't have to worry about X anymore. X went poof.

Voila, NC-17.

And now for the complete score: NC 17, Duke 6.

NC-17 poses a problem for hard-core porn movies, which now advertise as XXX. NC-17 NC-17 NC-17 takes up so much space on the marquee there's hardly any room left for John "Wadd" Holmes. They could advertise as NC-51, but the higher math would confuse their audience.

Why NC-17? A Double-R, or RR, rating was rejected, because it was feared too many people would step up to the ticket window and order roast beef and cheese.

(I'll let you in on the secret: X didn't really go poof. NC-17 is X with an expensive haircut. Under the old rating system studios were afraid to make Xs because there was no profit in them—they couldn't do saturation advertising because many mainstream publications wouldn't take ads for X-rated movies. But with this happy-face NC-17, newspapers will likely take the ads. You didn't realize this was all about money? Shame on you. Soon there'll be lots more moody, dirty movies for adults. Is this a great country, or what?)

What good are ratings? As a parent, I want to know how much cursing, how much sex, and how much violence there will be in a movie so I can make an informed decision whether to allow my children to go. If there's a lot of sex—is Laura San Giacomo in the film?—my children can't go, because I'm going, and it's embarrassing for all of us to be there together. Someone should stay home with my wife.

Wouldn't it help if ratings were more specific? For example, shouldn't we differentiate between external and internal violence? Typically, external violence is a pizza-faced kid who couldn't get a date for the prom putting on a hockey mask and slashing every living thing in Toledo. This is an HEV-163: heavy external violence, at least 163 mutilated body parts. (Do not confuse this with HOV-3, a rush-hour car chase film.) Internal violence is what happens to your duodenum if you watch this film. This gets a V rating, for vomit. *The Cook, the Thief, His Wife & Her Lover* would get a V-4 rating, indicating you would rrrrralph up not only today's meals but also those from the past few days.

In terms of sex, some people may want to distinguish between quantity and quality. (To them I say, Hey, who's got time for quality?) But for most of us, the simple MSH rating—More Sex than at Home—will suffice.

The MR rating warns people this is a Molly Ringwald film.

An S rating warns that Martin Sheen or one of his sons is in the film. Avoid S-3.

The VK rating is an insider's term referring to a film that has changed its content to soften its rating: In the original *Godfather*, it wasn't a horse's head in the bed, it was Victor Kiam, wiggling his waggle. This was considered too horrible, so the scene was rewritten.

NACL contains salty language.

UL-185 is the price of unleaded gas this week.

COD is the Chill Out Dad rating, which signifies that your children believe they can handle a movie that you wouldn't even take your wife to. *Blue Velvet* is a COD.

CG-35 is a movie you need your kid's permission to see.

NA, for No Adults, is a movie with any combination of skateboarding, ninjas, bicycle messengers, and Kiefer Sutherland.

BP-160 is a movie starring Julia Roberts, and is unsuitable for men with high blood pressure.

NO-83 is the temperature forecast in New Orleans.

BW-90 is a Bruce Willis film, requiring proof that your IQ is below 90.

SAT-450 is a Stallone film.

CSNY means the movie has a strong '60s content.

MIT: Strong Nerd Content.

The I rating means you have to come alone.

NG means this film is no good.

NFG is the NC-17 version of this film.

Witless for the Prosecution

If we're lucky, by now Kato Kaelin will be finally and forever off the witness stand, and pretty much out of our lives (unless you have a guest house). But the crucial questions about Kato are left hanging:

1. Where does he go from here?
2. How does he get his hair like that?

Let's take his hair first. It is dyed and streaked and layered and razored, and the ends are perfectly curled. It's a cascade of color and texture. It's as thick as Russian dressing; I suspect Kato uses mayonnaise on it. It must take him three hours a day to get it that way. America's best-loved feature writer, Mr. Henry, calls Kato's coif "Conan the Librarian."

Being un-haired myself (memo to Robt. Shapiro: The Rogaine isn't working for you either, pal), I called my friend Nancy as an expert witness. She stared at Kato's hair, and concluded, "I guess it's cleaned and moussed, as opposed to dirty and stringy. But it's a very thin line."

As to where Kato goes from here, well, he's a very hot property as a house guest. Kato is reportedly living in Charlie Sheen's house now—I guess Judd Nelson's guest room was booked. And there are *thousands* of guest houses to go through in L.A.

County alone before he begins freeloading his way east, so I wouldn't start stocking your refrigerator yet.

I'm assuming his future is either as a continuing character in a soap opera (art imitates life) or as a beach volleyball player. He's certainly got the name for it. Karch Kiraly, Sinjin Smith, Kato Kaelin, right?

I watched Kato on the stand. He was a very accommodating witness. He could perhaps become a professional witness if the house-guest thing falls through. But . . . and let me put this as gently and respectfully as possible: He is a moron. I have leftover lasagna that is better at abstract reasoning.

There was that anxious time when Shapiro asked Kato how many hours he spent in the police station talking with the detectives, and I was afraid Kato would have to take off his shoes to count that high.

Someone in my office speculated that after the trial Kato would write a book. My response was: "Write a book? Kato can't even *read* a book. He can't even use a book to stand on to screw in a lightbulb." (It would take four Katos, by the way. One to hold the bulb, two to brush his hair out of his eyes, and one to administer CPR when he accidentally sticks his finger into the socket.)

Kato's strength is clearly the "yes" or "no" question. When he is required to say anything more expansive, he knits his brow and closes his eyes and appears to be in real pain, as if he's trying to pass a kidney stone. All this thinking must be quite taxing.

Still, I have no doubt that he is telling the truth. I base this on my keen powers of observation, honed over years as a professional journalist, plus the startling fact, discovered by my friend Gino, that *Brian "Kato" Kaelin* is an anagram for *Kaka-Brain Not Lie.*

Has there ever been a more recognizable yet insignficant figure in American history than Kato Kaelin? Even Jessica Hahn had more on the ball.

What does it say about America that this guy has become such a star? His claim to fame is that he is peripherally connected to a double homicide. Other than that he's a house pet, a cockapoo. This is no joke. Kato used to live for free at Nicole's, and O.J. apparently wasn't pleased with the arrangement, so he and Nicole dealt with Kato like community property. In the end, Kato went to live for free with O.J., and Kato the Akita remained with Nicole. I thought Nicole got the better of the deal. The dog was smarter. Kato the dog at least had the sense to alert people that a murder had been committed. Kato the person simply sat up in bed, wondering what might have made a thumping sound roughly consistent with a man strangling a yak.

Here's what we know about Kato: He lives and eats for free. He does nothing. He's thirty-six, and the only thing he's got going is his hair. Don't tell me he's an actor. Have you seen him on the stand? He makes O.J. look like Laurence Olivier. But since he was discovered sleeping in O.J.'s guest house, he has an agent, he has a movie deal, he's hosted cable talk shows, he's been invited to the Radio & Television Correspondents' dinner in Washington, where the secretary of health and human services reportedly asked him for an autograph, and he's living in Charlie Sheen's house! Hello! Hello!

Maybe this reveals my East Coast bias, but as I sat there watching Kato, I kept thinking: Is this what L.A. is really about? (I mean, like, uh, rilly.) Do people actually go to court dressed that casually, in denim work shirts, like they're appearing on *Nick at Nite*? I half expected Kato to have sunglasses perched on his head, and zinc oxide on his nose. Am I the only one flabbergasted to hear testimony about how two men went to a McDonald's drive-thru in a Bentley? In a *Bentley*?

It took just one look at Kato to put my smart friend Martha in a nostalgic reverie. Kato reminded her of all the guys on the surfing team at Marina High in Huntington Beach, California, just an hour or so from the L.A. courtroom where Kato testified.

"Those were the days we sat on the beach with olive oil on the ends of our hair to cure split ends, and lemon juice on the top of our hair to lighten it—the whole vinaigrette . . . Can you imagine showing up with Kato on your arm? He's such a loser."

In this case, so are we all.

Chic Coffee:
Say It Ain't So, Joe

In the '50s, the craze was ice cream. Every weekend the family went out for ice-cream sundaes and banana splits, and then your dad dropped dead at forty-eight, his arteries all plumped up like kielbasa, and so we reconsidered our diets and opted for something less frivolous and more nourishing, and in the '60s, the craze was . . . pizza. Pizza was also horrible for your health, inasmuch as it consisted essentially of bread (for useless bulk) and cheese (for circulatory blockage), tomato paste (for color), yeast (for infections), and those red-and-yellow-flake peppers (for boils and blisters on the roof of the mouth). Eventually, diet gurus began to enter our lives, and in the '70s, the craze was salad bars, which featured "three-bean salad" (garbanzo, fatouli, and ganoozi beans) and other fine ethnic delicacies you would not feed a hamster. No one really liked salad bars, other than the manufacturer of Plexiglas sneeze guards. In the '80s, the fad was enterprises dedicated to the production and sales of fresh chocolate chip cookies, as though chocolate chip cookies were some product of great quality and sophistication in which absolute freshness was required for the true connoisseur, as opposed to some brown glob that tastes perfectly good when it comes in a bag from Keebler.

Now it's coffee.

People actually go *out* for coffee. Like it's a movie. Like it's entertainment.

All across America, every store that goes out of business is replaced by a Starbucks or a Quartermaine's or some other fancy coffee chain featuring this week's special: Peruvian Monkeyfoot Decaf. (Which comes, by the way, with a thick foamy head that would make Budweiser jealous, and takes up two thirds of the cup, so when you pierce the canopy of foam, you realize you've paid four dollars for two sips. Which is why they call it Star-BUCKS.)

All day long there are lines out the door for coffee!

What are they putting in it, heroin? Look, coffee is black and bitter and you drink it when your eyes are red and your tongue feels like it is coated with goat fuzz, and it makes you feel momentarily better. One thing coffee is *not* is entertainment.

Still, nowadays there are only three kinds of people standing on America's streets.

1. Smokers, who are banned from every building, and forced outside, like cattle in a pen;

2. People using ATMs (and the people waiting to kill them);

3. Trendoids who have bought a container of some idiot coffee like espresso macchiato and are congratulating themselves for knowing the difference between *foamed* milk and *steamed* milk.

In the old days, and by old I mean in those days before anyone compared Keanu Reeves to Laurence Olivier, coffee came in the following varieties: black, regular, or light; "wid" or "widdout" sugar.

There were no *flavors*. This was coffee, java, joe. People only cared if their coffee was hot, not where it was grown. People saw Juan Valdez, the Colombian who hand-picked the beans with a donkey, the donkey at whose shuffling side he trudged up and down the coffee fields, picking beans—and all they really cared about was if they washed the beans at customs.

Now there are at least four hundred different coffees. It's like going to Duron.

You say, "I'm looking for something to go with a mostly burgundy Persian rug."

They say, "How about a Ugandan kona hazelnut latte?"

You say, "With foamed milk, not steamed, right?"

They say, "What do we look like, peasants?"

If that isn't pretentious enough, at Starbucks they hand you a pamphlet with mechanical drawings that opens out like the blueprints for the Louvre and assures you of "the world's best beans, roasted to perfection, and prepared at peak freshness by our professional baristas."

Baristas?

Are they, like, women lawyers?

I remember coffeehouses from the old days, when you'd take a date (who always dressed only in black) and listen to some guy who looked like Maynard G. Krebs recite poetry and play the bongos. There were tables and chairs, and you could order stale doughnuts along with the coffee. The coffee they served was Turkish, and it was so thick you could stand up a paint brush in it. After one cup you began to grow a mustache. There was a sense of community. There was commerce. . . . often people selling drugs.

Today's coffeehouse has one window bench where people drink their coffee like parolees and stare out at the street watching buses go by. They sit there burning holes in their intestines at precisely 195 degrees Fahrenheit, as it boasts in the pamphlet. There's no food to eat, just *biscotti*, the fourteenth century's version of melba toast, which tastes like a pumice stone. Hot coffee and formaldehyde are the only two solvents that will soften *biscotti*.

No seats. No food.

So why are they there, spending outrageous sums of money on what is, after all, JUST A CUP OF COFFEE?

Obviously, to show off.

There's a coffee snobbery that rivals wine snobbery. You have your foam versus steam. Your mug versus demi. Your caf versus decaf. Your New Guinea Peaberry versus Ethiopia Yerga-cheffe. God help you if you ask for Costa Rica Tres Rios, and you can only name dos of the rios.

To help you decide which coffee is right for you, they hand you a bean to chew on. What is *that* all about. That's like asking someone to choose a computer by licking the keyboard. Why would you chew on the *bean*? The whole purpose of grinding the hard, bitter bean and brewing the coffee is to get *rid* of the bean. If coffee beans were for chewing, we'd all be drinking Dentyne.

Anyway, now it's coffee.

But what's next?

Maybe it's outdoor cafés that sell nothing but foam.

Maybe it's the crumbs from on top of the Entenmann's cakes. You go with a plastic bag and a spoon and serve yourself. Crumbs R Us.

Maybe it's the green slime inside the lobster.

My friend Ed says the next big thing is Toast.

Just Toast. Totally Toast. House of Toast.

Seventy-five ways to serve toast. Grilled over mesquite; popped up from an old-fashioned toaster; burned on one side, like your mom used to make it; roasted on a spit; the Colonel's xtra krispy; decaf.

Hey, you know what might go great with toast?

Coffee.

IF YOU'RE GONNA HAVE A SCANDAL, DON'T MAKE IT A *BORING* SCANDAL

*

What Has Four Wheels and Flies?

Remember when Bill Clinton announced he'd be taking a bus to the Inauguration?

A bus. A great populist statement.

Except Clinton had no intention of taking a real bus trip on a real bus. He took one of those buses the rock stars take, a Bonnie Raitt bus, with a VCR and a refrigerator. They call it a "motor coach." Nobody ever called the twelve-hour, thoroughly nauseating ride from New York City to Buffalo, with stops absolutely everywhere—and believe me, you've never seen Elmira, N.Y., until you've seen it from a bus station—a motor coach. They called it the Vomit Comet. In the theater of transportation, a long-distance bus is the gum on the bottom of the seat.

I want to know when the last time was Clinton took a real bus.

Not a commuter bus, where the worst thing that can happen is you have to stand for ten minutes and smell the hair of the people next to you. A real bus. Like in *Midnight Cowboy*.

Oh, and I'm sure Al Gore takes them all the time. Growing up in a hotel and going to St. Albans and Harvard, I'm sure Gore was a regular Ralph Kramden. The only thing he knows about Trailways is that he had the A stock.

A real bus:

a. smells bad.

b. smells real bad.

c. smells like Marge Schott's sneaker.

d. all of the above, and sometimes the person sitting next to you actually dies.

The main reason long-distance buses smell so bad is that people who buy tickets on long-distance buses tend to ride on those buses for long distances, and unless they have the bladder of a moose, there comes a point where they have to go to the bathroom, which is tucked in the very back of the bus (often next to a dead person). Have you ever opened the door and caught a whiff full in the face? Reportedly, Saddam Hussein has written a letter to Greyhound asking for the "recipe."

Have you been on a real bus lately? There isn't a trip you can take where after about three hours some walleyed maniac doesn't stand up in the aisle and begin shouting: "WHY ARE YOU PEOPLE TALKING ABOUT ME?"

People who ride the buses lately are either desperately poor, completely psychopathic, and repeat drunk-driving offenders, or people who are saving up to go to Las Vegas.

I'm telling you, Woody Guthrie wouldn't get on a bus anymore.

My friend Nancy remembers going to and from college on terrible, long bus trips (like there's any other kind). "There's always someone pretending to fall asleep on your shoulder, and the next thing you know, you've got some big fat guy's head in your crotch, and he's banking that you're too embarrassed to tell him to get the hell out of there."

Like most of you, my first experience with buses was a school bus. I think back to pleasant trips on my yellow school bus. I think back to those seats, where the leather had long ago been ripped away, so you were sitting directly on the springs, so that when the bus—which had no shock absorbers to begin with, and couldn't have passed inspection in Kuala Lumpur— went over a bump, you were impaled; you'd come home with coiled spring marks on your behind; your parents would wonder if you were tortured by a madman with a pogo stick.

I think back to how well behaved we were on the bus, how orderly: After we beat up the smaller boys, we threw pencils and pocket knives at the bus driver, hoping we would kill her, at the least wound her enough to where she'd lose control of the bus and plunge over an embankment—killing us all.

I bring my own children to the bus stop now, and wonder how it is that I can trust their fate to, and I mean this in the very best way, A DRIVER WHO LOOKS LIKE HE HAS LEFT A STRING OF BODIES CHAIN-SAWED TO DEATH FROM HERE TO EL PASO. I mean, the last time I saw anyone with a pallor like that was at Mao's Tomb. It was Mao.

The Packwood Papers

Dear Diary:

Routine day. Sponsored pro-choice legislation. Voted to save loopholes for timber industry. Attended surface transportation subcommittee hearing. Copped a feel from that blond page with the fishnet stockings in the mail room.

Dear Diary:

Watched tapes from the Clarence Thomas confirmation hearings. Pubic hair on the Coke can? God, that man is smooth.

Dear Diary:

The newspaper says I "made unwanted sexual advances to more than two dozen female aides, associates and lobbyists." Who said they were unwanted? *I* wanted them. What's this country coming to when a United States senator can't rub up against a young woman in the elevator and stick his tongue down her throat? What are we, in Russia?

Dear Diary:

Did a Q & A this morning at a fund-raiser. Someone asked me, "Senator Packwood, what's the secret of selecting a good staff?" So I told that great story about how I needed a legislative assistant: I interviewed three women. One from Harvard. One from Yale. One from Brown. Each one was smart as a whip. I said, "This is a very difficult choice, but difficult choices are what leadership is all about." Then I hired the one with the biggest hooters. Ha-ha-ha. God, that's a funny joke.

Dear Diary:
Read where Bob Hope was sleeping with all the bimbo starlets he took on the USO tours. Remind me to ask William "Not the Refrigerator" Perry how I can get on a USO tour.

Dear Diary:
I think I'm making progress with the big redhead with the lilac perfume who lobbies for cable TV. I spotted her in the Dirksen Building, and I asked her, "What's your sign?" She said, "Forty percent off everything on this rack." I told her I was a Taurus. She said, "I'm a Lexus."

Dear Diary:
Told Ethics Committee I kept a diary.

Dear Diary:
My God, they want to subpoena my diary. What do I do now?

Dear Diary:
Hmmmm: "I fondly remember the time when John Glenn was dead drunk on the balcony of the" . . . no, "I fondly remember the time when Pat Moynihan was down on all fours, buck naked, pretending" . . . no, "I recall with great glee when Strom Thurmond first suggested we run Nancy Kassebaum through the Tailhook gauntlet" . . . no, I've got it, "Who would have ever believed that Alan Simpson would dress up as a Taiwanese candy striper, and" . . . yeah, let's see them subpoena this.

Dear Diary:
Today I revealed that my diary was 8,200 pages long, single-spaced! And I've been working on it every day for twenty-five years. Well, one of my staffers calculated that's enough for thirty full-size books. Norman Mailer hasn't written that many words. That's longer than the Great Wall of China. Jeez, it's even longer than Clinton's health care bill. Uh-oh, now I have to wade through it all and get rid of any reference to cheating on my taxes, stuffing bodies in the trunk of my car, and removing the tag on my mattress. That's all I need, some two-bit Democratic senator screaming, "Criminal misconduct!"

Dear Diary:
Hit one out of the park today! Told the Senate I named names in my diary. You should've seen them scramble. Only Teddy Kennedy took it in stride; he got me in the cloakroom and said, "I bet Chris Dodd fifty bucks that my name is in there more than his."

Dear Diary:
Jesse Helms, in the Marble Room, with an air hose.

Dear Diary:
Someone asked me, given the lesson of Watergate, why I kept a diary. Why I put it all in writing. I said my diary included "the hopes, the dreams, the despairs of all of us."

Dear Diary:
Nixon sent me a telegram. Said I was a putz.

Dear Diary:
I assured the Senate this isn't blackmail. "The secrets in that diary are safe with me." They're afraid of leaks. I said: "Come on. Who in this chamber would leak anything?"

Dear Diary:
Maybe I should black out all the references to Barbara Mikulski coming over in that Daisy Mae outfit.

Dear Diary:
What is *Hard Copy*, and what do they mean by "Joey Buttafuoco says we're the only people who believed him"?

Dear Diary:
Why is everybody so upset with me? Doesn't everyone take extensive notes on his friends' sex lives?

Dear Diary:
I read Colin Powell got $6 million for his book. What's the best stuff he's got? Can he put Schwarzkopf in the Tidal Basin wearing only swim fins and a holster with the first three runners-up in the Miss Nude Cherry Blossom pageant? I can do that with two members of the House leadership!

Dear Diary:
Hired a literary agent.

By Land and Air and She

Sometimes you learn a new fact about someone you know, and instantly gain a perspective that explains everything.

Take Pee-wee Herman. You'd watch this alleged adult prancing around in his bow tie and white socks, looking like a badly drawn character from a 1952 Indonesian comic book, and you'd ask yourself: What gives? What is the *deal* with this schlemiel? Can anyone be that much of a loser? Then, illumination comes in the form of a solo performance in a darkened movie theater. Ladies and gentlemen, Misssster Pee-wee Herman! Thank you very much. Let's give him a hand, so to speak.

Or Lassie. You watch Lassie for years, and you love her daring and her intelligence, but there's something about her you can't quite put your finger on. Her courage at times seems almost excessive, almost . . . foolhardy. Also, she is never content to just save Gramps from the mineshaft, she then has to *gloat* about it in this deep, throaty triumphant bark. And she drinks water from a bowl like a slob. Then one day you find out something that puts everything in a new perspective: Lassie was a boy! A male dog. Which would explain why you never saw a fire hydrant on the set.

Anyway, I read an item in the paper last week that did the same thing for me about Hillary Clinton.

No, Hillary is not a boy. (Not to my current knowledge, anyway.) But suddenly, she seems to make much more sense to me.

It was puzzling: Here is the most competent member of the Clinton administration, who is not even technically a member of the Clinton administration, a strikingly handsome woman of astounding talents and with an awesome résumé, and yet she doesn't seem ever to be entirely satisfied with herself. She keeps changing. Her name. Her hairstyle. Her clothes designers. Her entire image! Remember the campaign? One week, she says she isn't some kind of stay-at-home wifey who stands by her man and bakes cookies. And the next week, she is *literally baking cookies* and handing them out to the press.

What gives, Hillary?

Then, last week, I was stunned to learn that in 1975 Hillary tried to enlist in the Marines. (Possibly she was looking for a few good men, as she was about to marry a man who was looking for a few good women.)

My first reaction was that it sounded like something that arose out of a drunken bar bet. You know, like when guys dare each other to do something stupid—say, take off their trousers, pull their underpants over their head and whistle the theme to *Gilligan's Island*—except this must have been a group of female lawyers. Imagine it. A bar scene. Hillary Rodham Clinton-to-be says, "Yeah, well, if you're so smart, I dare you to argue the pro-life position, that the state has the right to force women to carry unwanted pregnancies to term." And Camille O'Rourke-Lefkowitz responds, "Oh, yeah? Well, I dare you to shave your legs and join the Marines."

Hillary in the Marines? Hmmmmm.

Hillary reports that the recruiter looked at her, in her thick glasses, with her burgeoning crow's-feet, and said, "You're too

182

Pumping Irony

old, you can't see, and you're a woman"—proving almost anybody can pass a simple multiple-choice exam.

The recruiter also allegedly said, "Maybe the dogs would take you," apparently referring to the army, where soldiers are called dogfaces. But Hillary was new to Arkansas then, and may have misunderstood his dialect. He might have said, "Maybe the frogs would take you," implying Hillary should try the French Foreign Legion; or "Maybe the Hogs will take you," a reference to the University of Arkansas Razorbacks; or maybe instead of "the dogs would take you" he was saying "the dorks would take you," a reference to a possible career in the life insurance industry. Or he might have simply said, "You make my knees knock," and Hillary has chosen to repress that memory.

Note to copy desk: Have somebody call the White House and ascertain just how inebriated Hillary was at the time. When men enlist in the Marines, they're usually so drunk they attempt to sign the enlistment form with their tongues. Oh, and leave room for an insert when the White House assures us that Bill tried to enlist in the Marines also, and was turned down during the physical when he kept taking his pants off during the eyesight exam.

Anyway, then I got to thinking about it. Why did Hillary apply to the Marines? How does it jibe with her nearly neurotic compulsion to remake herself all the time?

When you think about the Marines, you think about what? The Look.

Marines look a certain way. They are steel-eyed guys wearing big, goofy lace-up boots and absurd camouflage gear that looks like a garbage man's uniform that has been vomited on by owls. Their hair looks like it has been cut by scorpions. In the Marines, every day is a bad hair day. (Oh, you do get a cool sword.) Here is the thing: As a Marine, you always look the same. You are supposed to look the same. So you don't have to worry about your clothes, or your hair, or anything. You're a Marine. You look like a wind-up doll. Any questions?

Anyway, that's my theory. Attempting to deal with her own insecurities, knowing that she faced a lifetime of personal grooming indecision, Hillary made a desperate bid for the kind of enforced structure only the Marines could provide.

They turned her down, and the rest, as they say, is history.

No More Puns on Whitewater. Oar Else.

They're breathing a sigh of relief in the White House over the most recent Whitewater poll, which found that:

a. 4 percent of Americans believe Bill Clinton did something terrible in Whitewater and should be punished.

b. 2 percent of Americans believe Bill Clinton is being unfairly blamed for what happened in Whitewater, and should be exonerated.

c. 94 percent have no idea what happened in Whitewater, don't care, and mostly just want to know more about this member of the British parliament who was found dead, hanging from a noose, wearing women's underwear, with an orange slice in his mouth.

I am in this last group. I like the Gory Tory Story a lot. I don't understand Whitewater, and don't care. (All I know is that the president ought to sign up Tonya Harding's lawyers—they haven't missed on a motion yet.) The only people who like Whitewater are Washington political geeks, who can only get excited about any scandal if it involves the unauthorized moving of a decimal point, and *Washington Post* headline writers, because it gives them an opportunity to use phrases like BILL'S UP

THE CREEK, or HILLARY SHOOTS THE RAPIDS. This only perpetuates the notion that Whitewater is actually about a log flume ride. It gives it a Mickey Mouse quality—which some would say it richly deserves.

In an attempt to understand Whitewater, I went to a newsman who has handled a major Whitewater story and asked him what it was all about. This is what he said, verbatim: "Bill bought some land in the middle of nowhere and got some loans or something, and there were friends and shady characters all over, and maybe the possibility of a sweetheart deal, and Hillary might have been the lawyer, I think."

This man considers himself one of the nation's leading authorities on Whitewater.

People ask, "Can Clinton survive Whitewater?" Survive it? Can he *explain* it?

Wouldn't that be something—if some two-bit land deal brought Clinton down? Here's a guy who has been so coated with Teflon you could fry an egg on his big behind. He survives dodging the draft. He survives that preposterous story about not inhaling the marijuana. He survives repeated allegations about a sex life that would make Heidi Fleiss blush. He survives the general impression that right before he became president, he was pledge master at Delta House; I mean, if there were a story tomorrow involving Bill Clinton, a vat of lime Jell-O, two orangutans, and the June Taylor Dancers, almost everybody in America would:

a. Believe it, and,

b. Not care.

He survives all that—and *this* might get him?

Apparently the horror in Whitewater isn't that the Clintons were so stupid that they bought land in the middle of nowhere, and lost their pants when even people *in Arkansas* weren't dumb enough to buy it—thus becoming the only people in the 1980s to not become filthy rich while speculating. That should be the appalling thing, because, my God, look at clucks such as Donald Trump who became zillionaires in that decade. No, apparently the horror in all this is that people in the Clinton White House have held *inappropriate briefings* about what happened! The crime is procedure. Not following the regs! This is such a nerdy, bean-counter scandal. It's like charging the Menendez brothers with not having a permit for the shotguns.

Some people (Republicans are people, aren't they? Well, except maybe for Newt Gingrich) are saying this is just like Watergate. That's not so. Yes, both scandals were quite technical and complicated, but that's where the similarity ends. At the center of this is a bunch of goobers who think *barium* is something you do when the patient dies. At the center of Watergate was something exciting: a group of Cubans sneaking around in the dark carrying monkey wrenches and bags of money, led by a maniac who ate rats and toasted his hand over a candle, like a marshmallow. Whitewater is nowhere *near* as cool as Watergate. Honestly, who's cooler, John Dean or Bernard Nussbaum? If you're drafting an all-cool team, the only No. 1 pick in the whole Clinton White House is that spiky-haired kid, Snuffleupagus.

Here's something to think about: This Whitewater land deal started about sixteen years ago. It predates Gennifer Flowers! It's ages ago. In the interim the American public has elected people to Congress who didn't even bother to pay their taxes for years at a time, and has made *America's Funniest Home Videos* a smash hit show. You no longer go to jail for killing your parents or slicing off your husband's wing-ding. And G. Gordon Liddy (his hands apparently healed) has his own radio talk show.

We have a tendency to drag these things out. Somebody in a suit promises full disclosure, and we begin dropping bread crumbs in the forest as we go from special counsel to congressional inquiry to independent prosecutor to blue-ribbon review commission. By the time we're ready to wrap up the whole thing, everybody's either dead or doing infomercials. The Packwood Diaries are far less complicated than Whitewater, and Julia Roberts will be a grandmother before anybody lays a glove on Packwood.

Americans simply don't know how to conduct a scandal.

It comes down to a difference of emphasis and style.

Take underwear. The sophisticated British politician is actually caught dead in someone else's underwear. What style!

Bill Clinton would never let that happen to him. He's too busy taking tax deductions on his . . .

How the Gingrich Stole Christmas

I think I can sum up the most volcanic American election in forty years in three words:

Congressman Sonny Bono.

Yes, we've got you, babe.

What was it exactly that persuaded Californians to elect a man who makes Tony Danza sound like Sir John Gielgud? Congressman Sonny Bono! What happened, Cher missed the filing deadline?

I could slap myself silly for not seeing it earlier; in retrospect, the seeds of Sonny's political career are obvious in his lyrics. The first indication of his designs on public service was evident when he told Cher, "There ain't no hill or mountain we can't climb," a clear reference to Capitol Hill. He staked out his political platform when he told her that their love wouldn't pay the rent, and that their money was all spent before it was earned, indicating a clear displeasure with big government overtaxing citizens to pay for failed social programs. And when he wrote, "Drums keep pounding a rhythm to the brain, la-dee-dah-dee-dee, la-dee-dah-dee-die" . . . well, obviously he is a proponent of the death penalty.

Congressman Sonny Bono was part of a Republican landslide that allows the aptly named Newt Gingrich to get a table at restaurants that would normally feed him from a dish on the floor. The *Post* ran this headline the other day: GINGRICH VOWS COOPERATION. Oh, please. This is like running the headline: DAHMER VOWS VEGETARIANISM. There wasn't an English-speaking person this side of Lichtenstein who believed Newt's claim that he felt "a sense of sadness" learning of Dan Rostenkowski's defeat; Newt would have gleefully stuck Rostenkowski's head in a toaster oven. He is the Zhirinovsky of American politics. Any minute now he'll lean out the window and start pouring hot soup on anyone who was ever in the Peace Corps. The very day he promises to be bipartisan, he calls Bill and Hillary Clinton "counterculture McGovernicks." This is Newt's notion of conciliatory? What would he call them if he were angry, "Julius and Ethel Rosenberg?"

Talk about losers. What's Clinton going to do next, quarterback the Buffalo Bills? Did this guy have the smell of poison, or what? Members of his own party were afraid to stand anywhere near him. When Clinton breezed into town, they all remembered dental appointments. The only Democrat who really couldn't run away from Clinton, his brother-in-law, Hugh Rodham, got so wiped in his Florida Senate race they ought to call him "Mr. Whipple."

Every single Republican ran against Clinton, regardless of how small or local the office: Somebody running for zoning commissioner in Toledo could stand up and scream, "Clinton wears a bra," and assure himself of a landslide. (And isn't it great that Strom Thurmond, at age ninety-two, will take over as chairman of the Senate Armed Services Committee? Thurmond thinks we're still using cannonballs. And Jesse Helms will be in charge of the Senate Foreign Relations Committee? His entire concept of foreign relations is "killing Commies."

(If this all seems a little anti-Republican, I have an excuse. The press is *supposed* to hate Republicans. It is our *job*. Wasn't it great watching the liberal media trying to cover this fantastic bloodbath as though they were completely objective? Subtle evidence of partisanship crept through, such as the lead headline in Wednesday's *New York Times:* OH, POOP. WE'RE TOAST.)

Clinton's predicament provides a very interesting lesson in the nuances of politics. Here is a man who solved the problem in Haiti, defused a potential crisis in Iraq, brought Israel and Jordan to peace, passed a sweeping crime bill, started reducing the deficit, and presided over an economy that's unarguably in the best shape it's been in years—yet head to head in popularity polls, he loses against every potential candidate, including O. J. Simpson, the late Ayatollah Khomeini, and those guys in the McDonald's ads who sit on lawn chairs in an empty football stadium parking lot and chew with their mouths open. The crack White House political staff (slogan: "Oh yeah?") has been analyzing the phenomenon and has come up with three possible explanations for why so many people hate Bill Clinton:

1. His cottage-cheese thighs;
2. That icky thing he does biting his lip;
3. The SCAN tattoo on his left biceps.

It has been suggested to Clinton that he is so unpopular with the electorate, the only way he can get Democrats elected is by becoming a Republican.

Democrats went down like dominoes. Marjorie Margolies-Mezvinsky was gone in less time than it takes to say "Marjorie Margolies-Mezvinsky." Ann Richards? Gone. Rostenkowski? Gone. Foley? Gone. Cuomo? Gone. Cuomo had been governor of New York for twelve years; it only seemed like thirty. Mario Cuomo had become the oldest Hamlet on Broadway. His administration was characterized by indecision; if he were asked today how it felt to finally be out of the public spotlight, he'd say, "Good and bad." Cuomo spent every day of the last twelve years in agony trying to decide if he should accept God's calling and run for president. Now that he has lost to someone named Pataki, Mario can run for a bus.

Not all Democrats were losers, though. Amid all this change, amid all this movement toward political and social conservatism, it's nice to see there's still room under the tent to eat, drink, and par-tay! Teddy Kennedy and Chuck Robb won—though Robb's victory might be somewhat tainted by the fact that he ran against Pinocchio. What does it say about the Democrats when their biggest stars are Teddy "Has Anybody Seen My Pants?" Kennedy and Chuck Robb-a-Dub-Dub? Who's their next bright light, Pee-wee Herman?

And lastly, how about a big round of applause for our own idiosyncratic Marion Barry, who bucked all the national trends about bashing liberals and cutting spending and getting tough on crime by running on a platform that called for letting prisoners out of jail early *and* giving them money. Yes, just like in Monopoly, you can get out of jail and collect $200. Darned few politicians were courageous enough to run on one of those planks, let alone both.

Kinda makes you wonder what Marion will come up with next time.

Let's see . . . You get out of jail, you get a bankroll—and a gun.

The Bogey Men

Of all the questions vexing mankind, and I'm thinking of questions about the origins of the universe, and the relationship between God and humanity, and the excruciating moral dilemmas imposed by modernity, right up there at the top is: "How can Gerald Ford *still* be such a bad golfer?"

Seriously, the man has done absolutely nothing but go skiing and play golf since he left office, and he left office, well, he left office immediately after the Ford administration, didn't he? That's almost twenty years ago. And he's still beaning people. You're safer crossing the Beltway on a skateboard than being in the gallery when this guy is playing golf. President Fore!

The other day, playing with Presidents Bush and Clinton, Ford whacked some woman in the finger, drawing blood. Bush was even worse; he sculled two people. He popped a guy in the calf, which was simply an appetizer compared with his shot that caromed off a tree and smacked a woman on the nose and knocked her down, leaving her prostrate and bleeding; I'll bet she was seeing a thousand points of light. Even plunking people Bush was eight strokes better than Ford. Ford couldn't hit a golf ball straight if he were playing inside a drain pipe. Playing golf with Ford and Bush is the closest Clinton ever came to combat.

The good news for Clinton is that he didn't actually kill any-one. (Of course, that's a fundamental difference between the two parties: Republicans hit spectators, Democrats hit on them.) The bad news is that Clinton wore a shirt that revealed where all the billions and billions of McDonald's hamburgers have gone.

I have no idea why presidents go out and play golf in pub-lic—especially with a gallery lining the fairways. Clinton can't possibly practice enough to hit the ball straight, unless he's out there with O.J. hitting sand shots in the middle of the night; golf isn't like politics, where Clinton can get to the center just by throwing Hillary over the side. Golf takes real work.

Believe me, I play golf as well as Clinton and Bush, and I would never even think of hitting a shot if there were a live body within two hundred yards of me. These people are stacked up ten deep, all the way down the fairway. If they were any closer, when they sweat you'd get wet. I'm never surprised when Ford stuns a member of the gallery; I'm surprised there's anybody left standing when he gets to eighteen.

Reading about the golf match made me think about an amazing coincidence: The human motor functions, which con-trol the complex series of coordinated actions necessary to play golf, are controlled by the brain, the same organ that permits writers to create transitional sentences fraudulently linking un-related subjects and thereby creating the illusion of coherence and competence. And that made me think about a story in the paper not long ago, about how scientists discovered that in some cases women use both sides of their brains, while men seem to use only the left side.

The left side traditionally handles language functions, and the right side handles visual-spatial functions, which would seem to indicate that men are using the side of the brain that allows them to articulate such profound thoughts as "Hey, baby, what's happening?'' but they are not getting much use out of the visual-spatial side, which would allow them to imagine naked women on Saturn.

I don't think it's news that a man's brain works differently than a woman's brain. For one thing, a woman's brain is actually in her head, and I think we know where we'll find a man's brain.

It was interesting to learn that the study (which was conducted at Yale, where Bush and Clinton dallied on their way to the first tee) found that on average ''women perform better on tasks that involve quickly identifying matching items from a group, or listing objects that are similar in color or words that begin with the same letter.'' I can see how matching items quickly would help in sorting laundry, but I'm wondering how far you can go with ''Shirley, Shirley, bo Birley, bo-nanna, fanna, fo Firley . . .''

Men, on the other hand, outscore women on tests ''where they have to find a hidden or embedded shape in a more complicated background,'' referring to our innate ability to always see a pair of breasts in a mountain range, ''and in some motor skills, such as throwing, that involve striking a target.'' Let me understand this. We needed to spend millions of dollars on a study to find that a man can throw a ball better than a woman? Anybody could have told them that. That's why guys say, ''Hey, Stanley, you trow like a gurl.'' What's next, a study to prove that fish can't speak?

MY BOTTOM-LINE
APPEAL

*

Just a Fancy Passing

A story caught my eye a while ago about J. R. Rider, a star basketball player at the University of Nevada–Las Vegas (a noted academic powerhouse whose motto is: "Dealer Must Hit on Sixteen and Stick on Seventeen"), who was involved in a grade-changing scandal. An instructor at a junior college—where Rider was taking a summer English course—grew suspicious of the authenticity of Rider's papers when three of them had his first name spelled incorrectly. (I have always thought *J* is one of the more difficult letters.)

But it wasn't the news of a college athlete getting his grade changed so he could maintain his sports eligibility that intrigued me. That happens all the time. Jocks' grades get lifted more often than Cher's butt. No, it was the reference to another course Rider was taking: Prevention & Management of Premenstrual Syndrome, which prompted me to ask:

1. What was a man doing taking that course?
2. What is a university doing *giving* that course?
3. Are you kidding me, or what?

(I take it you wouldn't cram for that final . . . you'd cramp for it.)

Initially, I was outraged at the lamentable state of modern

collegiate education. When I went to school we majored in big things, things of substance, such as history and chemistry and French. I know this is going to sound very provincial, but back then we couldn't major in Batman.

But on reflection, I love the fact that you can go to college now and major in the '60s. I'm thinking I can ace out—especially if the tests are short-answer, because I can name all the members of the Dave Clark Five. What an advantage, having lived through it. What a great break Charlemagne would have had if he took a course in the Life and Times of Charlemagne. It reminds me of a story about a journalist who'd won a fellowship at Stanford, and found herself in a class about the '60s, with an earnest group of students, one of whom actually asked about Malcolm X, "Why did he call himself Malcolm the Tenth?"

It's not that we didn't have gut courses back when I was in college, courses like Introduction to Egyptian Art ("Hi, I'm Art Farouk") and A Theoretical Approach to Mesopotamian Penmanship. College was hard. These courses were like lumbar supports. They were the soft sleeping couch in a room otherwise filled with Danish modern furniture. They were Abbott and Costello at an Ingmar Bergman film festival.

But I was one of those liberal arts snobs who disdained gut courses like Introduction to French Culture: From Fries to Toast. Instead, I took Existentialist Philosophy of Religion, which—don't get me wrong—helped me get a certain kind of babe, but which is of no practical use to me now that I have to remodel the kitchen. I used to laugh at the people who took the most notorious gut course of them all: Basket Weaving. As it turns out the guys who took Basket Weaving twenty years ago are getting $1,000 for fifteen minutes' work now. They make some sort of donkey-shaped bowl out of banana leaves, and all of a sudden they're *artistes*. Arnie Berger, who couldn't find his behind with both hands, let alone name any of the Three Musketeers, has a New York gallery that does nothing but show his cockamamie baskets. I get out of school with a 3.4 overall, and I subscribe to *Better Homes and Gardens*. Berger, a walking staph infection who thought Romulus and Remus were *planets*, is *in Better Homes and Gardens*.

My friend Gino has a friend who is dating a kinesiology major—a fancy term for phys ed. He takes a *bowling course*. He actually gets credit for bowling. Can you believe it? What's the difference between an A and a B, whether you pick up the ten pin on a 2-4-5-10 split? Do you get extra credit if the name on the pocket of your shirt is spelled correctly? It's just as well they didn't offer bowling when Gino went to school. He'd have cut it. He didn't go to any classes. One time he had a girlfriend take a class for him. There were no tests, only a paper. She went to class. She wrote the paper. Gino's only responsibility was to hand it in. How hard is that? M. R. Rider could do that. The day it was due, Gino walked to the lecture hall, stopped the first man he saw, and asked, "Where is Dr. Roussofsky's classical architecture class?" The man promptly replied, "I am Dr. Roussofsky." A one in a million, right? Gino was so ashamed, he didn't even hand in the paper. Got an F so big you could hang one of Berger's baskets on it.

I know people condemn B. R. Rider for having a tutor write his papers. But this is hardly new. I must admit I took a college journalism course for a woman whose shape made me weak. I was working at a New York daily newspaper at the time, and I was hopeful she might find a suitable way to reward my efforts on her academic behalf. I wrote all five papers for the course, including the feature story that was the final exam. The instructor, some broken-down hack who was editing a free weekly rag, gave me—or, rather her—a C-. Here I am writing for 650,000 people a day, over a million on Sunday, and I hooked an elementary journalism course at a college where most students' body temperatures are higher than their boards.

Well, I'm steamed. I'm having revenge fantasies about how I

will barge right into this moron's cubbyhole, look him right in his rheumy eyes and say, "How dare you presume to give me a C– in your lousy little course? *Do you know who I am?*"

Of course, he'd say, "No. Why, no, I don't. Who are you?"

And I'd have to say, "I'm, er, er . . . Marlene Keppelman."

The Oy of Sex

Recently I encountered two big stories concerning sex. One about the sex lives of men. One about the sex lives of cows.

In the first one, men between twenty and forty were surveyed as to how often they have sex, how many sexual partners they've had, and what varieties of sex they've experienced.

In the second one, we learn how a cow gets horny.

Being over forty, I was jazzed about the cows.

It seems that farmers want their cows to get pregnant because after giving birth they produce the most milk. So you need to know when they're in heat. So farmers have attached electronic beeping gizmos to cows' ankles and rumps, and they measure the cows' sexual excitement. (They actually record how often a cow is mounted, and for how long. Unfortunately, there is no way for the female cow to communicate the thought, "Oh, sure, thirty seconds. Do you ever think about my needs?")

Life for men in America would change irrevocably if humans wore these electronic gizmos. We wouldn't get away with anything.

She: ". . . and the defense reaction was to tell the judge I was completely out of bounds for even *mentioning* the defendant's

previous arrest, since it was thrown out of court because they
had no warrant. Don't you think his attitude was just a trifle
insincere and patronizing?"

He: *Beep*.

Which, of course, leads me to the survey of men's sex lives,
and it seems that some of us are doing better than others.

Black men, for example, tend to have their first sexual experience two years earlier than white men, and eventually, they
have 50 percent more partners. This is why, when I telephone
women for dates, I give my name as Jamal Kornheiser.

The average man between twenty and forty years old has
had seven sexual partners over his career—forgive the sports
term.

Seven.

A sportswriter friend of mine sniffed at seven. "That's a bad
year for me," he said.

"Bad year for you," I said. "That's a bad evening for Wilt."

Twenty-eight percent of the men said they'd had sex with
just one partner.

"Tell me you've had sex with more than one person," my smart
friend Martha said.

"Oh, sure," I said.

"Good," she said with relief.

I said, "That's counting myself, right?"

My favorite finding was about religion. The survey said con-
servative Protestants—I guess we're talking about Bush and
Quayle—reported an average of five sexual partners; other Protestants, seven; Catholics, seven; and people belonging to other
religions, or no religion, eight. Which would imply that Jewish
men were doing better than Joey Buttafuoco. And who's gonna
believe that?

The average twenty- to forty-year-old man is said to have sex
once a week. Men over forty were originally included in the sur-

vey but were later excluded after too many answered the question "How many times a week do you have sex?" by laughing and saying, "A *week*?"

The keys to understanding the survey are in the analysis of two seemingly unrelated results:

1. Only one man in a hundred said he is gay.

2. Twenty-three percent of all men said they have had sex with at least twenty partners.

These results, when analyzed carefully, have one thing in common. The respondents are—and I want to get the correct scientific terminology for this—lying. There are rugs in a basement in Marrakech that don't lie this bad.

Does one in a hundred sound right to you? Where are you living, in the Biosphere? One in a hundred? If that's true, then they're all already *in* the army.

The Kinsey Report, the bible of sexuality, which was published forty-five years ago, said one in ten men was gay. What, Kinsey misplaced the decimal point?

Now as for twenty or more partners . . .

The truth is that men have sex only one fifth as often as they say, and *want* sex only one tenth as often as they say.

After you deduct some rock stars, some actors, and the Los Angeles Lakers, that still leaves, like, 20 million guys who'd have to be bagging babes left and right. Most of the men I know can't even get a date.

The error in this survey is the respondent. Don't you know the kind of man who willingly signs up for a sex survey? He's a total dork. He lives with his mother . . . or he lived with his mother until she died—maybe a few weeks after she died. He hasn't had a date since 1972; outside of being interviewed for this sex survey, his only human contact is in a supermarket. You gonna *believe* this guy when he tells you he has women draped all over him like tinsel?

Men lie one way.

Women lie another.

When the survey about women comes out, it will say 95 percent of the women in America have had sex with two or fewer partners—the man they are currently with, and Joey Buttafuoco. The other 5 percent have only one thing to say: *Beep.*

Bok Choy? Leaf Me Alone! And That's Fennel!

Somewhere in America would it be possible for me to get a loaf of bread without sun-dried cherries in it? Or walnuts. Or basil. Or cheese. Or olives. Seriously, what bozo with a baker's hat is responsible for putting olives in bread? Would he drop a slice of toast into a martini?

I like bread the old-fashioned way—without the entire table of contents of the *Whole Earth Catalog* inside.

Whatever happened to Wonder Bread building strong bodies twelve ways? How many schoolchildren want peanut butter on tomato basil bread? What school do they go to, Our Lady of Cher?

My friend Mike walked into a deli the other day—excuse me, not a "deli," a "gourmet boulangerie"—and made the mistake of ordering ham on rye. The woman behind the counter glared at him and hissed, "Tourist."

My God, what if he'd ordered ham on *white*! Would they have called security?

Deliver me from all this food pretentiousness. When did food go from sustaining life to interior-decorating it? Have you seen what they've done to chicken lately? And I date "lately" from the time *spaghetti* was officially replaced in the language by *pasta*. You cannot get chicken salad anymore. You can get chicken tarragon, or chicken primavera, or chicken andouille, or chicken in pesto sauce. But if you ask for plain chicken, you will be hooted. They will tell you to come back when the Kmart closes for the evening.

If you want plain chicken, it has to be "free-range" chicken, which is a chicken raised by liberals. These chickens aren't cooped up in cages and pumped up with steroids. Allegedly, free-range chickens are healthier because they feed exclusively off the land. Well, have you *seen* the land lately? No way I'm eating anything that's been grazing on Route 1 near Hyattsville.

And no matter what you order, it comes with baby corn. How did baby corn become the Sinatra of Side Dish? I don't want to eat anything with the word *baby* in front of it. Not baby corn. Not baby carrots. Not baby peas. I don't even want to eat a Baby Ruth.

Man About Town Chip Muldoon is in from L.A., where you cannot order a meal without mangoes or beets—which may explain why Richard "Hello, Dalai" Gere is taken seriously out there. Mangoes you can ignore. But even if you don't eat the beets, the red stuff bleeds into everything else on your plate, and ruins it. It's like throwing a madras shirt into a white-underwear wash.

I hate beets.

The only time I've ever eaten beets as an adult was a few years ago at the world-famous Chez Panisse restaurant in Berkeley. We'd booked the reservation months in advance. Dinner was a flat eighty dollars per person. There was no menu. They serve one standard dinner a night, and the night I went, it had beets. For that money I wasn't passing on anything, so I ate the beets. They tasted like someone had opened a tin can of candied lima beans in the middle of World War I, and here I was, seventy-five years later, licking the lid.

California is the mecca of trendy eating. In California, even the public water fountains spout Evian. (And could somebody please explain to me how so many junk foods, bags of the greasiest, lardiest, straight-into-the-arteries globules, now claim to have "No Fat!" and "No Cholesterol!" How can this be? "Lite Ice Cream . . . with half the butterfat!" Half the butterfat of what, Dom DeLuise?)

Chip Muldoon says the big eating craze out there is a particular pizza, the Sunset Strip, a quintessentially L.A. concoction with pineapples, artichokes, strips of mesquite chicken, sun-dried tomatoes, porcini mushrooms, and chili peppers.

"That's a pizza?" I said. "It sounds like a Jackson Pollock painting."

I've tried to start eating healthy. I'm part of a weekly organic food plan. (I responded to an ad that I thought said "orgasmic" food. You know, when you get past forty you really should see an eye doctor.)

I pay approximately $399 a week, and I receive a pouch with enough fruits and vegetables to feed a family of one a light snack. But the food is very fresh. The dew is still on it. So are the bugs. An organic farmer doesn't use pesticides.

"Waiter, there's a fly in my soup!"

"Well, sir, you ordered the *organic* cream of tomato."

I was so excited about my first shipment. I felt like I was being made love to by Harry & David. I got the pouch and opened it. There were six items, four of which I recognized: spinach, broccoli, lettuce, and onions.

Bok choy, though, was new to me; I couldn't recall seeing it before—unless it was as a triple-word score in Scrabble. And fennel was a complete mystery. I assumed it was either ornamental shrubbery or organic road kill.

"Good thing you didn't get sorrel," someone told me.

Wow. Sorrel must really be scary.

Lips that touch fennel will never touch mine, so I gave the bok choy and the fennel to my friend Nancy, who quit the food plan when she felt inundated by root vegetables. "I want to be healthy," she said. "But not *that* healthy."

My children were devastated. (They go to a multicultural school; apparently, there was a bok choy and fennel festival last week. Go figure.)

The next day, just out of curiosity, I asked Nancy about fennel.

"It's like celery, but it has kind of a licorice taste. You braise it," she said. Not me. I come to bury fennel, not to braise it.

The Power of Money

Who *wouldn't* have picked 4, 8, 19, 28, 30, and 41?

Weren't they obvious?

The only hard one in the bunch was 28.

They're exactly the numbers I would have played in Power-ball, had I thought it made sense to stand in a line for three hours in the broiling heat to buy a ticket, standing ten deep around the 7-Eleven among people who usually wouldn't set foot in a 7-Eleven without an immunologist: painfully thin men with bad beards and hideous skinny legs in jogging shorts, and women with those precise blunt-cut power hairdos and no behinds, wearing linen shorts and expensive Joan and David flats.

So I'm sitting here typing this column, and somebody in Wisconsin who should rot in Hell has a $100 million of my money, and what're they gonna do with it—buy cheese?

Actually, I shouldn't disparage the person in Wisconsin, who, according to the rumor that just now crossed my desk, is an unmarried woman. I just hope the money doesn't ruin her. That can happen, you know. Yeah, a young woman, out on her own with tons of money. Before you know it, some unscrupulous viper will dance her and romance her and bleed her dry just for her money.

What a shame. I wish there was something I could do, because as you know I really respect women in general, and Wisconsin women in particular. Money means nothing to me personally. I spit on money. I don't care about her money. I care about her. I would do anything to protect her identity and her privacy. Nobody should take advantage of her. Nobody should even know who she is. The only way she should have to deal with the public is by making the call herself, by reaching out to talk to someone who isn't interested in money, someone older, someone settled and established, someone who doesn't care at all about money—money, feh! patooie!—someone warm and understanding, someone, you know, losing his hair. 202-334-6000.

Wait. I just heard it might be a man.

A *guy*!

Hmm.

Okay, same deal. We are talking $100 million here.

I asked some people what they would do with $100 million. Most people think small. They think houses and cars and trips to Europe, which still leaves them with $98,674,508. *Then* what do you do? One young woman I spoke to said she would "put my dog in day care, and buy a toaster oven." With $100 million, she could put her dog in day care in Nepal.

People should think bigger, like the redoubtable Captain Airwaves, who said, "At my age, I'd think seriously about a big memorial; real marble, some of the Italian stuff. Don't paint my name on the outside—carve it. I'm even thinking of script."

But even then he's still got $94,235,091 left.

Now, what would *I* do with $100 million?

1. End world hunger;
2. Buy a yacht with bathrooms the size of my boss's lawn;

3. Arrange to send Ed McMahon five hundred letters a week for the rest of his life that begin, in screaming bold type, YOU, ED MCMAHON, MAY HAVE ALREADY WON ONE MILLION DOLLARS, YOU FAT SUCK-UP NO-TALENT GASBAG;

4. Offer to give every poodle in Ohio a buzz cut;

5. Offer Donald Trump $11 million to cha-cha down Broadway wearing only platform shoes, a pink cummerbund, and a jockstrap (now, I know what you are thinking: Donald, of all people, wouldn't do it, because he's already filthy rich. But he knows a good deal when he sees it. He could not possibly resist, and if he did, his decision would bedevil him the rest of his life, which would be almost as good);

6. Buy some small country, like Vanuatu, and declare myself its Lord High Dermatologist. At the U.N. I would bang my shoe on the table and demand kosher hot dogs;

7. Hire mimes and instruct them to follow Sam Donaldson wherever he went;

8. Buy Cal Ripken a base hit, which he can't seem to get otherwise;

9. Hire completely hairless, shockingly obese people to hang around me all the time, making me look, by comparison, like Valentino;

10. Make a movie and then pay people handsomely to see it, so that forevermore the highest-grossing film of all time would be the documentary *Bean Farming in Uruguay (Part II)*;

11. Buy the house next door to Pat Buchanan. Give it to a nice lesbian couple;

12. Build, to the dimensions of the Lincoln Memorial, a gigantic shrine to Allen Funt;

13. Hire a full-time humor clipping service, so it wouldn't come as a surprise to me—as it did this week—that there has been, living and working in Virginia for *years*, unmolested by humor writers, a judge named Michael P. McWeeny;

14. Charter a 747, paint it blue and white, park it at LAX and hire Cristophe to cut my hair for 300,000 hours, thus freezing travel to Los Angeles for thirty-five years, thus killing the movie and TV industries, thus (eventually) eliminating violence in America.

Call Me La Ishmael

I am grateful to my parents for naming me Anthony Irwin Kornheiser because it gives me license to say anything I want about other people's names. What could be more preposterous than *Anthony Kornheiser?* This is like naming someone Moishe O'Hara. Or LaToya Teitelbaum. Or Wan-fu Piscatelli.

I have never heard of another Jewish Tony, other than Tony Curtis, whose real name is Bernie Schwartz.

All ethnic groups have their conventions for naming children. Jews often name their children after Great-Uncle Yitzhak or some other long-departed relative, which ensures that Jews often have anachronistic names that are hopelessly fuddy-duddy. The first girl I ever dated chewed bubble gum like a third-baseman, wore poodle skirts and bobby socks, and was named Bathsheba Berkowitz.

Presbyterians name their male children after their fathers, so they are all named John Porter Babblington III. The girls are all named Catherine, but that doesn't matter because they never use their real names. They are all nicknamed Muffin or Cookie or Jellybean or some other light, edible confection. Bathsheba Berkowitz's college roommate was Mallomar McPartland.

There is also a trend among Presbyterians to name their children after cold, inanimate objects, like Stone, or after manly occupations, like Hunter and Tanner. The perfect WASP name: Mortuary Slab Porter Babblington IV.

Many names are pretty much the same around the world: You've got John, Jean, and Juan. And Joe, José, Josef, and Giuseppe. Or Michael, Michel, and Miguel. Or Yasser . . . uh, I guess you're pretty much out there on your own with Yasser.

One ethnic group that can't seem to get too trendy with names is the Poles, since their alphabet consists of only seven letters—Z, X, I, Y, K, C, and S—and they can only name their kids Sczyski or Skzyzicky. Other groups using the same alphabet we do somehow wind up with names we recognize as ridiculous. At my local 7-Eleven—and I swear this is true—one clerk is named Meshmoo and another is named Saliva.

Italians name their children after saints, like Saint Salvatore "Sal the Septic Tank" Spunkatello.

Some of the most exciting names lately have come from black families, who either name their children after sounds (Shrieka) or for some reason precede their names with the syllable "La." There are LaKeisha, LaPhonso, LaBradford, LaToya, LaTrina, LaDeedah. In the hope that my son would be a good basketball player, I wanted to give him a "LA" name also, so I named him Los Angeles Kornheiser.

Today's most popular yuppie kids names are Alexander, Benjamin, Nicholas, William, Beavis, and Christopher for boys; and Ashley, Amanda, Demi, Leigh, Stephanie, and Tipper for girls. Thankfully, we appear to be out of the hideous *J* phase of the '70s and '80s, when every other child was named Jennifer, Jessica, Jamie, Joshua, Jason, or Justin. My nominee for the Cultural Totem Pole Hall of Fame is actress Jennifer Jason Leigh, who touches all the bases.

Parents ought to be more responsible for what they name their children. The sins of the '60s are haunting us now. I know the hippies meant well when they named their children after their favorite things, like Sunshine, Tranquillity, and Blotter Acid—yes, Blotter Acid Blumenthal, now a senior business-and-marketing major at Dartmouth. Face it, it's wrong to name your baby when you're so stoned you can swear the cover of the Moby Grape album just winked at you. Here is what happens when you do this: I know of a kid born in 1968—this is also true—who as a teenager would introduce himself to people this way: "Hi. My name is Caribou, but you can call me Mike."

A colleague of mine is named Athelia. It is a biblical name. Athelia tells me her name is routinely mispronounced—everything from Althea to Athleria—and her one regret is that she has been so accommodating over the years, answering to every mispronunciation, never correcting anyone. "I have an eighty-year-old aunt who still calls me Azalea."

Names are cyclical. Sometimes the name you least expect turns out to be insanely popular. When my friend Gino and his wife, Arlene, named their daughter in 1981, they thought they were being wildly adventurous, even foolhardy, by choosing the name Molly. *No one* was named Molly. It was as though they had chosen the name Frigidaire or Mel Torme's Greatest Hits. They worried that in later years, little Molly would hate them for their recklessness. Now, little Molly is in seventh grade, where every girl in her class is named Mollie, Molly, or LaMollie, and most of them have a pet cat or hamster named Molly. There is only one girl in the class who *isn't* named Molly. She is named Saliva.

Of course, in sixty years or so, no one will be named Molly anymore and little LaButthead will giggle at Grandma Molly's ridiculous name.

Lard Have Mercy

My boss is very depressed. He just found out that the "low-fat" muffins he has been eating for the past year weren't so low-fat after all. They were advertised as containing two grams of fat and 150 calories. In fact, they have eight grams of fat and 530 calories.

This means that for breakfast you can either eat one of these muffins . . . or a life-size sculpted swan made entirely of processed lard. Same difference.

"I'm very upset," my boss said. "I thought I could eat these muffins and be lean and trim, and live to be a hundred and ten."

"Not a chance," I said. "Almost everyone in the office would have killed you first."

I have seen these "low-fat" muffins. They are generally the size of an ottoman. If you get fatigued eating these muffins, you can *sit* on them, like Little Miss Muffin . . . uh, Muffet, Muffet. Even if they are low-fat, you have to ask yourself: Compared with what? George Wendt's huskier brother, Wally?

I watch supermarket shoppers studying the nutritional analysis on cereal boxes. I see the ones with young children comparing Count Chocula or Lucky Charms with shredded wheat, and putting the shredded wheat in their cart, thinking they've struck nutritional gold. Have they any idea how many tablespoons of sugar it will take to cajole their children into eating shredded wheat? Shredded wheat tastes like something a donkey has slept on.

Take cookies. One box of cookies will say LOW-FAT. Another box will say LOW-CAL. A third box of cookies will say LOW IN CHOLESTEROL. The low-fat box may be high in calories. The low-cholesterol box may be high in fat. It's so confusing.

Question: How do you know which box of cookies to buy?

Answer: What's the difference? They're cookies, you bozo. They're gonna kill you. Buy the ones with the most butter, and hope that before all your arteries ice over you get hit by a bus.

It's like people insisting they can load up on the "no-fat" ice cream they've found in the store. Oh, please. Actually I have seen "no-fat ice cream." It's called water.

Now that I'm working out, I have the appetite of a water buffalo. I am sucking up food like a Hoover. I have actually *gained* weight since I started going to a gym. My trainer tells me it is better to eat a lot of little meals than a few big ones. I ask him what he means by "little meals," and he says, "A couple of rice cakes." I tell him that if I wanted to eat a couple of rice cakes, I'd work out in a gym in Bangkok.

I'm grateful to *The Washington Post* for running a big story blowing the lid off some of these "low-fat" claims. (I'm particularly grateful for a small item that said a roast beef sub contained *less* fat and *fewer* calories than a vegetarian sub: definitive proof that there's a God. Tell the truth, wouldn't you be delighted if every vegetarian got as fat as a barn? Aren't you sick of people pinching their noses and telling you they don't eat red meat, like you're a cannibal for ordering a hamburger?) My favorite part concerned the owner of a restaurant that advertised a "low-fat" dim sum that should have had seven grams of fat, and actually had fifty-four! This is no small mistake; this is like taking off for Cleveland and landing in Kuala Lumpur. The restaurant owner explained, "I don't have that much knowledge about food or nutrition." Thank you for not opening up a hospital.

The article offered some tips on how to "eat out defensively." (Of course my question then becomes: If we're already driving defensively, and now we need to be eating out defensively . . . how should we go through the fast-food drive-thru, in a crouch?) One of the tips was how to recognize fat in foods. "If a dish glistens, it probably was cooked in oil or butter." Or hair spray, I guess. What does this mean? Should we eat only foods that look as if they've been rubbed in dirt?

Advertising That's Below the Belt

So I'm sitting there, watching the TV, not paying a whole lot of attention, when this thirtyish blonde comes on. She's got the Lauren Bacall look, she's leaning out on what appears to be a New York City terrace overlooking Central Park—it's a very sophisticated setting—and she says, "My mother always told me to look at a man's eyes first." There's a pause. Then, she knits her eyebrows in this hip, dismissive way, and purrs, "But what did she know?"

They go to a voice-over, and it turns out it's an ad for Sansabelt slacks. Men's pants. And I'm thinking, *huh?*

Several days later I'm watching TV. This time a late-twentyish, studious woman comes on expressing that same soft, come-hither mood. She's got the Carole King *Tapestry* look, holding a book, an NYU law grad maybe, and she says, "I always lower my eyes when a man passes . . ." Pause. A sly grin. ". . . to see if he's worth following."

Sansabelt.

Sansabelt? The pants Ed McMahon advertised for years. Your basic fat man golfer pants, right? What are those pants doing with these women?

I see another ad: Sitting on the porch of an Outer Banks–

type beach house is a windswept, milk-fed, apple-cheeked blonde, as fresh and clean as a barrel of rainwater. It takes a look like that to get away with saying, "I have always considered a man's lower half his better half."

Sansabelt.

A man's lower half.

I am not unaware that it is common practice for a man to peer at a woman's lower half. A car I see daily in my neighborhood has a bumper sticker pleading to approaching drivers, WATCH MY REAR END—NOT HERS. Size and contour are the subject of Spinal Tap's enthusiastic "Big Bottom," which proclaimed, ". . . talk about mud flaps, my gal's got 'em."

A woman's lower half; this, you'll admit, has been going on.

But gorgeous young women going on TV specifically telling men that they're looking at them, and looking specifically at their behinds, this is new. (At least I assume it's the lower *rear* half they're looking at. Am I mistaken?)

"What do you think this means?" I ask my friend Mike.

"It means you are in deep trouble," he tells me.

I'm over forty years old. I've had a tush all my life. Never once has it occurred to me that anyone is interested in it.

My tush is for grading.

Who knew?

"This matters to women?" I ask my wife.

"To some," she says.

"To you?" I ask.

She grins and turns away. When she reaches the stairs, she turns back and says, "The other day I was picking up Michael at school, and one of the mothers looked at him and said, 'That kid's going to have great buns.' "

"Buns?" I ask.

"Buns," she says.

"Michael's three and a half," I say.

Great buns!

That night I peeked at my own buns in the mirror.

I am in deep trouble.

Jerry McCann is vice president of marketing for Jaymar-Ruby, which produces Sansabelt slacks. He freely acknowledges his pants were floating face down in the water with everyone other than Ed McMahon. "Younger men had zero awareness of our product, zero." So to establish an image with younger men, they brought in younger women. "Young men are concerned with how they look to women. We are saying women look at men and the way they're dressed."

The lower half?

"There is a wink about that whole issue in our advertising," McCann concedes coyly.

The buns?

"I get nervous when people take it to the anatomical extreme," McCann says.

As you know, Sansabelt slacks (which now come—can you believe this?—with belt loops) are not the only product being marketed with sex. Calvin Klein sells perfume with incorrigibly naked, intertwined bodies. Sometimes, when he wants to sell designer underpants, he uses seminaked intertwined bodies. Blue jeans and cars are routinely sold with sex; many TV beer commercials are so sweaty, you have to towel off after thirty seconds.

However, this Sansabelt campaign is different. Not only is it a reverse seduction—what ad agency dared fuse women with lust before?—it's the deliberate slathering of sex in order to reposition a product. These were maximum polyester, middle-aged, convention-man pants. Sansabelt *was* your father's Oldsmobile! It's shivery enough to think of Sansabelt men as having behinds, let alone that any woman would be checking them out.

I peek again at my tush in the mirror.

It's lumpy and as large as a lampshade. I am way beyond buns—these are full loaves of bread. I vow to work diligently on the Stairmaster.

I am in deep trouble.

Second Thoughts
on Watches

My grandfather gave me my first watch when I was five. He made quite a ceremony of handing it over. It had been his own watch, and it apparently had great sentimental value. It had a silver expandable band, and its crystal face was faintly yellow with age. I slipped it around my left wrist, and admired it. Then I lowered my arm, and my grandfather's watch, which was much too big for a five-year-old, slid rapidly off my wrist, landed face down on the thick kitchen tiles, and shattered.

"*Que sera, sera,*" I said, that being a big song at the time.

"Get a load of this kid," my grandmother said. "He drops an heirloom, and he thinks he's Rosemary Clooney."

I didn't put on another wristwatch for thirty-five years.

Everybody else wore a watch; if I needed to know what time it was, I asked. If nobody was around, I turned on the radio. If I had no access to a person, or a radio, or one of those big clocks outside a bank, odds were I was probably on vacation, so what would it matter?

"Time," for $200:

Does anybody really know what time it is?

"Time," for $400:

Does anybody really care?

Last year, as a concession to middle age, I started wearing a watch. (What if I have grandchildren? What would I give them, my Left Banke albums?) And as soon as I did, I noticed all the other watches. They're everywhere. You pick up the Sunday paper, you'll see pages and pages of watch ads. Clearly, advertising reflects what people really buy—that's why you don't see pages and pages of ant farms.

The country has gone watch crazy. People own five, six, seven watches, even though they still have only two wrists. Like fancy-schmancy cars, watches have become a way of showing off how well you're doing. Rayful Edmond III wore a $45,000 Rolex. (It's understandable Rayful would be fussy about time, since he'll be doing so much of it.) I wonder what kind of watch Leona "Hard Time" Helmsley wears.

As most of you already know, digital is dead. (It's still big in Waikiki; *Digit Goes Hawaiian.*) If you have digital watches, get rid of them immediately. Do not embarrass your family further. Digital watches mark you as a hopeless boob.

Retro is in. Today's watches strive to evoke a simpler, long-ago time—apparently a time before watches were invented, since so many of these watches employ Roman numerals. (Except some Movados, which have no numbers. You're supposed to guess the time.)

Reconditioned watches are extremely in. Yuppies rummage around their attics looking for any old watch that's been buried in a trunk for at least seventy years, then pay out the wazoo to get it fixed. (Some of these old watches have radium dials, so after a few wearings, your wrist glows in the dark, which solves the problem of buying a night light.) Since this watch was built before batteries, it must be wound every day, leading to an appreciation of the expression: "I don't know whether to spit or wind my watch." The wearer of this reconditioned gem is deliriously proud until some seventy-five-year-old with a Seiko laughs and asks, "Sonny, where on earth did you get a piece of junk like that?"

As a consequence of this nostalgia for simplicity, the multifunction watch of the '70s is passé. It's difficult to buy a big chunk of a watch with nine hundred different dials and gizmos. This is bad news for people who think a watch ought to tell you at what temperature you can fry an egg on Mars, or the latitude and longitude of Madagascar. They can buy an almanac and strap it to their wrists.

Exactly what is the deal with all these half-moons on watches? Why should I care about lunar phases? What do I look like, a guy who's going to cross the Atlantic in a rowboat? This moon stuff escapes me, unless it's part of a plot to introduce a Roseanne Barr "Butt-Face" model.

Years ago all anyone asked of a watch was that it tell time. Then it had to be waterproof, then shatterproof; a common fantasy in the '60s was to smash John Cameron Swayze with a hammer, then throw him over the side of a tuna trawler to see if his infernal Timex was still ticking after they fished him out.

There are so many more things we want in a watch now. I asked a friend what she wanted in a watch. She said, "A date." I told her she'd have to get that on her own.

I want a watch with microwaveability; I want to be able to put it in a microwave, set the dial on high power for two minutes, and when I take it out, I want it to be dinner.

I want a watch with four-wheel drive.

I want a watch that every so often bursts into music by Zamfir, Master of the Pan Flute.

I want a watch where, instead of numbers, it has the faces of all the Eastern European Communist Party chiefs who have resigned in the last thirty-six hours.

I want a watch that cleans my house; it could be the maid's watch, I don't care.

I want a watch that informs me how many bowls of various

cereals I have to eat to equal the nutritional benefit of one bowl of Total. I want the watch to tell me what my cholesterol count is at all times, and to buzz whenever I go near a patch of oat bran. (I don't know about you, but I'm getting mighty sick of Wilford Brimley hectoring me about Quaker Oats. I want a watch that sends deadly gamma rays out at that old goat.)

I want a watch that'll make me attractive to the women in the Michelob Dry commercials.

I want a watch designed so that when your watch beeps while we're at the movies, my watch launches a nuclear missile that takes you out.

Actually, I want my grandfather's watch.

MY LIFE AS A DOG

*

Party Animals

When my son turned five, I decided to break tradition by not hiring a birthday party professional; the choice came down to two hours on Sunday afternoon or his freshman year at Yale. This was devastating news for the lady at Party Planners, who had counted on us to finance her vacation in France.

This would have been our third straight party with her. When Michael was three, she brought in a pony.

"Why does it cost so much?" I asked.

"It's a Lipizzaner. He's coming from Vienna," she said.

When Michael was four, she booked the cast from *The Heidi Chronicles*. All the kids got depressed and hid under the bed.

This year, we drew the line. She'd been planning a Gatsby theme. Cocktails and cigarettes on Long Island.

"It's a good way to introduce your son to F. Scott Fitzgerald," she insisted.

"But my son can't even spell F.," I said.

So we made him a pirate party. As the kids came in, we gave them each a pirate hat and a pirate eye patch, and sent them straight downstairs to the basement, where they began to scream. An hour later, we served cake. Now all the kids want to live at our house.

The crucial thing to understand is this was a party for boys. With girls, it's different. Girls want structure. They want activities. They want order.

Boys want to scream.

That's it. Dig a pit. Throw them in. Let them scream.

Granted, there's a risk. You throw ten boys in there, maybe only eight come out. But those eight will say they had the best party ever.

Is this just me? I tried my best to raise my children without audible oinks in the nursery. Did I blow it? Did I unconsciously set sexist roles in motion?

When my daughter was three, she began to play with Barbies. I swear this was not my doing. She'd sit for hours on the floor in her room, happily dressing and undressing her Barbies. She never looked at a truck or a gun, though I subscribed to *Off-Road* and *Ammo*. She was six years old before we ever heard the word *gun* in the house.

It was her brother who said it.

It was his third word.

First was *cookie*. Next was *Mommy*.

Then, *gun*.

One day when he was about four, he was playing with pipe cleaners, and I noticed he'd twisted one into an interesting shape.

"What's that, Michael, a pretty bird?"

"Mutant Ninja Killer Nunchucks," he said.

We gave our kids Legos. Personally, I hate Legos. Everyone who ever walked barefoot into his child's room late at night hates Legos. I think Mr. Lego should be strung up from a scaffold made of his horrid little pockmarked arch-puncturing plastic cubes. Anyway, my kids got Legos. Elizabeth built a graceful Spanish-style villa with a patio and a fountain.

Michael built a bazooka.

My daughter's favorite game is basketball. She wants me to play it with her every morning before school. I am happy to oblige.

My son's favorite game is called "I'll Kill You." I hide.

Apparently, it's the favorite game of all the boys in his class. (My friend Nancy tells me it has always been thus. She remembers recess at Blessed Sacrament almost thirty years ago, when the girls played basketball, and the boys—segregated behind sawhorses for the safety of others and confined to an alley— played something they called Maul Ball. "They'd take a hardball, and attempt to kill each other," Nancy recalled. "We simply assumed it was men's work.")

The principal of my son's school recently sent home a notice to all prekindergarten parents saying that the kids were specifically barred from bringing "weapons" to school for show-and-tell. This created a show-and-tell crisis in dozens of homes in our neighborhood, a frenzied 8 A.M. scramble for nonassaultive objects. For the last six Thursdays, my son has brought a hardboiled egg. His pal Adam brings a box of Tylenol.

Surely you must have noticed the difference between little boys and girls at parties. Most girls will stand quietly on line for games such as pin-the-scoop-on-the-ice-cream-cone. Boys, in the words of my smart friend Martha, "just barge in and grab the first thing that's longer than it is wide, and begin killing people."

The gifts are different, too. Girls will settle for dolls and notepads and board games. Boys want retro-rocket phaser guns with flashing lights that make twenty-four different kinds of high-pitched, whiny sounds, including one that exactly replicates the sound of a father going stark raving mad and smashing the gun to smithereens. Someone made the mistake of giving my son a notepad for his birthday. He picked it up and hurled it at the neck of one of the other little boys at the party. I asked him why he did that, and he grinned and said, "It was a Ninja Pizza Weapon." Go figure.

I can't vouch for this story. It may be apocryphal, but I believe it has the ring of truth: I'm told there is a group of radical feminists in San Francisco who formed a cooperative to raise their children. They were adamant about raising their children without stereotyped sex roles. They made sure all the children sang songs together, and played games together, and learned that each of them was equal and had equal opportunity and responsibility. They sought to make nurture triumph over nature. Among the gifts at a birthday party for one of the boys were a starter set of tools and a beautiful set of Barbie and Ken dolls. He was no stranger to dolls. He had many of them, as did all the boys in the cooperative. He took out the starter hammer and smashed Ken's head.

Your witness, counselor.

Oh Dud, Poor Dud

Last Thursday was Take Our Daughters to Work Day. And like any sane father I dreaded it. Isn't it enough that my daughter sees me around the house in my underpants? Do I have to be humiliated further by letting her see me at work, where I appear even less dignified?

So I came up with a scheme that would make my daughter think I was important: I seriously considered renting a hotel suite and hiring a secretary for the anteroom. Then I would sit inside, behind a big fancy desk, and as I was telling my daughter how important my work was, every few minutes the secretary would urgently come in and say, "I'm sorry to interrupt, Mr. Kornheiser, but this call really needs your attention."

"Okay, put the call through," I would say.

I'd shake my head in anguish as I listened to the voice on the other end (which in reality would be James Earl Jones saying "Welcome to Bell Atlantic"), and finally I'd speak angrily, and say something like:

"Look, just get on it right away. Don't make me fly out to-night and do it myself."

Or:

"What? That material was supposed to be in San Diego at

nine A.M.! You tell Moskowitz he'll be carving soap in South Dakota if this doesn't get done by three this afternoon!" (I'd then bang my fist on the desk, because why not, it's a rental.)

I'd let this go on an hour or so, and schmaltz it up by having somebody show up and make a big fuss over me for a huge charitable donation I'd made—the $650,000 for Bosnia I'd raised personally just by calling millionaires who owed me favors. Then I'd have the secretary come in to say apologetically, "I'm so sorry, Mr. Kornheiser, I know you were counting on spending your entire work day with your lovely daughter"—and I'd look at my daughter very lovingly—"but the White House just called. The president needs you there right away. He's got to give a speech tonight at the United Nations, and he says there's only one man he'd trust to write it on such short notice: Tony Kornheiser."

I'd pause dramatically.

"It's the president, Elizabeth; I've gotta go. I'd love to bring you with me, but you need security clearance, and there just isn't time."

Then I'd walk to the newspaper, where I'm treated by everyone there—my boss, my coworkers, the copy aides, the janitorial staff—like a dust bunny. At work, basically, I slink around meekly, like a panhandler, begging people for ideas for my column, offering them money and flattering them furiously, because I never have ideas of my own and, like Blanche Dubois, I'm totally dependent on the charity of others. I am afforded so little respect that even the random lunatics who come into the newsroom complaining that the CIA has implanted electrodes in their teeth call me "cueball head" and laugh at me.

I don't want my daughter to see that.

So take *your* daughter to work. Leave mine out of this.

I'm not even going to get into the notion of how politically incorrect it is to take our daughters to work, and not our sons. What do I tell my son when he asks if he can go to work with me—wear a dress?

It's one thing if you actually *do* something at work—if you build a house, or sell cars, or you're a neurosurgeon (where you are so important that people literally wipe your brow). But I type. That's what I do, sit and type. It isn't a real action job. It's unlikely Steven Seagal will play me in the movies.

Here's my day: I come in. I sit down at the keyboard. I wait for the muse to hit me. To mug me, actually.

When the muse doesn't come, I go eat.

I talk on the phone, desperately asking people for column ideas. (I've been known to call up foreign embassies and plead, "*Quien tiene una columno para yo?*" My Spanish is terrible.)

Sometimes I eat while I'm talking.

Must I go on?

Must my child see this?

I am not the same man at work that I am at home.

At home I'm a putz. But at work I'm a putz in a tie.

But anyway, it was Take Our Daughters to Work Day in America, and since I am a loyal American, I had to do it. Here is what happened:

Elizabeth, twelve, walked into my office, and the first thing she saw was my computer screen. Crawling across the dark screen in bright purple letters, again and again, was the sentence I had typed in many months ago to use as a screen saver—a quote from the movie *Animal House* that I thought summed up almost everything in life: "You fudged up, Dorfman, you trusted us."

Only it didn't say "fudged."

"Wow, Dad, who wrote *that*?" she asked.

"Er, the computer fairy," I said, and immediately booted up my machine to get rid of the screen saver. After a few seconds of beeping there arrived on the screen my pending messages, the top one of which was from Gino, my editor, expressing his forthright opinion of my most recent piece of writing. Gino wrote that I had royally fudged up and what was I, some sort of fudging idiot?

"Wow!" said Elizabeth.

So I sent my daughter to the cafeteria.

"They've got Gummi Worms down there," I said. "Here's some money."

I gave her sixty dollars.

I hoped that would hold her until five, when Take Our Daughters to Work Day was over.

Anyway, one very nice thing happened. I dropped in on my idol, Bob Woodward, and hung around his office like a starving puppy until he sighed and let me in. Even though he was busy, he regaled us with anecdotes about Watergate and other big stories he'd been involved with. He couldn't have been more cordial, and I thanked him profusely for being so kind. The one embarrassing moment came afterward when Elizabeth asked, "Dad, why did Mr. Woodward keep calling you 'Tommy'?"

A Bright and Shining Guy

Dwight Eisenhower. Robert Duvall. Burt Reynolds. Michael Jordan. Ed Koch. Frank Perdue. Willard Scott. Sean Connery. Sinead O'Connor. Winston Churchill. Kareem Abdul-Jabbar. Peter Arnett. Elton John. Bozo the Clown. Gandhi.

Bless 'em all.

Bald like me.

(Not sure you're losing your hair? Yul know, believe me.)

What makes us so damned cool?

Is it just the fact that our brains are closer to the surface, which makes us quicker on the uptake, or that we can stick our heads out the window and find out the weather without opening our eyes? Or is it that we're so good in bed?

Oh sure, you think I'm being defensive. I can hear women now, saying it's no big deal being bald. Like it's no big deal being flat-chested, I suppose? At least you have those high-fashion models and Audrey Hepburn to make you feel glamorous. Who do we unhaired have as role models? Fred Mertz and Louie DiPalma.

My hair began falling out when I was eighteen. I asked my doctor if there was any way to save it. He said, "Sure, put it in a

shoe box." So I switched doctors. I went to a famous hair spe-
cialist in New York, who began injecting my scalp with estrogen.
He said it would help me keep my hair. The treatments were
going okay until I began getting an uncontrollable urge to shop at
Loehmann's.

A few years later I bought a toupee. It was curly; it looked
exactly like the one Kevin Dobson has. It cost $400, and I wore
it outside the house for a total of five seconds. I was going to my
car when my neighbor saw me and said, "Don't move. I'm getting my shotgun. There's a yak on your head." I went back inside
and put the toupee in the shoe box with the rest of my hair.

I wouldn't say I'm overly self-conscious about having this
vast, blatant, blindingly reflective expanse on the top of my
head, unless you think removing all the mirrors from my house
or never sitting down or bending over in the presence of other
people is overly self-conscious. I grew so weary of having people
look at my head and say in their idiotically chipper tone, "Tony,
did you know you're going bald?" Did I know? Did I know?
Wow. I just thought I had an extremely robust and well-devel-
oped part in my hair.

I've compensated. I grew a beard. I wear a hat. (All the time.
Even inside the house. My kids think I'm a baseball player.) You
show me someone with a beard and a hat, I'll show you a bald
man underneath.

I hold on to my fantasies. I still have a brush. I still have a
hair dryer. I do my best to comb over; me and Sam Nunn. I still
go to a hairdresser; the fabulous Barbara, bless her. I overtip her
like crazy, out of gratitude for her using a scissors and not just a
buffing cloth.

(Did I tell you how much I hate my father? Oh, big time.
He's eighty years old, and he has a full head of hair. I look like *his*
father. He tells me being bald is nothing to be ashamed of, then
he whips out a comb and stands in front of a mirror and Fonzes
himself. He's eighty! He tells me my hair wouldn't fall out if I

didn't worry so much. I say, who died and made you Sigmund Freud? In fact, the genetic code for baldness is carried by the maternal grandfather. So I ask my Dad about my maternal grandfather. "Bald as a hard-boiled egg at fifteen," he says. *Laughing!*)

As you can tell I'm not completely at peace with my condition. I'm still in the Shame Phase. I'm not liberated, like Richard Sandomir, who wrote the book *Bad Like Me: Adventures of Baldman*. Sandomir, thirty-three, is gloriously bald. He doesn't attempt the comb-over, which he calls "turban renewal." Sandomir wants to establish the Bald Hall of Fame, and locate it in Morehead City, N.C. (Previously, he founded the Baldness Defense League. He held the inaugural press conference at the Astor Place barber shop in New York. Sandomir feared he'd "be assassinated by an overhaired zealot.")

Sandomir disdains all the rug wearers, weave dreamers, and minoxidil minions, such as Charlton Heston, Burt Reynolds, Rick Barry, and Bill Murray, who has hair patching to cover up a significant bald spot on his crown. Sandomir wants to "out" them. One of the Great Moments in Bald History was Ted Danson's recent shedding of his piece to reveal a nascent bald growth on top, a public self-outing.

"I wept," Sandomir admitted.

Among his other Great Moments in Bald History are: the scene in *The Fabulous Baker Boys* in which Beau Bridges spray-paints Rustoleum on his bald spot; Julius Caesar crossing the Rubicon; Telly Savalas's birthdate; *People* magazine naming Sean Connery the world's sexiest man ("Why did they make him wear a wig in *The Hunt For Red October?*" Sandomir asks. "Don't they think a bald man could steer a submarine?"); Benito Mussolini's head being paraded through the streets of Milan.

Sandomir is one of my idols. I wish I were as advanced as he is. Regrettably, I'm still trying for a miracle. A few years ago I got involved with a medical study, testing a drug called Viprostol. I rubbed it on my head twice a day. (I was careful to wear plastic gloves, for fear hair would start sprouting on my palms.) It didn't work. Then I tried Rogaine. It hasn't worked either. All I have to show for it is some fuzz, like you'd find on a plucked chicken. God, I hate those Rogaine commercials where some wimpy yuppie decides to do something about his thinning hair. How I wish I still had thinning hair. This guy has a bald spot the size of a dime and he's whining. I'd like to pop him in the labonza. Lemme give you some advice, pal: Get a shoe box.

Shop Till
the Mailman Drops

In the dream I am upstairs, standing in front of the linen closet, stacking the bars of soap. There are already forty-eight of them, and it's just July. An idiot has sent me a gift from the Soap on a Rope catalog: eight bars of bath soap per month for a year, ninety-six in all! Almond, ginger, and oatmeal soaps. We're not sure whether to bathe with them or serve them for breakfast.

My wife yells up, "Honey, dinner's ready."

"I can't eat," I say. "I have to take another shower."

"That's your third today."

"Fourth, actually—two more to go. I'm finally making a dent in this bar. Why would anybody make pralines-and-cream soap? Where did the guy work before he got this job, Baskin-Robbins? . . . Look, make sure to send the kids up for their baths after dinner."

"They refuse to take another bath. Kids in school are teasing them because their fingers are always puckered. We don't have kids anymore, we have baby prunes. Michael's science homework was to use the word *experiment* in a sentence. He wrote, 'I am part of a hydroponic experiment.' "

"Tell them this will stop soon. Tell them Daddy will soon

have enough rope to hang the people who manufacture the Soap on a Rope catalog.''

Every day more and more catalogs arrive at my house. They are left on my stoop because they are too thick to fit inside the mail slot. For Christmas I'm not tipping my mailman, I'm giving him a truss.

I am new to the Catalog Game, unlike my colleague Ronalie Peterson, who is legendary for getting EVERY CATALOG EVER MADE, an average of twenty a day this time of year! If there were a ''Michael Milken in Jail'' catalog, Ronalie would have had it five minutes after sentencing. When I was young, nobody I knew shopped by catalog. The only catalog I ever heard of was the Spiegel catalog, which they gave away on TV game shows. I know this sounds totally retro, but people in my neighborhood went to stores to buy their food and clothes. ''Who shops by mail?'' I asked my father. ''Farmers,'' he assured me. Now farmers are the only ones who don't shop by mail. If they're hungry and they want a pear, they'll go out and pick it off a tree. The rest of us dial an 800 number and wait for UPS. The good news is, the pears come exquisitely wrapped and gorgeous. The bad news is, they come in three weeks.

''Your pears are here, dear.''

''Fine, set them next to the ninety-dollar orthopedic pet bed and the one-hundred-seventy-five-dollar nostalgic Air Force leather bomber jacket with the hand-painted map of the Hapsburg Empire in the lining.''

Let me make my position on catalogs clear: If I am driving, and I see you walking down the street in L. L. Bean duck shoes, I'm going to try to run you over.

Enough is enough. How obscure and limited is our taste supposed to get?

Duncraft: gourmet birdseed catalogs. *Gourmet birdseed!* What, with little flecks of Brie in it? This is what we need during a recession, birds that only eat Omaha steaks?

Almond Plaza: thirty-six pages of almonds. Okay, eight pages, even fourteen, but thirty-six pages of almonds? The "Gettysburg Address" is written on the back of an envelope, and we get thirty-six pages of almonds.

Plow & Hearth: compost heaps for college grads. Here's something from this one: the Scoot-n-Do, a little green wagon you sit on while you do your gardening so you don't get grass stains on your catalog jeans. (Also in here is the Squirrel Spinner: "Train your squirrels to be acrobats." You put corn at the end of a wooden stake, the squirrels climb down for the corn and presumably spin around until they vomit. Great fun for the whole family.) Todd, who showed me the Scoot-n-Do, also told me about the Bug Sucker, a self-explanatory tube device used to rid yourself of household bugs neatly, without squashing them on your wallpaper.

Smith & Hawken: nature junk for the environmentally guilt-ridden, including an $85 "Sardinian Fire Tool," a long, steel, confusingly needless rod.

Mission Orchards (also, Harry and David): incredibly expensive fruit, like *one pound* of Medjool dates for $17.95! I've had less expensive dates that led to marriage.

The Cockpit: macho aviation fantasy wear for desk-bound chicken hawks.

Brownstone: serious clothes for female fogies of indeterminate age.

Hold Everything: empty boxes, all shapes, all sizes. Yuppie Tupperware.

Nothing doesn't come in a catalog anymore. One man at work told me he has a catalog devoted exclusively to Soviet military insignia—apparently they're liquidating now that the Cold War is over. One woman said she'd just sent away for the Robert Redford Catalog, undoubtedly a time-share deal. Another woman told me she has inherited the catalogs of the people who previously owned her house, including a Lesbian Music catalog and a politically correct children's game catalog. "Who'd you buy the house from, Gertrude Stein?" I asked.

Soon we'll see a "Keating Five" catalog that lets you order free, laundered money by discreetly calling the Senate Office Building, a "Trump Goes Bump" catalog for slightly soiled Georgia peaches and used airplanes, and a "What's Shakin' on H Street" catalog, where you can order huge new holes in the ground.

My smart friend Martha is partial to the Miles Kimball catalog, where she once ordered the indispensable rotary nose-hair clipper for a loved one, not to mention the personalized cocktail napkins with a picture of a backyard swimming pool that say "A Sip and a Dip With the [family name]." These, Martha explains, are for "people who drown drunk in their pools," the Orange County A-list.

I notice I'm getting a classier kind of catalog lately: Ever since I let my membership in Telly Savalas's Players Club lapse, they have stopped trying to sell me vinyl jackets and felt paintings. I kind of miss the catalog that tries to sell brown, nuclear-winter sausage and quasi-edible "cheese food" in the shape of a log cabin. Hand to God, who buys that stuff, and *whom* do they send it to? Thankfully, I still get my Lillian Vernon catalog, and just like you, I search for that cute Lucite bunny with a cabbage face I can monogram to use as either a key ring or a dinner plate, and of course I crinkle up my face and say, "Oooohhh, that's so pwecious, I want one."

I have come to view catalogs as windows to my soul. I'm the kind of guy who hopes for Victoria's Secret, and winds up with Lillian Vernon's.

Tony, Tony, Tony.

My name is Tony, and I'm an egomaniac and a TV whore. No TV appearance is beneath me. I would do the weather on the Food Channel; I'd do commercials for adult diapers. I would sing "I Love You, Pooky-Dooky" with Barney. I would even go on Sally Jessy Raphaël's show, even though she is so unbearably slimy that she has to wear spike heels or she'd slide across the floor.

I asked my dear friend Gino, who is known for his sensitivity, to help me come to terms with this problem. He said, and I am quoting this verbatim: "Your problem is that you are pretentious, bloated, and more self-absorbed than a sponge in a toilet"—I cut him off there, and told him we'd continue the discussion after I got back from lunch with Diane Sawyer's dentist.

So it will come as no surprise that last week I happily accepted hosting CNBC's *Equal Time* with Fave Rave Info-Babe Mary Matalin (the one whose lips don't move when she talks). I didn't ask who the guests might be—because I figured I could pretty much hold my own with anybody, since I got nearly 1142 on my college boards. Hey, I'm a sportswriter. Nobody's going to ask me to be a cohost and then bring on guests who are, you know, actually *smart*.

Unfortunately, when the night of the show came, I discovered the guests were:

1. A brilliant feminist author, lawyer, and Ivy League professor;

2. A genius political strategist, think-tank fellow, and PBS documentary filmmaker.

Wendy Kaminer has written a book called *I'm Dysfunctional, You're Dysfunctional*. Not only didn't I understand it, I couldn't even understand the reviews.

As a cohost I was expected to ask her intelligent questions.

One of Matalin's first questions to her went something like this: "Let's get right to the philosophical ramifications of your work, the correlation between the self-help recovery ideology and the disempowerment of women with regard to doctrinaire feminism."

Here is an actual question I asked: "So let's say you're on a bus, and you're looking at the people. How can you tell the functional ones from the dysfunctional ones? Is it something they wear?"

Wendy looked at me like I was from South Yemen and simply continued to answer one of Mary's previous questions.

I was hopelessly out of my league. I had that horrible, numbing feeling you get when the teacher calls on you to name all the provinces of Canada, and the best you can say is: "Manitoba, and, uh, the blue one."

Some people commented to me that my eyes appeared to wander during the show. I explained to them this was because I have the attention span of a prairie dog when a conversation isn't about me, and in this case not only wasn't it about me, but it wasn't even about anything I could understand.

I told myself to sit up straight and at least look like someone with a pulse. (What actually kept flickering through my head was that old Beach Boys song. I wanted to ask, "Wendy, Wendy, what went wrong, oh so wrong?")

When it came my turn to ask another question, I said, on live national television:

"So, uh, let me ask the question that every parent wants to know: We're in the supermarket. My daughter throws a tantrum because she wants Count Chocula, and I refuse to buy it for her because it's, you know, one hundred percent sugar, and this shames my daughter, and takes away her self-esteem. Years later, when she kills me with a shotgun, will a jury let her off?"

What was going through my head at this moment was: "Help. Get me out of here, God."

What was going through her head, I am reasonably certain, was: "Help, get him out of here, God."

So at least we were on the same wavelength.

My next question was:

"So many people are in Twelve Step programs now. Some people are in eight or ten of them at the same time, and that's like, what, a hundred and twenty steps? That's like a stairway to Heaven. Is there anything we can do to consolidate all their steps, so they can get out of the house before nightfall?"

Wendy thought I was kidding. People who watched the show told me they thought I was kidding.

Yeah, yeah. That's the ticket. I was kidding.

The next guest was Ben Wattenberg, the smartest man in the world. He has a job in a think tank. He thinks. This is his whole job description: Think. Someone pays him to think. Is this a great country, or what? He has come on to talk about his new PBS talk show. The only time I watch PBS is during Pledge Week, when they put on specials with Liza Minnelli.

"He's got a great sense of humor," Mary says.

I mention that I vaguely remember a column of his on the fertility crisis in sub-Saharan Africa—but I'm sure Letterman was all over that one, too.

"The man is brilliant," Mary says. "He'll love you."

So I say, "Ben, you're a real smart guy—who do you have in the NCAA pool? Your Final Four teams still alive?"

Then I ask him about his job: "Do you think with your shoes on or off?"

I press on: "Let's say you've had a real good day thinking and you come up with an idea. So you go down the hall to a colleague, and you say, 'I've got this great idea.' And you tell him, and he says: 'I already *knew* that, Ben. Everybody knows that.' Do you feel crushed?"

As soon as the show ended, I apologized to everyone in the crew for being a buffoon.

"No, you did very well with Wendy Kaminer," the producer told me.

"Oh yeah," I said. "And I suppose she'll dedicate her next book to me: *I'm Dysfunctional, You're a Moron.*"

I told the producer I had embarrassed myself beyond measure, and I was about to tell her I was done with TV forever when she said Mary was going on vacation soon, and would I cohost with Jane Wallace?

And I said sure.

The Man of Steal

Everything in here is 100 percent true. Not that funny, maybe, but true.

My car was stolen this week.

Right in front of my house in the District of Columbia. In broad daylight.

WHILE I WAS HOME!

It's probably my fault for not sitting out on the curb every second—or not hiring Peruvian illegal aliens for when I went to the bathroom. Silly me, I thought it was all right to park your car in front of your own home without consulting Steven Seagal.

At five forty-five my car was there. I saw it. Twenty minutes later, I opened my front door to drive to the bank, and it was gone.

I actually believed that either (a) my wife or (b) a neighbor had borrowed the car for a while. And I walked out to the curb to wait for the car to come back.

Which is when I started asking myself the following questions:

1. *Borrowed* the car?
2. Your wife has her own car, and her car is not here, and she

is not at home. So if she drove her car home and borrowed your car, then does that mean your car is safe and *her car* is stolen?

3. How did your neighbors get the keys to your car? You don't even speak to them.

4. Are you an idiot?

I then uttered the three words most associated with car theft, "Son of a . . ."

I called 911 to report my car stolen.

Then I called my colleague Mike "That Toddlin' Town" Wilbon, because he's from Chicago, so he's used to items being stolen—like elections. I always consult Wilbon on matters of urban terror. Last year we went to a boxing match, and there was a drive-by shooting outside the arena. I asked him what we should do if it happened again while we were on the street— should we run like hell? Wilbon insisted that we "should lie down on the sidewalk and pretend we're dead." He administered that advice as though it were obvious urban strategy, like not licking the seat of a taxicab, that should have been self-evident to anyone but a total hick.

I was still talking with Wilbon when my ten-year-old daughter came home.

"Where's your car, Daddy?" she asked.

"Stolen, honey."

"You're kidding, right?" she said, laughing.

"Nope. It was stolen."

"Daaaaaad . . ." she said.

I handed her the phone. "Talk to Wilbon."

Now my daughter believed it, and in that happy way kids have when they think they've wandered into a storybook, she said breathlessly, "Wow! This is just like Genevieve's mom. She has a Honda, and her car was stolen from in front of her house yesterday."

Just then my six-year-old son came around the corner. My

daughter gleefully ran out to tell him the news: "Daddy's car was stolen!"

To which my son thoughtfully responded, "Dad, can you make me a bologna sandwich?"

It was now six-thirty, maybe thirty minutes after the car had been stolen. The phone rang, and a woman said, "This is the telephone company operator. You should call this number right away," and she gave me a number.

I told the kids: "This is good, I may have won a lot of money."

I called the number. I identified myself and said, "So, have I won rumba lessons?"

A man identified himself as being from the U.S. Park Police and said, "Do you know the whereabouts of your 1991 Honda?"

"I do not," I said, sensing a breakthrough.

Of all the good luck in the world, the U.S. Park Police had already found my car abandoned about two miles from my house.

I asked if Hondas were stolen a lot.

Not as often as Acuras, he said. But more often than a 1974 Pacer.

"So what am I supposed to drive to be safe?" I asked.

"A Liberian tanker."

The police said the car was driveable, and I could come get it. We all piled into one car and drove over and met officers Michael Snowden and John Marsh, who brought me to my car.

"Anything missing?"

"I had a Bullets pass in the glove compartment," I said.

"They may have taken it."

I checked. No such luck.

"Nobody wants to see the Bullets," I smiled.

On the other side of my car was another Honda, and when my daughter saw it, she got tremendously excited.

"It's Genevieve's!" she exclaimed.

And so it was. I felt like I was on the set of *America's Most Wanted*. I mean, what are the odds of that? Of all the cars stolen in the entire city of Washington, that two would be recovered at the same time, side by side in a park, and they would belong to fourth-grade classmates? (Answer: Approximately the same odds as people named Zoe and Kimba being nominated for attorney general.)

"So what do I do now?" I asked Officer Marsh.

"Get the Club," he said, referring to that big metal stick advertised on TV that attaches to your steering wheel. It looks like a rectal thermometer for a brontosaurus. Come on, if this thing is so great, how come it only costs fifty bucks?

"Get it now," he said. "Before you get home."

So I drove to an auto parts store—thanking my lucky stars that my car was recovered before it was chopped into tiny pieces like fish food—and I told the clerk my sad story, about how my car was stolen from right in front of my house. In broad daylight. WHILE I WAS HOME!

"You're the fourth one today."

Alley Oops

For those of you who have breathlessly anticipated more about my son's birthday party, you're in luck.

You may remember my advice to parents who were planning a birthday party for their sons, age five or six:

1. Dig a large outdoor pit.

2. Throw all the boys in.

3. Every few minutes toss down some birthday cake and Fox's U-Bet Syrup.

4. After two hours, drag the boys out of the pit and hose them down.

5. Accept compliments.

Well, my son turned seven this year, and this time the old backyard wasn't good enough. He wanted a bowling party. I said fine, because he had fewer friends to invite this year—many of the regulars were in prison.

I was happy to take him bowling. I like bowling. I bowled as a yoot. Me and a lot of guys who grew up to be Joey Buttafuoco. They had back hair when they were twelve.

So I took ten boys, spread them over two lanes, and started keeping score.

Oh, I should tell you that it's duckpin bowling, with the real small pins, and the real small balls, and it's harder to keep score because you get three rolls per frame, not two—and the automatic pinsetter doesn't come down by itself, you have to press a button, which means that the kids have to keep track of how many rolls they've already had, and you have to keep track of the kids who are lowering the pinsetter just for laughs and trying to hit it with the bowling ball, and, well, this is what it sounded like . . . remember, I'm sitting in the chair, trying to keep track of ten small boys bowling, trying to see the lanes, add the scores, and maintain order:

"Your turn, Aaron."

"Daddy, can I have a drink?"

"I'm not your daddy, Billy. I'm Michael's daddy. . . . Aaron, how many pins did you knock down? . . . David, it's your turn on Lane Sixteen. Sixteen, David. On your right, David. Yes, David, the side with your blue sock. . . . How many, Aaron?"

"Forty-one."

"That's impossible. You can't count."

"I can too count. I can't read."

"That's three rolls, Nick. Press the pinsetter, you're done. . . . Nick, Nick, press the pinsetter on *your* lane, not David's. No, David, don't roll the . . ." *Bang* ". . . Yes, sir, I know it is expensive equipment and I will make every effort to ensure that these plucky young lads don't continue to . . ." *Bang*.

"I got four."

"Yes, Sean, I saw. Which ball was that for you?"

"This one."

"Yes, Sean, I mean, what number ball? How many times have you rolled the ball this frame?"

"Should I count the time that by mistake I dropped the ball off Nathaniel's ankle and it rolled all the way to the snack bar and the man there said you were a putz? What's a putz?"

"Daddy, I'm thirsty."

"I thought we established, Billy, that I'm not your daddy."

"Jason, how come all the other kids have bowled, and you haven't? . . . What? What do you mean, Daniel said you were too stupid to bowl? You're not too stupid to bowl. Lots of stupid people bowl. Did I ever tell you about my old friend Joey Buttafuoco . . ."

"What's my score?"

"After five frames, eighteen, Sam."

"Is that good?"

"Yes, it is very good if you were a famous bowling dog."

"What kind of cake is there? When can we eat?"

"Daddy, I'm thirsty."

"Billy, I am not your . . . Oh, Michael, I *am* your daddy, son. You're thirsty?"

"No, but Billy asked me to ask you."

I really wasn't doing well with this. The kids had bowled out of turn. Some of them had bowled twenty balls in a row and not hit anything. Others had deliberately lowered the pinsetters, and aimed at them. Few of the kids could add past ten, so scoring was impossible. All the food questions meant they were getting bored with bowling. And a few of them—my son included—had gathered around Jason and were watching him try to eat a bowling ball.

"Back here, guys," I announced. "We've only got two frames to go. Aaron, you're up on Lane Fifteen. Nick, Lane Sixteen. . . . We won't be taking any questions right now on the size or style of the cake, or the flavors of the drinks, do I make myself clear? And why, kids? Why? You got it! Because I'm the daddy and I say so."

It was at this point that a woman who is related to me by marriage came by and told me, "You know why they're acting this way? You're too structured."

"They've got two frames to go," I said. "I thought it was important that they post a score."

"Why?" she asked. "Why was it important that they post a score? They're seven. Were you thinking of sending the score to the American Bowling Congress?"

"That's good, Alice, that's good . . . *bang-zoom*, you know?"

Next year, I'm bringing back the Pit.

Mail and Female

My daughter came home from sleep-away camp, where she'd spent five weeks. She looked great. And I was so proud of her, going away by herself.

The first question I asked her was "How was camp?"

She began by saying, "Well, the day I left I got on the bus and I sat next to Ashley, and she brought Goldfish, which was good, because I forgot my Now and Laters, and then Shannon came over, and she's from Baltimore, and she gets her clothes at the Gap, and she had a Game Boy, but all she had was Tetris, which I have, so we asked Jenny, who was the counselor, if anybody had Sonic the Hedgehog, but . . ."

She went on like this for a few minutes, still talking about the bus ride up to camp five weeks ago, and I came to the horrifying realization that she was actually going to tell me how camp was MINUTE BY MINUTE. Because this is what girls do (and when they grow up and become women, they do it, too, as any man can vouch). They gather information and dispense it without discrimination. Everything counts the same!

It is not that women lack the ability to process and prioritize information, it is that they don't think life is as simple as men do, and so they are fascinated by the multiplicity of choices that they see. It is a little-known fact of American history that Paul Revere's wife, and not Paul Revere, was originally supposed to warn the Colonial militia about the British invasion. But she insisted that "one if by land and two if by sea" was insufficient. What if *some* were coming by land, and *some* were coming by sea, and some were wading in the water on horses, which is sort of both by land and by sea when you come right down to it, and what if some were being catapulted through the air . . . and finally Paul just put on his coat and galloped off.

This is why you have to be very specific about what you ask women. If, for example, you missed a Redskins game, and you know a woman who saw it, never, *ever* ask, "What happened?" Unless you have nowhere to go until Thursday.

Ask:

1. Who won?
2. What was the score?
3. Was anyone carried out on a stretcher?

You must get them to fast-forward.

Left to their own devices, girls go through life volubly answering essay questions. And boys? Multiple choice is *way* too complicated. Boys restrict themselves to true-false.

Boys do not gather and retain information, they focus on results.

My son went to camp for six weeks—one week longer than my daughter. As I had with my daughter, I asked him, "How was camp?"

He said: "Good. I busted Jason's nose."

Short and to the point.

This was followed by "Can we go to McDonald's?"

Did I mention the cheers? My daughter came back with cheers. About 187,640 musical cheers, all of which are accompanied by an intricate series of hand, feet, and hip movements. She went to camp a ten-year-old, she came back a Vandella.

It's amazing, the affinity of girls and cheers. If you've ever been to camp you know that girls have a special gene for cheers, and that even girls who have never been to camp before—or, for that matter, been to America or spoken English before—automatically know all the cheers the moment they step off the bus.

You give me a group of three or more girls at camp, and I'll give you the entire score of *Guys and Dolls*. Girls spontaneously burst into song. It's a gender thing, I guess.

As a boy at camp, I used to look at girls in amazement, wondering why they would waste their time practicing socialization skills, when they could be doing useful things like me, memorizing Willie Mays's doubles and sacrifice flys during an entire decade.

Boys don't cheer.

Even during "color war," that traditional camp competition when cheering is supposed to result in points, here's how boys cheer on the way to the dining hall:

They look at the other team and say, "Yo, Green Team, drop dead."

If I Had a Hammer, I'd Take Out an Eye

Last week, I moved. I got a house that was bigger in every area than my last house, except one—the stairwell from the lower floor to the upper floor. Unfortunately, I did not discover this until moving day. And that is why I am dressing in the dining room now. Because my dresser didn't fit up the stairs. Neither did my antique roll-top desk, which is now in the kitchen, filled with Froot Loops and Count Chocula. Neither did my box spring, leaving me with two choices: (1) buy a new bed, or (2) sleep in the dining room, near my clothes.

Humor writers sometimes make things up to be funny. Unfortunately, I am not doing that right now. The truth is, I am the kind of guy to whom this sort of thing happens *all the time*. There is a technical term for this kind of individual. I am an "imbecile."

For example, I am not particularly talented when it comes to everyday man work. (An everyday man, for example, would have used a tape measure to measure his stairwell. I do not use tape measures. I am afraid of "whiplash.")

I cannot change the oil in my car. I'm afraid to open the hood of my car because I don't know where to stick that hood-stand thingamajiggy to keep the hood from slamming down on the back of my neck and killing me.

I am the last person on earth who still goes to full-serve gas stations. Nobody goes to full-serve. They don't even call it full-serve anymore. They just nail up a sign that says TONY.

I don't go to show off. I don't enjoy paying sixteen times the normal price for a gallon of gas. If I wanted to pay sixteen times the normal price for something, I'd buy my milk at the 7-Eleven. No, I go to full-serve because I cannot use the pump at self-serve. The last time I tried, I couldn't fit the nozzle into the gas tank, and I had to get help from—oh, the embarrassment—a woman in a Volvo station wagon. The time before that, I couldn't get the nozzle out on time, and I got gas all over my pants. I couldn't go to work. I had to stop at Saks and buy a pair of pants. The salesman asked me what I did for a living. I said I was Emerson Fittipaldi.

I can't fix anything. I can't change anything. I can't build anything. The reason I don't take aspirin isn't that I can't open the childproof cap—I don't even *try* to open the childproof cap because I can always get a child to do that for me. No, it's because once the cap is open *I can't get the cotton out of the bottle.* (I once tried to use a shrimp fork to do this. I could show you the scar.)

My children are small now. But when they get older and they ask me for advice on how to make their way in the world, I will tell them simply: Belong to AAA.

I feel I have a mission in life. I was put on this earth to pay sinewy tattooed men to do simple things for me. Handymen *love* me.

To this day my eighty-two-year-old father doesn't send me a gift on my birthday. He sends me money so I can pay Ray to fix the toilet by putting a brick in it, and so I can pay Ed to hammer a nail into the wall, because when *I* do it I leave a crater the size of a large Armand's deep-dish pizza.

I can mow, but I cannot start the mower. The last time I tried I pulled the rubber thing so hard that the mower leaped into the air like a salmon, flipped over, and cracked the gas tank. So I pay Leon to cut my grass.

(By federal law, all handymen must be named Leon, Ray, or Ed.)

When I was young, I ached to be good with wood like the rest of the guys. But in wood shop I was barred from the jigsaw after a regrettable incident involving a stuffed woodchuck named Safety Sam, who was dressed up like a railroad engineer with a red bandanna and a sign around his neck that said, SAFETY SAM SEZ: I DON'T BELIEVE IN ACCIDENTS. I accidentally cut off his head.

For years I refrained from all do-it-yourself projects, until finally, when I was 24, I bought a stereo system and grew determined I'd build shelves for the speakers. I wanted each shelf to jut out twelve inches from the wall, and I went to a lumberyard and had the boards cut to the specifications. Then I went into a hardware store and asked for "four thirteen-inch nails." I had no concept of brackets. I figured you buy a nail a little bigger than your board, and keep pounding until you reach the other side. I explained this to the men inside the hardware store (Ray, Leon, and Ed, as I recall) and they laughed in my face. So deep was my shame that I haven't walked into a hardware store since, except to obtain batteries for the flashlight I keep next to the phone, in case the lights go out and I need to call Ray to change a fuse.

Fortunately, I am not the only imbecile out there. A few weeks ago, my friend Gino got a new living room couch. The night before it was to be delivered, he decided to put the old couch down in the basement. He also decided that he and his wife could do this by themselves. Like me, Gino is afraid of tape measures, and so it was not until the couch was actually *in* the stairwell that Gino discovered the couch was *bigger* than the stairwell. It got wedged so tight that it could not be budged. At the high end of the steps was Gino's wife. At the low end, in the basement, was Gino. In between: *le couch*, jammed like a cow in a phone booth. With mounting panic, my friend realized three things:

1. There was no way to get back upstairs.

2. The basement was underground, with no doors to the outside, and it was midnight. He was going to spend the night in that basement, which . . .

3. Had no bathroom.

An hour later, Gino was still in the basement, contemplating bodily functions, and nervously eyeing the washing machine.

Suffice it to say that he eventually managed to squeeze over the couch by removing most of his clothing and suffering severe couch-tack abrasions. The next day the three delivery men arrived with the new couch, and Gino did what he should have done in the first place: He slipped them thirty dollars to get the old couch downstairs. It took Leon and Ray about nine seconds. Ed would have helped, but he was busy collapsing against a wall, laughing.

Wo Fat

Every Sunday night at seven, Mom, Dad, and I would pile in the car and drive to the Bamboo Inn for dinner. In my faith, this is called a pilgrimage. Catholics have the pope. Protestants have those silly golf pants with ducks on them. Jews have moo goo gai pan. This is true: The only night all year the Bamboo Inn closed was on Yom Kippur, the one day Jews fast.

I've been eating Chinese food religiously for over forty years. I used to wonder where Chinese people ate on Sunday night, Katz's Deli? But it's not just Jewish people who adore Chinese food. All Americans love Chinese food. As a parent I love it because it's a way I can sneak vegetables into my children's dinner. They're not like the vegetables my kids reject when I cook the meals. Chinese vegetables are sliced up and coated with sauce and indistinguishable from meat or fish or noodles. It is all attractively iridescent, like the suits that Dion and the Belmonts wore on Ed Sullivan.

For a long time the only reason to stay away from Chinese food was the vast amount of MSG used in cooking it. MSG was widely thought to be the cause of everything bad in the world— other than the Village People. Women would come out of Chinese restaurants complaining about a headache or a small speck floating in one eyeball or a flare-up of hemorrhoids, and they would refrain from having sex that night. And since a lot of guys had sprung for the dinner, well, MSG had to go. Soon Chinese restaurants had signs on the walls that said: WE DON'T USE MSG. Actually, these signs said: NOTICE TO PLEASE: MS IS NO LONGER EMPLOYED HERE. RESPECTFULLY, FINE, GOOD. Chinese restaurants never really got the hang of English. But it didn't matter because they made great food that everyone loved. And now that the MSG scare was done, America was happy eating Chinese food.

Until last week, when we found out Chinese food has a higher fat content than Rush Limbaugh. The Center for Science in the Public Interest said last week that a container of kung pao chicken—a personal favorite—(the translation of *kung pao chicken* from the original Szechuan is, "giant lumpy mound of poultry grease")—has almost as much fat as *four* Quarter Pounders!

Fat in the fried rice. Fat in the beef with broccoli. Fat in General Tsao's chicken. (The corpulent General Tsao became a hero of the Ming Dynasty by exploding at the Imperial dinner table, a sign of great respect to the hostess.)

Chinese restaurant owners are throwing themselves off bridges. They spent a lifetime learning to say, "Oy, gevalt!" Now it's wiped out with one study.

I am devastated by this development. How can I give up Chinese restaurants? All I really need to know I learned at a Chinese restaurant. I learned how to drink tea from those small cups that got so hot you had to hold them with a napkin—and I admit I always wondered how people smart enough to come up with sweet and sour pork weren't smart enough to invent the handle. I learned how to read by cracking open fortune cookies. The only problem was that the first time I gave an oral report in school, the subject was "making friends," and I said, "Man who opens heart to friend builds gentle breeze to hang wash on."

(Am I the only one who remembers back in the Cantonese-only days, when Chinese restaurant menus always had a page of "American" food, which resembled American food in an eccentric sort of way, the way a lithograph of *Dogs Playing Poker* resembles *Guernica*. The American food was oddly prepared; for example, there were olive garnishes in the Jell-O. And speaking of desserts, there would always be (1) litchi nuts, which tasted like chilled eyeballs, and (2) ice cream, which was served in metal dishes and had chunks of ice in it, and which came in two recognizable flavors, such as chocolate and vanilla, and a third wildly exotic flavor, like "mung bean.")

I am so devoted to Chinese food that I spent years "seasoning" my wok. You "season" a wok by treating it with oil and then baking it. Granted, I may have used the wrong kind of oil—I rubbed in neat's-foot oil because it did such a good job on my Tommy Tresh autograph model baseball glove. As a result my wok had a rather substantial rust spot, which made it look like I was cooking in a hubcap. It took me awhile to perfect the art of using the wok. First you have to heat up the wok to the temperature of Three Mile Island, and *then* you drop in the oil. I kept getting "oil backfire," which would burn my face and hands. I now realize why the Chinese are so svelte: They run away from the wok. Hence the expression "Wok—don't run." Ha ha.

Getting back to that statistic that one container of kung pao chicken has almost as much fat as four Quarter Pounders—well, this is terrible news for McDonald's, which had cornered the fat market for so many years.

What I love about McDonald's is that they hang up a nutritional chart on the wall, breaking down the various contents of their foods. This is what I call "chutzpah": selling you for breakfast a cholesterol-laden egg, a slice of melted cheese substance, and a hunk of pork sausage on a greasy muffin and making believe you won't drop dead by the time you reach your car. If you look at this nutritional chart carefully, you'll see that the healthiest thing you can buy at McDonald's is a salad. Let me ask you something: When was the last time anybody ever said to you, "Hey, you wanna go down to McDonald's and cop some *salad*?" No way. When I go to McDonald's I'm going for something that I'd be afraid to eat with the lights on.

So in order to compete with the Chinese restaurants for the fat market, I believe we'll see McDonald's introduce Phat Foo Mac, which, translated from the original Hunan, is: "Bucket o' Angioplasty."

How Men and Women Click

Now, we have another install-ment in Differences Between Men and Women. As before, I warn you I could be wrong, I often am.

Today's topic: the TV remote control.

Women hardly click at all.

Men click incessantly.

Women consult the TV guide, decide what they want to see, and commit to it. They click with civility on the hour or half hour. Their clicker is a tool.

Men grab the clicker and start zapping. Like gnats, they alight for only a few seconds, then skip away. Their clicker is a toy. Men are very big on toys. Who do you think is buying all the CDs?

My friend Nancy tells me, "Women do this: They say, 'There's an interesting movie from nine to eleven tonight, dear, let's watch it.' We sit. We watch. If it was me, I'd watch straight through, even the commercials—I don't even mute them. I commit. Of course, that's not possible when my husband's around. He starts at Channel Two, goes all the way up to the top, through fifty or sixty channels, and then goes around again. He calls it rolling through: 'Honey, I'm going to roll through.'

We see five seconds of a tractor pull, five seconds of a fox family in the wild, five seconds of motorcycles on ice, five seconds of British drama. There's absolutely no thread to hang on to. We're rolling through."

(A woman standing nearby heard this and said, "Men always hog the clicker, there's no point in watching TV with them. But another problem is they'll never read aloud with you." Dumb-struck—nobody ever asked me to do that—I asked her to hold that thought for a later column.)

I click. I'm clickaholic.

I see everything, but watch nothing.

I can't help myself. It's like when I'm in New York City, and I don't go to sleep because I'm afraid I'll miss something.

Before I had cable and a clicker, I stood near the TV and turned the dial. I went around once, then shut off the TV. Life is much better now with a clicker—less strain on the legs. I sit and go around and around like a Ferris wheel. My wife hasn't sat in the TV room with me in eight months.

I cannot watch anything live anymore; I have no patience. (Even on tape—as soon as I don't see lips moving I'm on fast forward.) It used to be I had trouble staying with a baseball game for a full inning. Now I can't even last through a full at-bat.

My friend Josh tells a story about a man who was clicking like crazy, going from HBO to Showtime to two movies on network TV—all running concurrently—until his girlfriend thought her eyeballs were going to explode, and she smacked him. "It wasn't the first time," Josh reported with great empathy. Recently, after a frenzied episode of clicking in which he wheeled among an NBA, a CBA, and four college basketball games "trolling for anyone in midair going up for a monster dunk," Josh's fiancée took a hammer to his clicker. Luckily, he had two in reserve.

(They make a TV now where you get the main picture with sound, and around the border of the picture tube, in neat windows, up to nine other channels—like a menu—and the nine other channels keep rotating up the dial. Technology creates some great cocktails: The *Post*'s art critic, Paul Richard, watched Bill Moyers interview poet W. S. Merwin on PBS with the sound, and live boxing from Atlantic City in one of the windows. I'm told the Japanese are working on a holographic TV where you'll watch a movie and feel like you're actually in it. This excited Josh. "Sign me up for *Caligula*.")

What are men looking for on these clicking tours?

Control.

Oh, give me a break, the truth.

The truth?

Okay, but it's off the record. I'll deny I ever said it.

It's naked women, isn't it?

Yes.

Men! You're all alike.

(No, not all of us. Some are like my friend Henry, who is "always shopping for a better evangelist." But many of us . . .)

"It's the whole point of having cable." Josh says he's "always hoping I'll find Emmanuelle. But as soon as she puts her clothes on, I'm back to Dick Vitale."

Now, why do men click incessantly, and not women? I asked a psychiatrist, a clicker himself. He said women are able to be more attentive, to focus in depth, while men are inclined to be many places at once. He offered some anthropological supports—that men are nomadic by nature; they were the hunters, and had to be ever vigilant, ever responsive to change. It sounded good. I hope to use it someday on PBS.

"Women are always complaining that men are unable to be intimate with them. The way men use the clicker—no sustained intimacy, no real commitment—that's how they are with women," the psychiatrist said. "Men are as inconsiderate of the TV as they are of women. They get distracted easily, and they're rude."

Women appreciate what they have.

Men believe in More, Better, and Different.

"What's interesting," the psychiatrist says, "is what happens to a man when a woman grabs the clicker. He can't stand it. He goes crazy. It's like trying to sit in Archie Bunker's chair."

Stifle the thought.

A Man's Home Is His Hassle

I often find myself reflecting about why I spent so much money for rooms I never use—like the, ahem, "powder room" off the kitchen.

This is a woman's room. Gather a group of women together to talk about what they want in a house, and you'll hear "powder room on the first floor." When you ask why, they'll say, "Because it's so convenient."

However, should a man actually ever *use* this convenient room, he would be punished. ("Can't you use the upstairs bathroom?" she'll say. "I thought this was supposed to be convenient," he'll say. "But not for us," she'll say.) Particularly forbidden is the use of the soap and hand towels, which are museum pieces and not meant for human hands. Visiting women intuitively understand this, and bring tissues. God forbid you should get water on the miniature soaps and ruin the pristine detail of the small Italian shepherd eating angel hair pasta on the back of a goat.

This is life in the '90s: A couple buys a house and immediately the man finds himself banned from it.

The other day, my research department telephoned a friend

of his, a real estate agent named Eric, and asked what men and women look for in a house.

"Women are interested in the neighborhood, like if there are kids in the neighborhood, and how close the schools are, and they are looking for *flow* to a house—nice, warm, open family areas where you can keep an eye on your kids and still carry on adult conversations."

And what do men want?

"A bar in the basement."

No woman will let a man decorate a house the way he wants—black Naugahyde couches (so the food stains don't show), a big pile of newspapers in the middle of the floor, a stuffed moose head, one of those small refrigerators that you could use both as a footstool and a place to store the beer, and a urinal in the corner.

Women are completely unaware of what a man wants. It's not a den, an office, or a library. (Men over forty are very big on getting libraries, until it is pointed out to them that they can no longer read anything smaller than the big, green PHILADELPHIA 160 MILES on I-95.)

No, ask a man who lives with women to list which rooms of his own house are important to him. And he lists:

1. Garage;
2. Basement;
3. Backyard.

What these rooms have in common is that none of them are actually *inside* his house. The only real room a man values is that one small bathroom that no one else uses—the one place in a houseful of women and children where he can truly be left alone. (As his favorite room, my friend Nancy's husband listed "refrigerator." Nancy thinks this is because he stands in front of it with the door open and the light on so often that he has come to think of it as a small den.)

Let us say a house needs to be painted—and a man would recognize this only if great gobs of paint chips were falling from the ceiling and landing in his Cheerios. A painter will come and ask, "What color do you want the rooms?"

And a man will answer, "I don't know, whatever. . . ." Which means: white.

Poor schlub. It never occurs to him, as it would to a woman, that there are *hundreds* of shades of white, including, just to name four from the 1,200-page catalog of Duron paint chips, Polar Bear, Navajo, City Lights, and, so help me, Snickerdoodle.

Men fear color because they have a vague dread that it means the old furniture won't work, and they'll have to buy new. Men don't buy furniture. They inherit it from their grand-mothers, and pass it along, uncleaned, to their sons—as I will proudly do. (Didn't you ever wonder why so many big, strong men with tattoos and back hair have threadbare velvet Victorian living-room couches with doilies on the back?)

Women like to buy new furniture. They like to go through those books of swatches. It usually takes them seven to eight years to decide which couch they want. By then a man wants to move. Men loathe new furniture, because it means they will no longer have a place to sit. Men know they are dirty and disgust-ing and will ruin the new furniture with their potato chip grease and their beer foam and their general crustaceous ooze. Every room with new furniture is more time spent in the garage for a man.

Men do not know from furniture. Take chairs. To a man there are only two kinds of chairs: comfortable and uncomfort-able. A man has no idea what a Queen Anne chair is—other than it is probably unavailable unless Queen Anne and her grand-mother are dead.

According to Eric the real estate agent, men are completely inflexible when buying a new house. They cannot envision change. Entire deals have been lost because a man doesn't like the wallpaper in the foyer, and when it is gently pointed out to him that he can replace the offending wallpaper for, like, a hundred bucks, he explodes. "What am I, Bob Vila? I came here to buy a house, not build one from the ground up!"

Women, on the other hand, are comfortable with change. They can see changing the wallpaper. They can see changing the furniture. They can see changing the rugs. They can even see changing husbands. But keep your hands off the soap in the "powder room."

How My Garden Groans

My tomato crop came in the other day. Five tomatoes. All ripe on the same day. I picked them, and held them up in front of my face to admire them. One had a huge, dark soft spot on the underside. One had a deep, forbidding gash along the top that looked like a tire track. One had what appeared to be a nose. So that left me with a total of two usable tomatoes, the size of kidney stones.

That's my entire yield.

It's pathetic. I feel as if the whole world is one large salad, and I'm a chickpea.

The man in the house behind me has four hundred tomatoes on six plants. They don't all ripen on the same day. He gets tomatoes from July through September. I think it goes without saying that I hate this guy.

The other day he looked over at my meager plants and said smugly, "I guess not everyone has a green thumb."

I tried to come up with a withering rejoinder. Unfortunately, all I could think of was: "Oh yeah? Well, at least I don't have to live next to *me*!"

I am so jealous of people who can grow fruits and vegetables.

I believe this is called "greenis envy."

I buy those packages of seeds, with the beautiful color pictures of what my vegetables should look like when they come up. I'll see these leafy carrots on the package, but what I grow are horribly deformed tubers that look like human pinkies. Whose seeds did I actually get, the Dahmer collection?

My friend Joel has a huge cantaloupe patch. You haven't seen melons like this since, um, a time when I could have safely completed this joke. I asked Joel how he did it. He said, "I scattered the seeds on the ground and walked away."

I knew there was a trick to it.

I probably shouldn't be so depressed about my inability to have a garden. I write a newspaper column. What do I know about digging? To me, good dirt is finding out that Dan Rostenkowski was a woman. Had God wanted me to farm, he'd have given me a better body for overalls and a name like Norbert or W.J.

Suburban gardening is about ego—like, which guy's got the biggest squash? (I believe that is called "zucchinis envy.") I'm clearly not doing it to save money. Because when all is said and done, with the tools you buy to prepare the soil, the fertilizing, the mulching, the spraying, and the dusting, each edible tomato has cost approximately $16.75. If you're gonna spend that much, Safeway will send a limo for you.

Still, I don't understand why I have no tomatoes, and my neighbor can be a wholesaler for Contadina.

"It's because he gets full sun," I told my friend Gino.

"It's because he's not *you*," Gino replied.

By the way, Gino has a wonderful vegetable garden, which is astounding when you consider this is the same guy who got his couch wedged into his basement staircase, and had to remove all his clothes and smear himself with Mazola oil to get back up the steps. Who'd figure a bozo like him could grow anything but fingernails?

"We have so many tomatoes, we use them to play catch with the dogs," Gino bragged.

The reason Gino's garden is so bountiful, it turns out, is that his wife is the gardener. Gino's one contribution to the garden was building a picket fence around it. I have seen the fence. Think about a wino who has been down on his luck since 1957, scrounging meals from Dumpsters and consuming no liquids other than peach schnapps. Now think about the wino's teeth. That's Gino's fence.

Hearing that Gino's wife was the gardener eased my spirits. Maybe gardening was a chick thing. Maybe all a man is supposed to do is dig the holes, then go play golf . . . and when he gets back, the salad will be grown. I went to a couple of women I knew for confirmation.

"Tell me about your garden," I asked Liz, a writer who is so sensitive that she cries when a tree falls in the forest and there's no one there to hear it.

She frowned. "It's too painful. . . . I planted a lot of seeds. They came up. It was gratifying, it renewed my belief in rebirth. Then everything died."

"What happened?" I asked.

"The same as every year. I start out very excited at seeing all these green sprouts. But then it gets hot, and I stay inside in the air conditioning, and I don't water. And the plants die."

"Why do you think they died?" I asked.

"Because I'm not a good person."

Bulletin: The wires just reported that Ivan the Terrible is in fact merely Ivan the Very, Very Bad. Thank you. We now rejoin this column, already in progress.

". . . no way," said the orangutan. "Because you don't know where that banana's been!"

Anyway, my boss Mary, who wishes to be called Mitzi in this column because she's afraid she will come across as a ditz, told a similarly harrowing story, which goes like this: "I'm really unhappy. I had a beautiful garden. Then my husband went away for a month, and now the garden is gone, and I see now that it must have been because he watered it."

Are we to assume that "Mitzi" didn't water the garden?

"Well, I thought that was the whole point. You don't have to water because they're *outside*. God has dew and rain. The plants are supposed to get down to the water under the ground, aren't they?"

You can see why she wanted to be called Mitzi.

"And anyway," she continued, "the hose doesn't reach. So maybe that's the problem. Maybe we need a longer hose, a hose that reaches the plants."

Getting an Earful

A few weeks ago I began to no-
tice that something was wrong with my hearing. The tip-off was
that one night when the children were watching *The McLaughlin
Group*—not *my* children, mine were watching reruns of *The
Patty Duke Show*; I bring in other people's children to make it
appear that we are an intelligent household in case *Life* magazine
sends a photographer over—and I couldn't hear John McLaughlin. He was talking and gesturing animatedly, but no words were
coming out. It was as though he were choking on a can of Ajax,
the Foaming Cleanser.

No such luck.

I ignored the problem the first night, because it didn't seem
like a problem, if you know what I mean. But the next night,
when I couldn't hear *America's Funniest Home Videos*, I went
batzoid.

After repeated, sophisticated testing procedures (I covered
one ear with a thirty-two-ounce *Last Action Hero* souvenir Slur-
pee cup), I found I couldn't hear a thing in my right ear. It was
apparent to me, as I knew it would be to any physician with a
degree from an American medical school, that a brain tumor the

size of a fully ripened Big Boy tomato was encroaching on my brain and would kill me by Thursday.

I called my doctor, and described my symptoms, and asked him to recommend a neurosurgeon. He sent me to an ear doctor. What a moron! As though a problem with hearing could possibly be related to the ear!

The ear guy (technically, an "ornithologist") looked in my right ear and asked, in the same disapproving voice a person might use to, say, inquire whether I regularly inject heroin directly into my carotid artery, "Do you use Q-Tips to clean your ears?"

What do you say to that?

I sensed, by the way he asked the question, that Q-Tips weren't good. But I felt that if I told him the truth—that I do not use Q-Tips because they are so prissy, and instead I regularly dig my fingers into my ears and grind around in there until I relieve the itch, and that there are times when the itch is so annoying that I will gladly shove anything in there, even a shish kebab skewer—he would find me hygienically repulsive, as you are undoubtedly doing at this particular moment, poised as you are with that spoonful of Wheatena frozen at your lips. It was easier to live with his judgment that I was stupid than that I was a cave man. So I said:

"Yeah, I use Q-Tips."

He frowned.

"They're not for the ears," he said.

Q-Tips are not for the ears?

What exactly are Q-Tips for? To paint the foyer? The doctor told me to lie still. He said, "I'm going to take something out of your ear the size of the Washington Cathedral."

Ear doctor humor, I presumed. Here's another: Did you ear the one about . . .

After a few twists he removed something the size of an

eraser—no, not the small tip of a No. 2 pencil, the big, arrow-head-shaped eraser that you fit *over* the small tip—from deep inside my right ear.

He showed it to me triumphantly, holding it up like it was a bone fragment from Zachary Taylor. I feared it was alive.

I didn't know whether to step on it or put it on a leash. Have you ever seen a banana that had been lying in the street since 1989, when it was run over by an oil truck, then some dog had gotten hold of it and dragged it around, and then, in the heat, it had begun to bubble and ooze? You would sooner frame *that*, and hang it in your newly painted foyer, than look at what came out of my ear.

"I'm so embarrassed," I said.

He smiled, then worked on my left ear—my *good* ear!—and removed something similarly revolting.

"This is humiliating," I said.

The doctor assured me that he sees this all the time.

I made him promise not to tell *Washingtonian*.

"You'll be amazed at how much sharper your hearing is now," the doctor told me.

"Why are you yelling?" I asked him.

Some will wonder about the lesson in all this. (Most people won't even get this far, however. They quit when I mentioned "ooze.") There are two lessons, and they are wondrous:

a. The human body is a miraculous creation of God.

b. God has a shockingly adolescent sense of humor.

Animal House

Earlier I wrote of my son's fifth birthday party and how—despite all the preparations I had made for an orderly, intellectually challenging party with a magician and a well-orchestrated supply of board games—the boys had reverted to their natural state, which is to say feral brutes whose idea of a swell time was to attempt to gouge one another's eyes out with a stick.

The next year, because he and his friends were one year older, one year more civilized, one year closer to becoming polite, sensitive men, I had grander hopes for his party. The party would reflect this new gentility.

As a symbolic gesture I went out to buy a tablecloth.

"I'm having a party for six-year-olds. There will be fifteen of them," I told the saleswoman at the party store. "Can you recommend a tablecloth?"

"Red," she suggested. "The blood stains won't show."

As the boys arrived, I sent them down to the basement. When I followed them down, I saw they had quickly made themselves at home—if their home was Beirut. Some were using the sleep sofa as a trampoline. Some were playing hide-and-seek *inside* the dryer. The rest were climbing the walls, literally.

I noticed one boy by himself, intently constructing something out of wooden blocks.

"What're you building there, son?" I asked. "A fort?"

"A gamma death-ray hydrogen bomb," he said proudly.

I'd been warned to pay particular attention to Martin and Gil. "Do not take your eyes off Martin and Gil," I was told. "They will wreck your house."

"They're only six," I protested.

"They can strip a car."

So I was keeping my eyes on Martin and Gil . . . when Brian crashed through the window. Luckily, it was a warm day; the window was up, so he went through the screen, not the glass.

"My God!" I shouted, as I ran to him.

"Did you see that, Dad?" my son asked. "Wasn't Brian totally awesome?" And the kids gathered around Brian and sang, "Doo-doo-doo-doo, BAT-man!"

At this point I went upstairs, because somebody was at the door—it was the scientist whom I had gotten to come over to entertain the kids by making slime and exploding volcanoes out of household chemicals—when I heard my son call out urgently:

"I need ice, Dad!"

"I told you guys, no drinks in the basement."

"It's for Jerome's eyes. Stuart hit him with the big bottle of Liquid Tide . . . by mistake."

(It's always "by mistake." When you come home and see six eggs cracked on the kitchen floor, you know it's "by mistake." Or you come home and find the goldfish dead; it's "by mistake." I once saw my daughter strangling my son, and wasn't the slightest bit surprised to learn this was "by mistake.")

I'd left the boys alone for less than one minute—and gotten off easy. The other day, my friend Gene got a telephone call from the principal in his son's school, telling him to come quickly and take seven-year-old Danny to the doctor to patch up his eye.

Danny's teacher made the mistake of inadvertently leaving four second-grade boys alone in a study group, unsupervised, for three minutes, while she took a phone call.

Three minutes.

If they were second-grade *girls*, they'd have sat together quietly and stitched a quilt for world peace. If they had any time left over, they'd have washed up for lunch.

What the boys did was hastily locate the only life-threatening object in the room—remember, this is a second-grade classroom; they're not storing hand grenades in the gerbil cages.

The boys managed to find some wooden dowels about two feet long, and then quickly organized themselves into an impromptu game of Death Javelin, which consisted of the three larger boys lining up on one side of the room and flinging the dowels at the smallest boy—who happened to be Gene's son, Danny.

Danny's assignment was to hold a jacket up in front of his face and ward off the Death Javelin. Sadly, Danny's reach wasn't quite high enough. The Death Javelin came hurtling over the top and bonked him in the eye. After the doctor, the eye patch, the scratches, the punctures, and the tears, Gene adopted a grave tone, like Ward Cleaver, and formally inquired of Danny, "What have you learned from all this, son?"

Speaking like a true boy, Danny replied, "I should've been taller."

My son's party provided no such epiphany. After leading them in a primal scream—much to the chagrin of the moms upstairs, who imagined their sons being initiated into some sort of weird Robert Bly beans and barf cult—I brought them outside, where the scientist instructed them in the manly art of making slime. The slime was a clear, gelatinous hodgepodge they smeared all over themselves and each other. (It's guaranteed nontoxic, because every scientist knows that a child's first question, *after* he puts something in his mouth, is, "Can you eat this?'') Eventually, it came time to wash off the slime, and I motioned them to the garden hose, and, just for laughs—because, hey, I needed some fun, too, I was a boy once—I hosed them down.

And they loved it.

They came running over, screaming to be soaked.

I checked for moms, and found the coast was clear, so I soaked them all, then led them in another primal scream. (A neighbor told me he hadn't heard anything like it since an Iron Butterfly concert.) Then I took them inside and fed them a gooey cake covered with ice cream and hot fudge.

It wasn't until late that night, when I was cleaning up, that I realized the only thing in the room that wasn't smeared with fudge, the only articles that were still in the same pristine condition as when the table was set, were the napkins.

Pa for the Course

Once again we revisit the tug-of-war between men and women, and what better place to do it than on the golf course.

Recently, my friend Doris was at the driving range practicing her long irons. "I was minding my own business," she said. "I had my golf bag and my beer—I felt a beer would make me look more guylike, don't you think?"

So Doris is out there hitting golf balls—like all of us: some straight, some veering off the way our Atlas rockets fell off the pad in the 1960s—when suddenly a small boy, maybe ten or eleven, walks up to her and says, "Keep your eye on the ball."

" 'Keep my eye on the ball,' " fumed Doris. "Like I'm a complete moron."

The kid wasn't the only one who offered Doris unsolicited advice. While Doris was practicing, a steady parade of people volunteered golf tips. And do you know what those people all had in common?

They were men.

"I don't know what it is about men that they think they can walk right up to you and give you advice," Doris said. "A woman would never invade your privacy that way." (And it's true. I have yet to see a woman stand by the loading bay of a moving van and direct the movers in and out of a house; men do that all the time—even when it's not their house.)

After five or six of these men—including an eighty-year-old who told her she was foolish for hitting off a mat and that she should hit off the dirt—Doris could take no more. So when some man who couldn't hit the ball out of his own shadow, a man with a swing that belonged in a sausage casing, said to Doris, "Excuse me, can I give you a tip?" Doris fired back, "No!"

"But I think you should know . . ."

"No!" Doris said.

"Listen, I can help you," the man persisted.

"No!"

"But . . ."

And Doris turned on him and glowered. "If you try one more time to give me a golf tip, I'll cleave your head with a two-iron," thereby ending what had been a pleasant conversation. (Isn't that just like a woman to get hysterical?)

"Why do men always think they know more than women?" Doris asked me.

I, of course, immediately corrected the poor dear. "We don't think we know more than women. We *know* we know more than women."

This is why men are always so generous with free advice. For example, you'll see a couple at a restaurant, and the man will be a big fat slob who has to be lowered into his seat with pulleys. And the woman will order a hamburger and fries, and this guy who looks like a china hutch with feet will say disapprovingly, "You sure you need those fries, hon?"

Men feel it is their duty to give unsolicited, unwanted advice. I know a man who tells his wife how to arrange plates in a dishwasher, like there's some sort of science to it.

My friend Tracee is an assistant sports editor at the *Post;* she knows more about sports than I'll ever know, even if I swallow the *Baseball Encyclopedia.* But every time a man calls the sports desk and she answers, the man says, "I'm looking for the *sports* department," as if there must be a mistake because a woman answered. What does he think he dialed, the lingerie department?

Not only do men give out unsolicited, unwanted advice, but we think we're doing people a favor. We feel this way because we were raised—by our mothers, I might add—to believe we're infallible. I am afraid to fly, terrified of being in the air; if you saw me on an airplane you would assume by my behavior that I had the emotional stability of a Jell-O mold. But I actually believe that if there were an emergency on board, say the pilots got food poisoning and died, I could land the plane. If there were a skilled female pilot on board, I would expect her to move aside while I flew the plane; she could, you know, get me a cup of coffee.

I told this to my friend Nancy, who has actually flown with me and has seen me cower like a Chihuahua on takeoff. Nancy said, "If there was an emergency on board, you would have your head so deep in the vomit bag, you'd look like Mr. Potato Head."

(Nancy is not feeling kindly toward men on planes lately, because she was recently on a plane and a man was unbelievably patronizing toward her. She had the aisle seat, and the man who held the window seat wanted to switch with her. But instead of asking straightforwardly, he said, "I'm sure you'd be more comfortable by the window, dear." To which she replied, "Oh, you're such a big, strong, protective man, I'm sure you're right, hee-hee-hee-hee. And I really would take the window seat, so I could stare aimlessly at the puffy clouds like I didn't have a brain in my head, but how would I be able to stretch my legs in the aisle and harass the stewardesses for more double Scotches, smoked almonds, and hot towels, and complain that my wife doesn't understand me like you would?'')

Nevertheless, I believe I could fly the plane because of in-born male superiority.

And now I would like to thank my friends Doris, Tracee, and Nancy for helping me with this column, and I'd like to caution Nancy, who's fair-skinned, not to go out in the sun without a hat, and remind Tracee that you at least need a runner on first base with fewer than two outs to enforce the infield fly rule, and advise Doris to keep her weight on her front foot while hitting out of a sand trap. And since it's summer, if any of you need to know the best way to light charcoal, call me.

Geezer Pleaser

An old friend invited me to dinner the other night with the promise of good food, good wine, and good company. My response was: How *late* is dinner?

I won't go if they're serving after seven, because then they won't be finished until at least eight-thirty, and then they'll expect me to chitchat until ten . . . which is out of the question, because by ten I'll be face down in the kiwi compote.

I've written before about creeping fogyism—that condition of becoming old before your time.

Now I think it *is* my time.

I can't stay up anymore.

Letterman is just a rumor in my life.

I'm basically done after "Final Jeopardy."

"Don't you understand that all the good things happen late at night?" my smart friend Martha asked me. "You're missing them. Yet you're still alive. What should we call this horrible life you're living?"

This is my day: I get up at five-thirty, pad around downstairs while waiting for the newspaper—I like being able to wander through my house before *they* wake up. The one thing I can't

figure out is: How did all those dirty dishes get in the sink between the time I went to sleep and now?

I'm up so early that when I turn my lights on, my neighbors
think I'm just getting home. It's pitch-black outside. I spend the
rest of the day waiting for the darkness to come back so I can go
to sleep. I think I'm the victim of some mad scientist's trans-
plant, and I wound up with the soul of a Norwegian.

Most people look forward to Thanksgiving and Christmas. I
look forward to the end of daylight saving time.

I don't even bother to read about the new season on TV,
because the last show I watched until eleven was *Hill Street
Blues*. Tell me, is Joyce Davenport still in that bubble bath?
That's the way I want to remember her.

I guess I'm beginning to take after my father more than I
realized. My father, who's eighty-two, now goes to sleep so early
that he's wide awake for Bob Costas. My father is the only person I know who flew to China and had no jet lag.

A few weeks ago my friend Nancy and I went to see an ac-
claimed production of the notoriously long *Richard III* with Ian
McKellen. It began at eight, and ran past eleven.

At intermission, I said, "Superb, isn't it?"

"Stunning," she said.

Then casually I said, "I know how it ends."

And she said, "So do I. More important, I know *when* it
ends."

We left without hesitation.

My friends ask me how come I look so tired all the time?

I say it's because I *am* tired all the time.

So they say, "You must be depressed."

I say, no, just tired.

They say, "Well, you must be having a midlife crisis."

And I say, then please let me spend it on a Sealy Posture-
pedic.

For a while I was embarrassed by how early I went to sleep—

especially when I started going to sleep before my kids; oh yeah, my nine-year-old is still doing her homework when I go up to bed. (It's beginning to make me puke when she says, "Daddy, can I tuck *you* in? And read you *Goodnight Moon?*")

But I'm not embarrassed anymore, because I know I'm part of a growing trend of Fortysomething Fogies who can't keep their eyes open. You can recognize us because we:

1. Need to agree on when we're leaving a party before we get there;

2. No longer stay more than six innings at a baseball game and never sit through a rain delay;

3. Think sex is something you awake from a deep sleep to have;

4. Live dangerously by drinking coffee after 5 P.M.;

5. Have Arseniophobia, defined as the fear of Arsenio Hall's audience whoop-whoop-whooping and waving their fists in that strange way, because something is happening and we don't know what it is.

I'm part of that trend. And as America's best-loved feature writer, Mr. Henry, points out, "If you are part of a trend, all your sins are absolved by *USA Today*. By the middle of next week you'll see it on the front page: 'We're *All* Going to Sleep Early.' "

The problem with going to sleep so early is that I am totally out of the loop when it comes to late-night TV, and friends, after eleven-thirty is where the popular culture is made and transmitted. All the new words come from late-night TV—all the new stars, all the new 900 numbers, all the cool diseases. I have seen my children contort themselves until they literally fell off their chairs, and I thought they were having seizures until they explained they were simply imitating Arsenio interviewing Sir Mix-a-Lot, whoever that is.

I am hopeless. I don't know L.A. hip because I don't watch Arsenio. I don't know N.Y. hip because I don't watch Letterman. I don't know what's happening in the world because I don't watch Koppel. Apparently the show for fogies is Carson. I must really be a fogy, because I think Carson is hip. I don't watch Carson, though. (I tape, of course. Unhappily, I never watch anything I've taped. That's how we'll all die eventually— our houses will collapse under the weight of unseen videotapes, and we'll be crushed by the first five years of *Nightline*.)

I am constantly waiting for the "best of . . ." to be on TV, so I can understand what everyone's said for the past five years.

I never heard of Wayne's World until the movie.

What do you mean, Carson's gone?

Jay who?

Well, Your Daddy Don't Rock 'n' Roll

Go ahead and exhale. You've earned it. You had your folks over throughout the holidays. And they're finally going home.

They ask if you could take them to the airport.

"What time's your flight?"

They say it's two-thirty. "But I think we should leave here by ten."

By ten? By *ten*? "Dad, the airport's only twenty minutes away."

They say, "We like to get there early, just to be sure."

"The terrorists don't get there that early. Why do you want to get there four hours ahead of time?"

They say, "It'll give us time to get settled."

"Settled? It's an airport, not the West Bank."

These are the facts of life between grown-ups and their aging parents: You invite them to stay with you because *you* think it's the right thing to do—even though you don't really want them, because they've become wildly eccentric and do things like invite the mailman in for a cup of Metamucil. They come because *they* think it's the right thing to do—even though they'd rather stay in their own home where no one will consider it strange when they walk around the living room in a mink stole and swim fins.

Your parents come in, immediately remark on how ratty your house looks—and how they can't believe *anyone* could live like this. Then they look at their grandchildren, joyfully exclaiming how much they've grown and how wonderful they look. Then they ask for a cup of coffee (if it's not too much trouble) and announce they're ready to go home. The problem is, their flight isn't for five days. The Era of Good Feeling is over. It has lasted ten minutes. The rest of the visit goes like this:

Your dad gets up at 4 A.M. every day. ("I can't sleep," he tells you. "Is it the bed? Is it something you ate?" you ask, assuming it's your fault. "No," he tells you. "I can't sleep because I'm eighty-two years old. The older you get, the less you sleep, the more you go to the bathroom. I've reached the point where I spend more time in the can than Spam.") Since he's wide awake, he wants breakfast, and he ambles into the kitchen to fix some. This is particularly frightening because he has no sense of modern technology (he still calls the refrigerator "the icebox," calls the CD player the "hi-fi," and tries to dial Cleveland on the microwave.) You vaguely hear him poking around in the cabinets and come in just in time to stop him from shoving a banana into the coffee grinder.

Your father's breakfast is interesting. It consists of juice, one piece of dry toast, and 392 pills.

"Lots of pills, Dad," you say hesitantly.

"Oh, these? They're just maintenance."

Maintenance? You're reluctant to pry, but you can't help noticing his set of monogrammed acupuncture needles.

"So, uh, Dad. You're feeling okay?"

He smiles reassuringly. "Don't worry. It's nothing," he says, inserting two small red pills under his tongue.

Your mother is not a problem at mealtime, because she hasn't eaten anything in twelve years. Nothing.

"Anything you want, Mom, just tell me," you say.

She hands you a grocery list. Everything on it seems to be "extra-strength" and "extra-absorbent."

Another weird thing about your parents is the strange prejudices they have, insane unsupportable generalizations that you tolerate because they're your parents—but it would be mortifying if they were to say these things in public. Like, your mom might say, "Hungarians drink like fish." Naturally, you wonder what possesses her to say such a thing. "Your father says he learned it in the war," she says. You are astounded. "Ma, Dad's never been to Hungary. He was stationed in Fort Dix. Hungarians are fine, sober people." And your mom says, "Well, maybe it's Romanians."

My father attributes his eccentricities to growing up in the Depression. He explains this is why he is reluctant to throw anything away—because he remembers when he didn't have anything. So he reuses things. Unfortunately, one of the things he reuses is Saran Wrap. He calls this "recycling." I call it "awww, Dad . . ."

He has no china anymore, just plastic plates he steals from the airlines. He is obsessed with the supermarket Styrofoam they sell the meat in. He has them stacked up in his closet. He must have four hundred of them. He tells me he saves them because he can cut them down and use them to store individual portions of meat in the freezer. He says you never know when you'll need one. I ask, "But when will you need four hundred? Who are you having over for dinner, Up With People?" I point out he doesn't have to save them, because every single cut of meat in America comes with its own Styrofoam tray. It is an endless supply. I tell him he should throw out all the Styrofoam trays he has collected—if only to make room for his glass jar collection.

And I ask him to drive us to the airport.

And Baby Makes 2 + 1

A newspaper headline caught my eye the other day, and I will repeat it here to see if you have the same reactions to it that I did:

FIVE-MONTH-OLD BABIES CAN ADD, SUBTRACT SMALL NUMBERS, STUDY INDICATES.

In rapid order, I thought:

1. Nonsense. Absurd. Don't make me laugh.

2. What's wrong with my kids?

I have a nine-year-old and a six-year-old. It is possible that my nine-year-old, whom I will call Corinne because maybe Dan and Marilyn Quayle will read this and think she is their child and teach her some family values, since all she seems to have learned in my house is how to burp on demand, a talent much admired among her friends—it's *possible* that my nine-year-old can add and subtract small numbers. I don't know for a fact because I have never seen her add anything more complicated than ketchup to a french fry.

I feel confident saying it's completely impossible that my six-year-old can add and subtract small numbers—my six-year-old, whom I'll call Michael because he won't care if I use his real

name, since he can't read anything that isn't in giant capital letters, let alone add and subtract small numbers—because the last
time I asked him what time it was, he said, and I quote, "forty-
three-eleventh thousand."

Until I read this story I was relatively comfortable with my
children's intelligence. My son was a typical six-year-old boy. He
could take all his clothing out of his drawers, and throw it into a
big pile on the floor and announce he had built a volcano. And
my daughter was right in step with all the other nine-year-olds.
She could:

1. Change her clothes seven times a day, throw all the dis-
cards in the general direction of the hamper, and then complain
the next morning that she didn't have anything to wear because
all her clothes were dirty;

2. Argue passionately that *America's Funniest Home Videos*
was actually an educational show, because it taught you valuable
lessons about behavior—like you shouldn't let your dog drink
from the toilet bowl;

3. Identify the Soviet Union as a "supermarket chain."

But the study really threw me for a loop when it said that a
psychologist had proved that five-month-olds could add and
subtract—or at least distinguish the difference between correct
and incorrect addition and subtraction. The proof was they
would stare longer at a wrong answer than at a right answer.

In the test, if you put one rubber duckie in front of them,
then put a screen in front of the rubber duckie, then ostenta-
tiously added another rubber duckie—which should make two
rubber duckies—then removed the screen to reveal three rubber
duckies, they would stare longer at the three rubber duckies
than they would have had there been two rubber duckies in
front of them. The study showed they would stare *almost two
seconds longer* at the wrong amount of rubber duckies. The con-

clusion was that the third rubber duckie was not what they expected, and their prolonged reactions proved they knew how to add and subtract.

Now, I don't know about you, but I'm not inclined to trust any scientific experiment conducted with rubber duckies. I don't recall J. Robert Oppenheimer explaining the theory of the atomic bomb by pointing to a rubber duckie.

This is scientific proof?

Two seconds of staring?

Look, when she was one year old, my daughter stared at chocolate pudding for half an hour, and she couldn't tell the difference between it and a pile of dog poop. On the other hand, it's things like this that always make me worry that my kids are stupid. When I read about a nine-year-old chess champion I always say, "There goes my kid's seat at Harvard." So I rush up to his room with a chess set and say, "If we hurry, maybe you can still get into Dartmouth." And he takes his finger out of his nose, and looks up at me, and says, "Daddy, if I drop my troll into the fish tank, will it explode and will it get fish guts all over the walls?"

I worry that I'm not diligent enough as a parent, that I've been too lax with my kids. I should have enrolled them in advanced Portuguese. My cousin's child asked for a nuclear-powered telescope for Christmas when she was seven. My kid asked for a Barbie Pez dispenser.

Maybe I overrate these things. I was a smart kid myself. I could read when I was three. I read from my grandfather's law books. He nearly dropped dead. He called all the relatives, and told them his grandson was a genius, and he would make enough money to take care of the whole family. I ended up writing a newspaper column like a thousand other slobs. His neighbor's grandson, a schlemiel who couldn't find his *pupik* with both hands, dropped out of high school and got a job stuffing stems into Styrofoam in a florist shop, where one day he met and later married an heiress, and is now retired, at forty-five, and living in Beverly Hills. His children are idiots. If they need to add or subtract, they can use a gold-plated calculator.

The Little Car That Didn't

Some people test well. I envy them. In high school I failed every math and science test. My math boards were so low, the colleges I applied to assumed I was a basketball player. I even failed a litmus test.

The one test I did well on was the essay. If the first three words were, "Compare and contrast . . ." I was golden. I could compare and contrast just about anything. The Magna Carta and the Declaration of Independence. The Roman Empire and the Greek city-states. Sonny and Cher. I could, as they say, really air it out: write long, and write illegibly—an unbeatable combination.

Unfortunately, yesterday's test wasn't an essay.

It was my car inspection.

We flunked it.

I took the test lightly. I should have prepared more. I should have gone to a D.C. Auto Inspection remedial course. The things I did were so obvious: spray the tires with Armor All, hang an air-freshener tree from the rearview mirror, put on an I BRAKE FOR D.C. AUTO INSPECTORS bumper sticker, and refill my windshield washer fluid with some old Perrier; the natural carbonation is great on glass, and who cares if the benzene poisons the wiper blades?

Actually, I should have taken the test in someone else's car. I didn't have a chance in a Chevette. Even the cab drivers were laughing when I drove up, and most of their taxis didn't even have bumpers. One station wagon, the whole right side was smashed in, and what looked like a person's leg was hanging out of the trunk, okay? So not only should this car be impounded, the driver should be facing a felony rap. He zipped through. Afterward, this same guy tells me, "Last year they flunked me. Best move I ever made was trading in my Chevette on this wagon."

It goes without saying that owning a Chevette has its ups and downs (shock absorbers are not standard in a Chevette; the Chevette owner likes to think of driving as a test of physical endurance). And it does teach you about humility. True story: I was leaving Capital Centre a few months ago, opening the door to my Chevette in the parking lot, when a young man in his early twenties and his friend stopped me.

Pointing to my Chevette, the young man said, "That's a rent-a-car, right?"

"No," I said. "It's mine."

"You *own* that car?" he hooted.

"Yeah. I own a Chevette."

He was grinning as he walked to his car, a late-model Toyota. He high-fived his friend delightedly and howled, "I'm doing better than Tony Kornheiser."

It's bad enough owning a car people laugh at. It's doubly humiliating when the inspectors slap a scarlet diamond-shaped sticker on the windshield—and they do it with such glee—to tell the world you've flunked the test, and you've got thirty days to correct what's wrong or you'll be shot on sight.

It's so embarrassing, failing your car inspection. It's like flunking out of Clemson. What's worse is having to sit in line for two hours to take the test.

Oh sure. You don't just breeze through. You really should bring a book. Not to read—to translate. They flunked me because one of my taillights didn't work. I bet it was working when I first got in line. It probably rusted in the interim. (Though it could be worse. It could be the DMV. That's the land of lost souls. You're lucky to get out of there the same age as when you walked in. And talk about friendly service. Where did they work before the DMV, Panmunjom?)

I was surprised when they got me for a taillight. I figured they'd nail me for bad tires. After all, I had to drive through D.C. to get to the inspection station. People say our streets aren't safe; hey, most aren't even paved. These aren't mere potholes—you can drop into them and disappear forever. Generations from now archaeologists will dig under the Whitehurst Freeway and uncover a fleet of fully preserved Dodge Omnis. If any of our mayoral candidates declared war on potholes, he or she would win in a landslide.

They flunked the guy in front of me, too. He was driving a black BMW sedan with tomato-red leather seats and vanity plates: DUN GR8. I assume they flunked him for tackiness. I thought my taillight was a bad rap. It was the third taillight, the one above the rear window. It's like I'd answered the extra-credit question wrong and they flunked me for the whole exam. They just started making those taillights in 1986. If they're so important, why didn't Henry Ford put them in the original blueprint? My wife's car only has two taillights; she passed. I don't feel any safer with a third taillight. I wouldn't feel safe in a Chevette if it had armor plating.

I tried to have this conversation with the inspectors, but they're not a real talkative bunch. They just hand you the punched card with your violations and paste on the scarlet sticker. This isn't "Metro Week in Review."

Fortunately, I was able to find a bulb for a third taillight at a Capitol Hill gas station on Pennsylvania Avenue. They were nice enough to fix the light on the spot, and give me a valid inspection sticker before any of my neighbors learned I'd failed the test and disgraced the block. I'm good for a full year. And next time I'm coming back in a Yugo.

Plenty of Nothing to Do

Now that the school year is over, and my children are home all day long . . . I'm thinking of smashing my head through a plate glass window.

Stop me if this sounds familiar:

"Dad, I'm bored."

Wait, let me try it again the way it really sounds:

"Daaaaadddd, I'm booorrrrrred!"

My kids are eleven and eight, and they're always bored. Everything bores them, including the brand-new $39.95 Sega video game I bought them this morning that they traded to the kid down the street because it was so borrrrringgg. They traded it for a stick. A *stick*! I asked them what the attraction of a stick was that they thought it was worth $39.95? They told me, and I am quoting verbatim here, "It was once alive."

I tell them there's so much to do: They can read, they can play the piano, they can ride bikes, they can watch TV, they can bury the cat up to its head in the backyard and fire up the lawn mower. (It's okay for me to joke about such things because I'm a professional humorist. Do not try this yourself.)

I tell them when I was young we didn't have anywhere *near* as many options. I tell them when I was young my diversions were pretty much limited to reading comic books about GIs in World War II (where machine guns went "*Budda Budda Budda,*" and soldiers with cigars in their teeth and comical cross-hatching on their faces that was supposed to look like stubble kept saying things like, "Eat lead, you lousy Krauts") and watching black-and-white TV with sitcoms such as *The Stu Erwin Show,* starring, obviously, Stu Erwin, who, to tell you the truth, I couldn't pick out of a lineup with the Andrews Sisters. There was no Nintendo, I say. The only thing remotely interactive with TV was *Winky Dink,* which featured a plastic screen that you were supposed to put on your TV and draw on with crayon—except you kept forgetting to put the screen on, and so your dad hit you with a belt or a baseball bat, which dads used to do fairly regularly (maybe Stu Erwin even did it), AND KIDS WERE BETTER OFF FOR IT, I point out menacingly.

They tell me the story bores them.

I ask them what they want to do.

"There's nothing to do," they say.

(What they're saying is that you, as a parent, are responsible for their entertainment. If you buy into this, they begin stringing you out. Say you take a deep breath, and against your better judgment you offer to make the deadly three-hour drive, and spend the $1,480 it takes to placate your family at a big-deal water slide amusement park like Busch Gardens, your kids will immediately say, "Do we have to go to Busch Gardens *again?*")

I tell them to call a friend.

None of our friends are home, they say.

What are you talking about, I say. Your friends are nine years old. Where did they all go at that age, to the Crusades? Are they celebrating D-Day by parachuting into the Le Havre–Cherbourg peninsula?

"Can you buy me X-Men cards?" he says.

I bought you X-Men cards two days ago. They were six dollars a pack, and you got five cards. Who drew these cards,

Picasso? These are not collectibles. There are no X-Men rookie cards.

What about all your toys, I say. What about those games?

"Games are for kids," she says.

Excuse me, Jessica Tandy, I say. What about playing ball? There are 368 balls in the house. There are tennis balls, foot-balls, basketballs, golf balls. There's that soccer ball you have on a string, I say, the one you've almost shattered the TV screen with. There's that ball the dog ate and barfed back up that no one will go near. There's that "vortex," the football with wings that some idiot invented as though it will help a kid learn to throw a football if you put wings on it; I mean, why not invent a golf club with a pogo-stick head, for those *really* long drives? Or a basketball the size of a watermelon seed so any shot goes in?

Both my kids like sports, and I try to get them to play sports with the kids on the block. But there's no league on the block. Sports have been taken over by some league with at least nine letters in its name, like the MCFPSPBFD 7-10 Gender-Equal T-Ball Workshop. Kids don't play ball unless there's an orga-nized league with a trophy for everyone. My son is eight, and he's already got more trophies than Willie Mays. Every time he puts on his sneakers, someone hands him a trophy. If Rodin were alive today, he'd be making plastic baseball players.

And if you put your kids into leagues, you have to drive them there, then watch them play. There were no leagues when I was a kid. I played stoop ball. My old man didn't stand around watching me play stoop ball; he did what all fathers did in the 50s—he finished the basement. (To this day I can't look at knotty pine without having flashbacks.)

If you don't stay and *applaud* your kids, they will grow up with a self-esteem problem. According to America's best-loved feature writer, Mr. Henry, that's the beginning of the end: Peo-ple are going to see grades fall, and cats being tortured, and fires being set, and eventually someone's sitting in a doctor's office recovering a memory. And who are they going to blame?

You.

Which is why when my kids are bored, I immediately rush out and buy them ice cream.

Smitten

Being a shameless TV hound, I eagerly accepted the invitation to cohost *Broadcast House Live* for a couple of days last week. It never occurred to me what a tragic mistake I had made until I saw myself on the monitor sitting next to the first guest, Jimmy Smits.

Jimmy Smits used to be one of the hunk lawyers on *L.A. Law*. Now he is the hunk homicide detective on *NYPD Blue*. Eventually, if his career lasts, he will be the hunk shuffleboarder on *Miami Beach Condo 33139*. Just how hunky is Jimmy Smits? He's the kind of guy you see, and then have to blind yourself with an ice pick.

I met Jimmy Smits briefly before the show. He was in the greenroom, where the guests and staff hang out. His body was obscured by a clutch of women in various categories of personal arousal, ranging from "squealy schoolgirl" to "yes yes yes yes YES YES YES." But I could see his head towering above theirs— because Smits is a big guy, six foot three, and not your typical twerp shrimp of an actor—and I elbowed my way through to introduce myself.

I felt empowered, being the cohost and all; I could walk right up to Mr. Big Shot TV Star Jimmy Smits and say anything I wanted. I have read all the classics of literature and philosophy and am equally well versed in American popular culture. I had a veritable library of information both arcane and profound from which to draw for my meeting with Jimmy Smits. So I walked up to him, pumped his hand, and said the first thing that came into my mind, which was, I swear:

"So, do you go to a gym?"

"You said *what?*" my friend Gino asked as I proudly related the story of my encounter.

I have to admit, it didn't sound quite so brilliant, repeating it a second time, down there in the company cafeteria.

"Why did you say *that?*"

"Well, ah, I go to a gym. . . . I thought we'd have something in common."

"So if you were introduced to Gabriel García Márquez, would you ask him, 'So, do you pee in a toilet?' "

Anyway, that's what I asked Jimmy Smits: "So, do you go to a gym?"

(It made sense to me. He's a big, strong guy, you know. What should I have asked—"Do you think we're acting prudently converting our naval fleet to nuclear propulsion?")

And Smits said, and this is his verbatim answer: "No, thanks. I'm fine."

A very enigmatic answer, I thought. Until I realized he obviously (1) had not even listened to anything said by someone who looks like me. And he (2) assumed I was some kind of water boy, and I was asking if he wanted me to get him a sandwich.

I would have clarified my role, but by then the women had eased me out of the way and were back buzzing around him, as close as the shell to the peanut. Grown women actually buckled at the knees near Smits: He would walk by, and the line of women would actually undulate as their knees gave way. I've had women react strongly around me, but it's usually more of a shudder.

One of the women on the show's staff told me her friend was so excited to hear Smits would be on the show that she pleaded, "Just rub against him, and tell me what it feels like."

(Men would never do that. If Claudia Schiffer walked through an insurance office, all the men would poke each other in the ribs and ogle her, and they'd find some reflective glass and station themselves in a way to surreptitiously catch her reflection from an angle, or they'd simply squat on the ground trying to look up her dress. But they wouldn't directly approach her. Women are much more honest and direct. They go up to a hunk like Jimmy Smits and swoon in his presence. They say, more or less, Here is my heaving bosom, take me and ravish me on the linoleum, but get done before five-fifteen because I have to get to the supermarket and pick up a brisket for my fat load of a husband, who sniffs his food like a dog and wouldn't notice if I walked into the living room totally naked unless I passed in front of the TV set and blocked his view of that Olajuwon fellow, whatshisname, Raheem?)

So later I'm sitting there next to Smits, and I'm supposed to interview him. And I have all these really intelligent questions prepared, you know, about the recent shift toward conservatism among the electorate. But we start showing a film clip of the humblingly muscular Smits doing push-ups buck naked, with a big, blue TV dot covering his heinie, which makes it hard to gracefully slide into a question about the efficacy of our foreign policy in Bosnia. And it was then, coming out of the clip, that I saw myself in the monitor—this fat, bald, marshmallow-pale geezebag sitting next to this unbelievably gorgeous man. And I thought to myself:

Gaaackk! Who is that toadstool interviewing Jimmy Smits? It's bad enough to be fat, bald, and forty-five—but now I'm sitting next to a guy who's much bigger than I am, and his skin is clear, and his eyes are bright, and he's filling up the TV screen like something Cézanne painted, and next to him I look like that putz Marty Allen who says "Hello dere," AND WE'RE ON TV FOR GOD'S SAKE AND EVERYONE CAN SEE HOW PA-THETIC I AM!

At this point I offered to move and let Jimmy Smits sit next to the host, my friend, the fabulous Robin Young, who had recently fainted and fallen off her stool.

"Maybe you want to sit next to Robin," I said.

Recognizing that I felt old and useless and ugly in his aura, Jimmy Smits did the kindest thing—he put his arm around me. Right there, on TV, Jimmy Smits put his arm around me.

And I have to admit, ladies, I felt a tingle.

Girth of the Blues

Photos from my college reunion came back the other day. There has to be some mistake. Everybody else looked just the way I remembered them, but somehow the pictures of me got distorted.

What kind of lens does this, gets everybody else in focus and makes one guy appear irretrievably fat?

From the front I'm pear-shaped. I look like something you win at a carnival for knocking milk bottles off a table.

From the side I look like the third leg of an isosceles triangle.

I should write Fotomat. Something must be wrong with their developer. This can't be me.

Where did that mudslide of a stomach come from?

What a lousy time I've picked to look like Dom DeLuise.

Next weekend's Memorial Day. The pools open. I'm going to have to take off my shirt. I can't afford to do that. The kids'll see me and think I'm some sort of inflatable rubber Shamu.

Luckily, I don't have any dimpling on my thighs yet, and none of that crepey skin under my arms. My midsection is a disaster. I sit down and I look like a shar-pei. Talk about love handles, this is some serious baggage here—the entire New York City subway ridership could hang on.

I guess it sort of snacked up on me.

I was never fat as a kid. I was one of those jerks who made fun of the fat kids. I truly didn't think I was fat now until these horribly distorted photos arrived. Okay, I'd noticed a couple of changes: I couldn't button the collar of my shirts, but I assumed it was the laundry putting in starch—I'd told them I hate starch. Then I couldn't button my suit jackets, and I told my wife, "Can you believe the laundry is putting starch in my *suits?*" She made a crack about how I'd better stop talking about buying a Miata, because they'd have to lower me in with a crane.

It's all come together.

My age.

My waist.

The amount of pounds over what it says on my driver's license.

Looking back, I should have paid more attention the night we all sat around watching *Designing Women*, and I made the comment how Mary Jo was such a foxy little thing, and three people in the room turned to me and said at exactly the same time, "I'd have thought you'd prefer Suzanne." Hmmmm, Ms. Avoirdupois. Anyway, I looked at those preposterously out-of-focus pictures— perhaps it's Kodak's fault, because I'm certain I was wearing a belt, and you can't even see it below my gut in the photos—and I wrote this song to the tune of "I'm Henry the VIII, I Am":

> *I'm fat as a whale, I am*
> *Fat as a whale, I am, I am.*
> *I'm much fatter than the people next door*
> *I can't fit into my pants no more*
> *And every day I eat gobs of sweets*
> *Two eclairs, a pudding, and some jam*
> *I am infinitely larger than a porpoise*
> *Fat as a whale, I am.**

*© Tub O'Lard Tunes 1990

I've started running.

Well, not really running, more like creeping.

And wouldn't you know, as soon as I started, I got hurt. Unfortunately, it's nothing sexy like shin splints or a stress fracture—my thighs got chafed, the inside of my thighs. All that fatty tissue rubbing against itself. It's a good thing my son's only recently out of diapers; we had some Balmex at home. My thighs looked like round steak. I'm surprised people didn't stop me on the side of the road and ladle me with barbecue sauce.

"Vaseline," advised the jogger pals.

I'm so slippery when I run now that if I fall down near a storm drain I'm likely to slide all the way to Maine Avenue.

Not that jogging is going to do me any good. Because it makes me hungry. I get home and eat twice as much as before. I'm down to only one big meal a day, but I'm eating it from eight to midnight.

Around the turn of the century, those were the good old days. If a man had an ample middle then, it meant he was prosperous. Girth was respected as a sign of accomplishment. William Howard Taft, all three-hundred-plus pounds of him, was elected president. Today he couldn't win. Today he couldn't even fit inside the voting booth.

I guess I'll go on a diet.

My wife doesn't trust me when I say that. I've gone on diets before, and never even made it through one full day without cheating big time. (My idea of a diet is: I eat with a small fork.) She'll bring home diet rice cakes, and I'll slather peanut butter and jelly on them.

"You're supposed to eat them plain," she says.

"Dick Gregory wouldn't eat these plain," I answer.

My former best friend, Mike, recently went on a diet, the one Tommy Lasorda and Ed Koch shill: You drink a couple of milkshakes and eat one "modest" meal a night.

"There's a slight difference of opinion," Mike says. "My

'modest' is, I stop after four rolls and one dessert. Their 'modest' is three hundred calories. It's somewhere between three leaves of romaine lettuce and one lick of white chocolate chunk. They claim you feel full on their food. I don't. I'm living on the memory."

Mike is my former best friend because he's lost thirteen pounds on this diet and will soon blow away in the wind. My only joy comes when I ask how he feels, and he complains, "Extremely hungry."

Our mutual friend Dave Kindred, whose prose once graced the *Post*, is tinkering with the thought of attempting this same diet, and has already begun experimenting with the milkshakes. "I like them," he is pleased to report. "After meals, I have them for dessert."

ACKNOWLEDGMENTS

My special thanks to my smart friend Martha Sherrill; America's best-loved feature writer, Henry Allen; Norman Chad, who is the real Man About Town Chip Muldoon; Jeanne McManus, who said I could call her my friend Nancy, and she would call me Ramon; my friend Gino, better known as Gene Weingarten, the editor of the Sunday "Style" section of *The Washington Post*. Gino wrote much of this book, including all the columns, the introduction, and this paragraph. That's my picture on the cover, though.